W9-BBW-431

A Cook's Tour

BY THE SAME AUTHOR

Bone in the Throat

Gone Bamboo

Kitchen Confidential: Adventures in the Culinary Underbelly

Typhoid Mary (an Urban Historical)

A Cook's Tour

in search of the perfect meal

Anthony Bourdain

BLOOMSBURY

Copyright © 2001 by Anthony Bourdain

All rights reserved. No part of this book may be used or reproduced in any manner
whatsoever without written permission from the Publisher except in the case of brief
quotations embodied in critical articles or reviews. For information address
Bloomsbury, 175 Fifth Avenue, New York, N.Y. 10010

AUTHOR'S NOTE: I have changed the names of some of the individuals
and some of the restaurants that are a part of my story.

Published by Bloomsbury, New York and London
Distributed to the trade by Holtzbrinck Publishers

Cataloging in Publication Data is available from the Library of Congress

ISBN 1-58234-140-0

First Edition 2001

10 9 8 7 6 5 4 3 2 1

Typeset by Hewer Text, Edinburgh
Printed in the United States of America by
RR Donnelley & Sons Company, Harrisonburg, Virginia

To Nancy

CONTENTS

Dear Nancy,

I'm about as far away from you as I've ever been – a hotel (*the* hotel, actually) in Pailin, a miserable one-horse dunghole in northwest Cambodia, home to those not-so-adorable scamps, the Khmer Rouge. Picture this: a single swayback bed, a broken TV set that shows only fuzzy images of Thai kick-boxing, a tile floor with tiles halfway up the wall and a drain in the middle – as if the whole room were designed to be quickly and efficiently hosed down. There's one lightbulb, a warped dresser, and a complimentary plastic comb with someone else's hair in it. In spite of the EZ Clean design features, there are suspicious and dismaying stains on the walls. About two thirds of the way up one wall, there are what look like bloody footprints and – what do they call it, arterial spray? How they got there, so high up, I can only guess. The wall opposite has equally sinister stains – evidence of a more opaque substance – these suggesting a downward dispersal. Having seen the bathroom, I can't blame the perpetrator for anything.

There are no smiles in this town, just glares of naked hostility. The clothing of choice is the moldering remnants of military-issue fatigues. There is a 'karaoke' booth in the lobby, next to the standard pictogram of an AK-47 with a red line through it (NO AUTOMATIC WEAPONS IN THE LOBBY). 'Karaoke' means, presumably, that the bison-sized women lounging around by the front desk with their kids are available for purposes of sexual diversion. The best-looking one is a dead ringer for Hideki Irabu. (We traded that lox to Toronto, didn't we? Or was it Montreal?) My Khmer translator, who has hardly opened his mouth since we entered Khmer Rouge territory, says that the last time he stayed here, during the last coup, he got a terrible skin rash. He intends, he says, to sleep standing up. Now he tells me . . .

Could you maybe make a doctor's appointment for me for when I get back? I'm thinking a full workup, to be on the safe side. I've been wading in water – and drinking it – from the kind of worst-case scenarios you read about in the guidebooks and travelers warnings. Needless to say, some of the food I've been eating – well, the food handling has been . . . dubious, at best. Is liver fluke curable? I don't think they gave me a shot for that. I miss you. I miss the cat. I miss my own bed, *The Simpsons* at 7:00 and 11:00. I could really go for a cold beer. A pizza. Some chopped liver from Barney Greengrass. Toilets that don't double as showers. I'll call you when I get back to Phnom Penh or Battambang.

Love you.
Tony

INTRODUCTION

I'M SITTING CROSS-LEGGED IN the bush with Charlie, deep in the Mekong Delta, drinking Vietnamese moonshine from a plastic cola bottle. It's dark, the only light coming from a single generator-powered lightbulb, and on the tarpaulin of stitched-together fertilizer and rice sacks laid out on the hard jungle floor in front of me, dinner has just been served: a humble farmer's meal of clay-roasted duck, duck and banana-blossom soup, salad, and stuffed bitter melon. My host, affectionately referred to as 'Uncle Hai,' sits to my left, his right hand clutching my knee. Every once in a while he gives it a squeeze, just to make sure I'm still there and that I'm having a good time.

I am having a good time. I'm having the best time in the world. Across from me, a ninety-five-year-old man with a milky white eye and no teeth, who's wearing black pajamas and rubber sandals, raises a glass of the vicious homemade rice whiskey and challenges me to yet another shot. He's a war hero, I have been assured. He fought the Japanese, the French; he fought in the 'American War.' We exchange respectful salutations and both hammer back a shot.

The problem is, nearly everybody at this meal is also, apparently, a war hero. The delta was an incubation chamber – a hotbed of VC activity during our country's time here – and everybody, one by one, wants to have a drink with me. Grampa, directly across from me, his legs tucked comfortably under his body like a supple sixteen-year-old's, has raised his glass in my direction six times already, fixing me in the gaze of his one

I

unclouded eye, before knocking back another shot. Almost immediately, someone else tugs on my sleeve.

'Please, sir . . . the gentleman down there . . . he is also a great war hero. He would like to drink with you.'

I look down the length of the makeshift picnic blanket to a tough-looking guy, fortyish maybe, with thick neck and forearms. He's staring right at me, not shy at all, this one. He's smiling, too – though not exactly the same warm, friendly smile Grampa's been giving me. This smile says, I've killed a few of your kind, you know. Now, let's see if you can drink.

'I'm right here, Cool Breeze,' I say, trying not to slur. 'Come and get me.' Then I give him my baddest-ass Dirty Harry, jailhouse stare while I drain another glass of what I am quickly coming to believe is formaldehyde.

Three Communist party officials from the Can Tho People's Committee, picking at salads with chopsticks, watch with interest as the silly American, who came all this way – by plane, by car, by sampan – to eat clay-roasted duck with a rice farmer and his family, slugs back his twelfth shot of the evening and looks worriedly around the clearing at all the other war heroes waiting to do the same. There are about twenty-five men crowded around the tarpaulin, sitting with their legs folded tightly, tearing at duck with their chopsticks and watching me. The women serve, looming up out of the darkness with more food, more liquor, and the occasional sharp word of advice.

Don't make him carve the duck! I imagine they're saying. He's American! He's too stupid and clumsy! In America, everything arrives carved already! He won't know what to do! He'll cut himself, the idiot, and shame us all! A paper plate arrives with a small paring knife and another sizzling-hot duck: head, feet, bill, and guts intact. I position the thing as best I can with burning fingers, wrestle not too gracefully with it for a few seconds, and manage to remove legs, breasts, and wings in the classic French tableside style. I crack open the skull so my friend Philippe can scoop out the brains (he's French; they like that stuff) and offer the first slice of breast to my host, Uncle Hai.

The crowd is pleased. There's a round of applause. Behind me, children are running around, playing in the dark. A while ago, there were only a few of them. But as news of the American visitor and his French friend spread, their number has swelled – as has the number of dinner guests. They've been arriving all night from surrounding farms. In groups of two and three, they've been coming from the river, pulling up in their narrow boats and disembarking at Uncle Hai's tiny landing. They've walked single file down the packed-silt riverbank, the dried-mud causeway that serves as both jungle highway and levee, part of an intricate, centuries-old irrigation system that extends for hundreds of square miles. Occasionally, a small child will appear at my elbow to stroke my hand or pinch my skin, seemingly amazed at the color, the hair on my arms. There is a look of absolute wonder and confusion on his face, as if, perhaps, older friends dared him to go pinch the Giant American Savage who once bombed and strafed the village, but now comes in peace to eat duck and drink rotgut with these patriotic heroes. A while ago, I had my Sally Struthers moment, posing for a photograph with about twenty of them, before allowing them to chase me around the clearing with a lot of fake Hong Kong martial-arts moves, then letting them tie me up with a length of twine – to much squealing of delight.

The duck is a little tough, and smoky-tasting from the mound of burning straw it's been cooked in; and the Mekong whiskey is going down like drain cleaner. I'm worried about what I'm going to do when all this alcohol hits me, how I'm ever going to get back on that narrow, wobbly boat in the middle of the night, make my way downriver through the absolute blackness of the jungle, disembark (while still retaining verticality) across a bamboo and mangrove monkey bridge to a sleepy Stone Age hamlet, then, in a shared car, bounce over twisting narrow jungle track and shaky wooden bridges to Highway 1 and Can Tho without blowing chunks all over the three representatives of the People's Committee.

I don't want to disgrace my clan. I don't want my gracious and genial hosts to see me stumble or fall. I don't want to get hauled away from this meal on a stretcher, my head hanging over the side of the sampan, drooling bile into the black water. I've got something to prove. We may have lost the war. We may have pointlessly bombed and mined and assassinated and defoliated before slinking away as if it were all a terrible misunderstanding – but, goddamn it, we can still drink as good as these guys, right?

Looking across at Grampa, who's refilling his glass while a toddler crawls onto his lap, I'm not so sure. Screw it. I'm having a good time. I smile at the old man and hold up my glass. I like him. I like these guys. Since coming to Asia, I've never met such a great group of people. It's been food, folks, and fun like I've never experienced. These are, by Vietnamese standards, party animals – warm, generous, thoughtful, kind – occasionally very funny, sincere in both their hospitality and their fierce pride. I don't want to leave. I want to do this all night.

One of the younger war heroes at the other end of the tarp suddenly stands up, and the other guests stop chattering as he breaks into song. Accompanied by a clapped-out guitar, he sings, his palms held together as if praying, looking out over our heads, as if singing to someone in the jungle. It's beautiful, a heartfelt, sweet-sounding, absolutely haunting invocation, and in the dim light from the single bulb, he looks angelic. No one makes a sound while he sings, but I manage to whisper a question to the translator on my right.

'What's he singing about?' I ask.

'It is a patriotic song,' he says, 'about the people of this village, the farmers and their families who hid the soldiers and helped them during the American War. About the difficulties they faced. And their courage.'

'Oh,' I reply.

I know the song is basically about killing my kind – and not too terribly long ago – but I'm absolutely riveted. I'm charmed. I'm flattered. I have been treated, in the last few hours, with never-before-encountered kindness and respect. Uncle Hai gives my knee another squeeze. The old man across from me smiles and raises his empty glass to me, summons a younger man to refill it, gestures that he should do the same for me. A swollen moon appears from behind puffs of cloud, hangs heavily over

4

the tree line beyond the river. Other guests are arriving. I can hear them in the distance, their sandals and bare feet padding softly along the hardened silt, emerging from the darkness to take places around the tarpaulin.

I wanted the perfect meal.

I also wanted – to be absolutely frank – Col. Walter E. Kurtz, Lord Jim, Lawrence of Arabia, Kim Philby, the Consul, Fowler, Tony Po, B. Traven, Christopher Walken . . . I wanted to find – no, I wanted to be – one of those debauched heroes and villains out of Graham Greene, Joseph Conrad, Francis Coppola, and Michael Cimino. I wanted to wander the world in a dirty seersucker suit, getting into trouble.

I wanted adventures. I wanted to go up the Nung River to the heart of darkness in Cambodia. I wanted to ride out into a desert on camelback, sand and dunes in every direction, eat whole roasted lamb with my fingers. I wanted to kick snow off my boots in a Mafiya nightclub in Russia. I wanted to play with automatic weapons in Phnom Penh, recapture the past in a small oyster village in France, step into a seedy neon-lit *pulquería* in rural Mexico. I wanted to run roadblocks in the middle of the night, blowing past angry militia with a handful of hurled Marlboro packs, experience fear, excitement, wonder. I wanted kicks – the kind of melodramatic thrills and chills I'd yearned for since childhood, the kind of adventure I'd found as a little boy in the pages of my Tintin comic books. I wanted to see the world – and I wanted the world to be just like the movies.

Unreasonable? Overromantic? Uninformed? Foolhardy?

Yes!

But I didn't care. I'd just put down a very nice score with an obnoxious and overtestosteroned account of my life in the restaurant business. Inexplicably, it had flown off the shelves. I was paying rent on time for the first time in my life. I had, amazingly, health coverage at long last. I actually had money in the bank and the goodwill of a publisher on my side. After a few months of traveling the English-speaking world, flogging my book, giving the same witless three-minute interview over and over and over again, I was no longer a useful factor in the day-to-day operations of my kitchen. My cooks had long since begun calling me 'Pinchay Famoso' and making fun of me when I'd show up slathered in TV makeup after yet another segment showing me warning the public about 'fish on Monday' and the 'perils of hollandaise.' I needed something to do. I needed another idea for a book – preferably while I was still in good odor from the last one. I may love cooking, and I certainly love the life of the professional chef, but I did not, at age forty-five, forty-six, or ever again, want to find myself slopping out brunches in some West Village café when my knees went completely and my brain turned, finally, to mush.

'How about this?' I suggested to my editor. 'I travel around the world, doing whatever I want. I stay in fine hotels and I stay in hovels. I eat scary, exotic, wonderful food, doing cool stuff like I've seen in movies, and looking for the perfect meal. How's that sound?'

That sounded like a good business plan, right? I'd comb the world looking for the perfect mix of food and context. Upriver in Southeast Asia to eat snakes and bird's nests, back to La Teste for a bowl of *soupe de poisson*, scale the mountains of the new haute cuisine – the French Laundry in Napa Valley, I hadn't eaten there yet! That Arzak guy in Spain – all the cooks are talking about him. I'd look and look, and eventually I'd find the best meal in the world – according to me anyway – and I'd write about it.

Of course, I knew already that the best meal in the world, the perfect meal, is very rarely the most sophisticated or expensive one. I knew how important factors other than technique or rare ingredients can be in the real business of making magic happen at a dinner table. Context and memory play powerful roles in all the truly great meals in one's life. I mean, let's face it: When you're eating simple barbecue under a palm tree, and you feel sand between your toes, samba music is playing softly in the background, waves are lapping at the shore a few yards off, a gentle breeze is cooling the sweat on the back of your neck at the hairline, and looking across the table, past the column of empty

Red Stripes at the dreamy expression on your companion's face, you realize that in half an hour you're probably going to be having sex on clean white hotel sheets, that grilled chicken leg suddenly tastes a hell of a lot better.

I talk about these mysterious forces all the time with my chef cronies. Nothing illustrates them more than the Last Meal Game. 'You're getting the electric chair tomorrow morning. They're gonna strap you down, turn up the juice, and fry your ass until your eyes sizzle and pop like McNuggets. You've got one meal left. What are you having for dinner?' When playing this game with chefs – and we're talking good chefs here – the answers are invariably simple ones.

'Braised short ribs,' said one friend.

'A single slab of seared foie gras,' said another.

'Linguine *pomodoro*, like my mother used to make me,' said another.

'Cold meat loaf sandwich,' said another, shuddering with pleasure. 'Don't tell anyone.'

No one I've ever played this game with came back with 'The tasting menu at Ducasse.' No one remembers their best meal ever as being consumed jacketed and tied, in a starched dress shirt, sitting bolt upright in a four-star restaurant. That particular combination of skill, technique, prime ingredients, and artistic genius was not really what I was looking for – though I was determined to give it a shot now and again. There are other forces at work in the enjoyment of a truly great meal. Nice crystal, mood lighting, squeeze-bottle-applied sauces, good china, attentive service, spectacular wine – I was already well aware of their strange and terrible powers to seduce and delight. Though not always capable of fully harnessing them myself, I was fully conscious of them. I knew how those things worked, the classic interplay between food and service, the effects of low-wattage peach-tinted lightbulbs, the sound of well-polished sommelier's shoes gliding across a dining room. The entire food business as show business is what my friends and I have been doing our whole lives. I knew about that like I knew about the physical forces at play in the kitchen: gravity, decay, coagulation, fermentation, emulsification, oxidization, reduction, caramelization. I didn't want to think about those things. I wanted to detach myself from the hard wiring, the way my whole nervous system becomes aware of every movement in a crowded restaurant, habitually monitoring the busboys' progress in the neighboring station, eyeing an overflowing bus pan, a backed-up service bar, listening for the sizzle as my fish hits a hot pan in the kitchen.

I wanted magic. When is food magic? What are the common denominators? Certainly, when food is the result of a brilliant and obsessive personal vision, it can take on mystical, magical aspects. At their best, chefs like to consider themselves alchemists, and some of them, particularly the French, have a long and glorious tradition of turning lead into gold. For what is a humble shoulder or shank or strip of gut if not leaden and unlovely, and what is daube of beef Provençale or osso buco – when every bit of flavor and texture has been coaxed gently by skilled hands – but pure gold? And it's not just magic for the person eating. It can be magic for the chef as well, seeing that tough, veiny, uncooked hunk of meat and bone going into the oven, swimming in purplish and not very distinguished red table wine, then seeing it, smelling it, tasting it only a few hours later, the sauce reduced, a hearty, thick, mellowed, and wonderful witches' brew – transformed.

It's an understanding of this process that raised the French (and Italians) to the forefront of classical cuisine. It's why we love them – even when we hate them. Few sane persons enjoy French pop music – or even the French much – but they know what to do with every scrap of hoof, snout, entrail, and skin, every bit of vegetable trimming, fish head, and bone. Because they grew up with that all-important dictum. *Use everything!* (And use it well.)

Why is that? Why them and not us?

The answer is, in many ways, to be found elsewhere in the world – in Vietnam, Portugal, Mexico, Morocco – because they had to. It was not – in eighteenth- and nineteenth-century France – as it is not today in much of the rest of the world, an option whether to use the nasty bits. You had to.

8

They damn well better have figured out something to do with calf's face, pig's feet, snails, old bread, and all those cheap cuts and trimmings, or they'd go broke, starve, never be able to afford the really good stuff for special occasions. Sauces, marinades, stewing, charcuterie, the invention of the quenelle, the sausage, the cured ham, salted fish, confit – these were strategies, the results of necessity and countless experimentation. Coq au vin? Tough oversized bird, marinated in red wine and braised long enough to be able to be chewed. Pot-au-feu? Boiled tongues, tails, bones, and cheap root vegetables. Pâté? Scraps and trimmings and fat, ground up and seasoned and decorated until somebody was interested in putting it in his mouth. *Confit de canard?* I got no refrigerator and I got no freezer and all these damn duck legs are going bad! Those shrewd and wily French toiled mightily over the years, figuring out ways to make just about everything that grazed, creeped, swam, crawled, or hopped, and every growing thing that poked through soil, rotted on the vine, or hid under dung, into something edible, enjoyable – even magical.

Long after the arrival of the refrigerator, while Americans ate plastic-wrapped fluffy white chicken breasts and denied even the existence of legs or giblets, secure in the certain knowledge that sirloin, filet mignon, and prime rib were really the only 'good' parts of the steer, that everything else was hamburger, the French kept at it like nothing had happened. They'd come to love their hooves and snouts. They'd found something to love in every little bit – if it was done right – and, as with so many cultures on this big planet, they'd come to value, to cherish, the humble, poor man's fare of their past. Merchandising, once a necessary device for the transformation of the inedible to the edible, had fostered an entire cuisine, an approach, a philosophy, a way of life. And magic was the mainstay of the process – a valuable arrow in any cook's quiver, even one playing with thousand-dollar-a-pound white truffles and torchons of foie gras.

Respecting the ingredient may no longer be an economic necessity in much of the emerging world; it is now a pleasure, to be experienced and enjoyed at one's chosen time and place. When everything is just right, a well-made *tête de veau* can be not only a thing to be savored for its challenging yet simple combination of flavors and textures; it can, with the haunting power of sense memory, remind us of times and places long past.

Think about the last time food transported you. You were a kid, had been feeling under the weather all week, and when you were finally getting your appetite back, after a long, wet walk from school in the rain, mom had a big steaming bowl of homemade minestrone waiting for you. Maybe it was just a bowl of Campbell's cream of tomato with Oysterettes, and a grilled cheese sandwich. You know what I mean.

Your first taste of champagne on a woman's lips . . . *steak frites* when you were in Paris as a teenager with a Eurorail pass, you'd blown almost all your dough on hash in Amsterdam, and this slightly chewy slab of *rumsteck* (rump steak) was the first substantial meal in days . . . a single wild strawberry, so flavorful that it nearly took your head off . . . your grandmother's lasagne . . . a first sip of stolen ice-cold beer on a hot summer night, hands smelling of crushed fireflies . . . leftover pork fried rice, because your girlfriend at the time always seemed to have some in the fridge . . . steamer clams, dripping with drawn butter from your first family vacation at the Jersey shore . . . rice pudding from the Fort Lee Diner . . . bad Cantonese when you were a kid and Chinese was still exotic and wonderful and you still thought fortune cookies were fun . . . dirty-water hot dogs . . . a few beads of caviar, licked off a nipple . . .

Nostalgia aside, good ingredients are not to be discounted. One tends to remember vividly one's first really fresh piece of fish, one's first taste of top-quality beluga, an early encounter with truffles, fresh baby peas right out of the pod, a perfectly marbled prime *côte de boeuf*, an introduction to fresh morels, or stuff you'd just never tried before and maybe didn't even know existed, like a hunk of raw *o-toro*, or sea urchin roe. I wanted more memories like these. New ones. I knew time was running out. I was forty-four years old and I'd been basically nowhere. I was becoming a little slower as a line cook, a little bit crankier. When I got swamped on my station, when it seemed sometimes like every order was coming off my sauté station, I began thinking it a conspiracy. The waiters were sandbagging me! Loading up Pops with sauté items, just to see him sweat. Listen to his knees snap crackle pop when he bends down to that lowboy. Look at him, snarling and cursing under his breath – he's losing it! While my Mexican *carnales* soldiered quietly on under mountains of orders, I would rail at the powers that put me in this awful spot. It was getting to me: the pressure, the relentless nature of feeding that bottomless pit of hungry public, of every day sending out food into the Great Unseen Maw in the dining room, only to have to do it again and again, with no end ever in sight. Even my expediting was suffering. I hate admitting this. Because when you're done as an expediter, you are truly fit only for the glue factory (or a consultant's job). The realization came on a busy night at Les Halles, when after screaming loudly, 'Fire table eight!' my Bengali runner, Mohammed, gently nudged my arm and whispered tactfully, even pityingly, 'No, Chef, it's table seven.' I almost cried. My eyes actually filled. I was losing it.

What the hell. I'd eat my way around the world, right? Fearlessly, I'd look for magic in Vietnam, Cambodia, Portugal, Mexico, Morocco – and anywhere else that occurred to me. There would be nothing I would not try. Okay: one thing. My wife, Nancy, already unhappy about me leaving her behind while I flew around the world, told me flat out, 'I hear of you scooping the brains out of some cute little monkey's head while he's still alive? It's divorce court. Got it? And try to lay off the dog and cat. You do still have a conscience, right?'

No problem. The novelty value of tormenting a little monkey (not to mention the risks of some simian spongiform bacteria) did not, to my mind, offset the cruelty factor. I don't know if that even qualifies as a meal.

I would, however, revisit Japan. Do it right this time and try that poisonous blowfish I'd heard about. In France, I'd eat an oyster, fresh out of the water, from the same oyster beds where I'd had my first as a kid – and see if there wasn't some magic to be had there. I wanted to find out if all my cogitating on memory and context was on target or not. I'd go to rural Mexico, to the little town in the state of Puebla, where all my cooks come from, maybe have their moms cook for me, find out how come they're all so damn good at what they do, what the roots of their particular kind of magic powers might be.

When I told my boss at Les Halles, José, about my plans, and that we'd be needing a new chef de cuisine while I bopped around the globe, there was not the weeping and rending of garments and the 'Oh my god! No! Noooo! What will we do without you?' that I'd been secretly hoping for. The first words out of his mouth were, 'Ah! Then you must go to Portugal. I will call my mother and tell her to start fattening a pig.' I cleared my schedule, prepared to cut myself loose from everyone and everything I knew and loved.

Full Disclosure

Here's the part where I reluctantly admit to something about which I'm deeply conflicted – even ashamed. I'd lie about it if I could. But you're probably going to find out about it anyway, so here's a little preemptive truth telling: Almost the entire time I would travel, there would be, somewhere in the vicinity, at least two people with digital cameras. They'd be wearing head-phones. One set of phones would be recording, or at least monitoring, every word, curse, and belch issuing from my mouth. When I went to the bathroom, I would have to remember to turn off the little clip-on mike attached to the transmitter on my hip. I had, you see, sold my soul to the devil.

'We'll follow you around,' said the nice man from the tele-vision production company. 'No lighting equipment, no boom mikes, no script. It'll be very inobtrusive. Just be yourself.'

'It'll be good for the book,' said my editor.

'We'll take twenty-two episodes,' said – God help me – the Food Network.

Okay, it would make things easier. In Russia, for instance, when I wanted access to a Mafiya nightclub, it helped to have television producers from New York Times Television making the arrangements. The words *New York Times*, particularly when traveling in Communist countries like Vietnam, or in de facto dictatorships like Cambodia, tend to open doors that might otherwise remain closed.

But you want to know what it's like making television? Even a completely nonscripted, cinema verité, make-it-up-as-you-go-along travel and food show, where you do whatever the hell you want and hope the cameras can keep up? It's being poked in the head with shotgun mikes so often, you feel like the leading lady in a late 1970s Ron Jeremy flick. There is no halfway. You don't, it turns out, sell out a little bit. Maybe you thought you were just going to show a little ankle – okay, maybe a little calf, too – but in the end, you're taking on the whole front line of the Pittsburgh Steelers on a dirty shag carpet.

There's a punch line to a joke – 'We've already established you're a whore. Now we're just haggling over price' – that fairly describes my predicament. I sold my ass. When I signed on the dotted line, any pretense of virginity or reluctance – of integrity (I don't even remember what *that* is) – vanished. It means when the shooter says, 'Wait a minute,' you wait to enter the restaurant, jump in the river, or light a cigarette, so he can get the shot. When they want you to enter the restaurant again, shake hands with the owner, tell him how delighted you are to be eating fish head at his establishment – even though you just did that five minutes ago, when you meant it – you do it.

I've had a lot of fun trashing Emeril and Bobby and the Food Network's stable of stars over the last few years. God, I hated their shows. Now I've gone over to the dark side, too. Watching Emeril bellowing catchphrases at his wildly barking seal-like studio audience, I find myself feeling empathy for the guy. Because I know, I think, how it happened. One sells one's soul in increments, slowly, over time. First, it's a simple travel show ('Good for the book!'). Next thing you know, you're getting dry-humped by an ex-wrestler on the Spice Channel.

I don't want you to think I don't like the camera crews that followed me around the world. As TV people go, they were pretty damn cool. Most of them had been shooting documentaries in hospital emergency rooms and trauma units before coming aboard my project, so they knew how to stay out of the way in crowded kitchens and how to behave around people with knives. They ate the same terrifying food. They stayed in the same at-times-septic hotels I did. They braved minefields and roadblocks to get their shots. They stood close, cameras running while, drunk off my ass, I wildly and irresponsibly discharged automatic weapons and high explosives. They froze when I froze, suffered the antimalarial drugs, the food poisoning, the bugs, the vegetarians that I had to. When challenged by locals to contests involving tequila, they did not let the side down. As I, from time to time, crawled, vomiting into some drainage culvert, so did they. They, too, were showered with blood, watched pig-fisting, throat-slitting, force-feeding – and filmed every second. They managed to shoot all day in Gordon Ramsay's kitchen without causing injury to themselves or others. And they did it with considerable good humor. But when you hear me carping about how lonely and sick and frightened I am, holed up in some Cambodian backwater, know that there's a television crew a few doors down the hall. That changes things.

All told, however, the writing of this book has been the greatest adventure of my life. Cooking professionally is hard. Traveling around the world, writing, eating, and making a television show is relatively easy. It beats brunch.

WHERE FOOD COMES FROM

'THE PIG IS GETTING fat. Even as we speak,' said José months later. From the very moment I informed my boss of my plans to eat my way around the world, another living creature's fate was sealed on the other side of the Atlantic. True to his word, José had called his mother in Portugal and told her to start fattening a pig.

I'd heard about this pig business before – anytime José would hear me waxing poetic about my privileged position as one of the few vendors of old-school hooves and snouts, French charcuterie and offal. Chefs adore this kind of stuff. We like it when we can motivate our customers to try something they might previously have found frightening or repellent. Whether it's a stroke to our egos or a genuine love of that kind of rustic, rural, French brasserie soul food (the real stuff – not that tricked-out squeeze-bottle chicanery with the plumage), we love it. It makes us proud and happy to see our customers sucking the marrow out of veal bones, munching on pig's feet, picking over oxtails or beef cheeks. It gives us purpose in life, as if we've done something truly good and laudable that day, brought beauty, hope, enlightenment to our dining rooms and a quiet sort of honor to ourselves and our profession.

'First, we fatten the pig . . . for maybe six months. Until he is ready. Then in the winter – it must be the winter, so it is cold enough – we kill the pig. Then we cook the heart and the tenderloin for the butchers. Then we eat. We eat everything. We make hams and sausage, stews, casseroles, soup. We use' – José stressed this – 'every part.'

'It's kind of a big party,' interjected Armando, the preeminent ball-busting waiter and senior member of our Portuguese contingent at Les Halles.

'You've heard of this?' I asked skeptically. I like Armando – and he's a great waiter – but what he says is sometimes at variance with the truth. He likes it when middle-aged ladies from the Midwest come to the restaurant and ask for me, wanting to get their books signed. He sidles over and whispers in confidential tones, 'You know, of course, that the chef is gay? My longtime companion . . . a wonderful man. Wonderful.' That's Armando's idea of fun.

'Oh yes!' he said. 'Everyone does it in my town. Maybe once a year. It's a tradition. It goes back to the Middle Ages. Long time.'

'And you eat everything?'

'Everything. The blood. The guts. The ears. Everything. It's delicious.' Armando looked way too happy remembering this. 'Wait! We don't eat everything. The pig's bladder? We blow it up, inflate it, and we make a soccer ball for the children.'

'What's with the soccer ball?' I asked David, also Portuguese, our bar manager and a trusted friend. He shrugged, not wanting to contradict his countryman.

'That's in the north,' he said. 'But I've seen it.'

'You've seen it?'

David nodded and gave me a warning look that said, You don't know what you're in for. 'There's a lot of blood. And the pig makes a lot of noise when you . . . you know . . . kill it. A *lot* of noise.'

'You can hear the screams in the next village,' Armando said, grinning.

'Yeah? Well, I'll bring you the bladder, bro,' I said, deciding right then and there that I was going to do this, travel to Portugal and take part in a medieval pig slaughter. Listening to José's description, it sounded kinda cool. A bunch of villagers hanging out, drinking, killing things and eating them. There was no mistaking José's enthusiasm for the event. I was in.

Understand this about me – and about most chefs, I'm guessing: For my entire professional career, I've been like Michael

Corleone in *The Godfather, Part II*, ordering up death over the phone, or with a nod or a glance. When I want meat, I make a call, or I give my sous-chef, my butcher, or my charcutier a look and they make the call. On the other end of the line, my version of Rocco, Al Neary, or Lucca Brazzi either does the job himself or calls somebody else who gets the thing done. Sooner or later, somewhere – whether in the Midwest, or upstate New York, or on a farm in rural Pennsylvania, or as far away as Scotland – something dies. Every time I have picked up the phone or ticked off an item on my order sheet, I have basically caused a living thing to die. What arrives in my kitchen, however, is not the bleeding, still-warm body of my victim, eyes open, giving me an accusatory look that says, 'Why me, Tony? Why me?' I don't have to see that part. The only evidence of my crimes is the relatively antiseptic boxed or plastic-wrapped appearance of what is inarguably meat. I had never, until I arrived on a farm in northern Portugal, had to look my victim in the face – much less watched at close range – as he was slaughtered, disembow-eled, and broken down into constituent parts. It was only fair, I figured, that I should have to watch as the blade went in. I'd been vocal, to say the least, in my advocacy of meat, animal fat, and offal. I'd said some very unkind things about vegetarians. Let me find out what we're all talking about, I thought. I would learn – really learn – where food actually comes from.

It's always a tremendous advantage when visiting another country, especially when you're as uninformed and ill-prepared as I was, to be the guest of a native. You can usually cut right to the good stuff, live close to the ground, experience the place from a perspective as close to local as you're likely to get. And José Meirelles makes the word *foodie* or *gourmet* woefully inade-quate. José comes from a large family that, like its prodigal son, loves food. He went to New York, became a cook, and chef, and then made a rather spectacular success in the restaurant busi-ness. José may be quite comfortable, even passionate, about dining at Ducasse or swapping recipes with Boulud or cooking at James Beard House or trying out hot new restaurants in Manhattan, but you've got to see him at his family's dinner table, eating *bucho recheado* (stuffed pig's stomach), to see him at his happiest and most engaged. From my vantage point behind the line at Les Halles, I was always intrigued by the look of pure joy on José's face as he'd plow through my kitchen (usually leaving a wake of destruction), hurriedly assembling a Portuguese-style cassoulet: a heap of *boudin noir*, chorizo, pig's feet, pork belly and jowl with white beans baked in a pastry-topped earthenware dish. I was disarmed and bemused by his insistence on buying salt cod for our *brandade de morue* only from the Ironbound section of Newark, where there's a large Portuguese population, and presumably they know about such things. His mania about top-quality fresh codfish (I'd never seen José yell until a seafood purveyor sent us cod that he found wanting), his love of high-test canned tuna in olive oil, white anchovies, costly sea salt, specially chiffonaded kale, dried chorizo, fresh and only fresh, wildly expensive whole cumin seeds from Kalyustan – all this made my food costs jump every time José walked through the door. He'd insist I buy specialty items for a rigorously French brasserie, things I'd have no idea what to do with; he'd get sudden compulsions to call D'Artagnan in the middle of the night and buy whole free-range pigs. For the first few months working with the guy, it used to irritate me. What was I going to do with all that quince jelly and weird sheep's milk cheese? What the hell is Superbock beer? José would go into these fugue states, and the next thing you knew, I'd have buckets of salted codfish tongues soaking in my walk-in. You know how hard it is to sell codfish tongues on Park Avenue?

And he talked continually about the pig slaughter – as if it were the World Series, the Super Bowl, the World Cup, and a Beatles reunion all rolled into one. I had to take his enthusiasm seriously. Not just because he's the boss but also because along with all that Portuguese stuff that would mysteriously arrive came food that even I knew to be good. Food I could identify and understand as being part of a tradition of glorious excess, French-style: fresh white asparagus, truffles in season, Cavaillon melons, fresh morels, translucent baby eels, Scottish wild hare, gooey, smelly, runny French cheeses, screamingly fresh turbot and Dover sole, yanked out of the Channel yesterday and flown (business class, I think, judging from the price) to my kitchen doors. I had more than enough evidence that José knew how to eat. If he told me that killing and eating a whole pig was something I absolutely shouldn't and couldn't miss, I believed him. It's very hard to not be hungry after talking to José for any length of time.

So it was with a mixture of excitement, curiosity, and dread that I woke up on a cold, misty morning in Portugal and looked out the window of my room at orderly rows of leafless grape-vines, the fires from distant hearths issuing smoke into a gray sky over the valley. Where I was staying was a bed-and-breakfast, a seventeenth-century *quinta* (a private home turned country inn) about half a mile from the Meirelles farm. It was set back from a twisting country road, past an arbor, surrounded by fields and orange groves and mountains, looking in every way as it must have four hundred years ago. Three young women looked after a few guests. There was a chapel, and a large dark country kitchen with a constantly burning wood fire and a long table. A vast carbon-blackened hooded chimney allowed most of the smoke to escape. The predominant smell in Portugal, I had quickly found, is wood smoke. The only source of heat in the large house – in my room, as well – was a burning fire. When I'd arrived late the previous night, there was one going in my room, creating a nice toasty zone, just large enough to undress and climb into the high four-poster bed. José's family, in addition to their farm, have a home in nearby Amarante, and another residence in Oporto.

By the time I'd arrived here, I'd already gotten the picture that Portugal has plenty of good stuff to eat. I'd eaten head of *merluza* (a sort of oversized whiting), roast kid goat cooked in an old wood-burning oven, the doors sealed with plaster (they used to be sealed with cow dung), an incredible octopus risotto, and, of course, *bacalao, bacalao, bacalao* (salted cod-fish). I'd spent a night in a roundhouse on a mountaintop in the Douro Valley, awakened in a torrential rainstorm to descend quickly (before the roads washed out) to a *quinta* at the bottom, where I had roast loin of pork, potatoes roasted in pork fat, and azeito cheese. I'd visited the open markets in Oporto, where I'd met fishwives whose skills with profanity would put any cook of my experience to shame. With José translating, I'd listened for a while to the back-and-forth between fishwives and customers, amazed that sixty-five-year-old ladies who looked like Martha Washington could make me blush.

On the day of the slaughter, we drove to the Meirelles farm, a stone and mortar farmhouse with upstairs living quarters, downstairs kitchen and dining area and adjacent larder. Across a dirt drive were animal pens, smokehouse, and a sizable barn. José's father and cousin grow grapes, from which they make wine, and raise a few chickens, turkeys, geese, and pigs. A few hectares of grapevines and multiuse plots of land stretched over gracefully sloping fields beneath tree-covered hills and mountains, a few church spires and smoking chimneys just visible among leaves and branches.

It was early morning when I arrived, but there was already a large group assembled: José's brother Francisco, his other brother, also Francisco (remember the wedding scene in *Goodfellas*, where everybody's named Petey or Paul or Marie?), his mother, father, assorted other relatives, farmhands, women and children – most of whom were already occupied with the early preparations for two solid days of cooking and eating. Standing by the barn were three hired assassins, itinerant slaughterers/butchers, who apparently knock off from their day jobs from time to time to practice their much-called-upon skills with pig killing and pork butchering. They were a likable bunch: a red-cheeked old man in vest and shirtsleeves, sporting a black brim hat and dapper mustache, two younger men in sweaters and waterproof boots. Looking amiable and unthreatening, they shook my hand over early-morning glasses of *vino verde*, a barely fermented white wine made from the family grapes.

Cousin Francisco positioned a sequence of bottle rockets and aerial bombs in the dirt outside the farmhouse and, one after the other, let them fly. The explosions rocked through the valley, announcing to all who could hear news of the imminent slaughter – and meal to follow.

'Is that a warning to vegetarians?' I asked José.

'There are no vegetarians in Portugal,' he said.

The mustachioed man I took to be the chief assassin – he was holding the knife, a nasty-looking blade with a slot in the middle and a wooden handle – began his approach to the barn. Everyone joined in the expedition, a look of neither sadness nor glee on their faces. Only José's expression was readable. He was watching me, a wry smile on his face, curious, I was guessing, as to how I'd react to what was about to happen.

At the far end of the barn, a low door was opened into a small straw-filled pen. A monstrously large, aggressive-looking pig waggled and snorted as the crowd peered in. When he was joined in the confined space by the three hired hands, none of them bearing food, he seemed to get the idea that nothing good was going to be happening anytime soon, and he began scrambling and squealing at tremendous volume.

I was already unhappy with what I was seeing. I'm causing this to happen, I kept thinking. This pig has been hand-fed for six months, fattened up, these murderous goons hired – for me. Perhaps, had I said when José first suggested this blood feast, 'Uh no . . . I don't think so. I don't think I'll be able to make it this time around,' maybe the outcome for Porky here would have been different. Or would it have been? Why was I being so squeamish? This pig's number was up the second he was born. You can't milk a pig! Nobody's gonna keep him as a pet! This is Portugal, for Chrissakes! This porker was boots and bacon from birth.

Still, he was my pig. I was responsible. For a guy who'd spent twenty-eight years serving dead animals and sneering at vegetarians, I was having an unseemly amount of trouble getting with the program. I had to suck it up. I could do this. There was already plenty in my life to feel guilty about. This would be just one more thing.

It took four strong men, experts at this sort of thing, to restrain the pig, then drag and wrestle him up onto his side and onto a heavy wooden horse cart. It was not easy. With the weight of two men pinning him down and another holding his hind legs, the main man with the knife, gripping him by the head, leaned over and plunged the knife all the way into the beast's thorax, just above the heart. The pig went wild. The screaming penetrated the fillings in my teeth, echoed through the valley. With an incredible shower of fresh blood flying in every direction, the shrieking, squealing, struggling animal heaved himself off the cart, forcefully kicking one of his tormentors in the groin repeatedly. Spraying great gouts of blood, the pig fought mightily, four men desperately attempting to gain purchase on his kicking legs, bucking abdomen, and blood-smeared rearing head.

They finally managed to wrestle the poor beast back up onto the cart again, the guy with the mustache working the blade back and forth like a toilet plunger. The pig's movements slowed, but the rasping and wheezing, the loud breathing and gurgling, continued . . . and continued . . . the animal's chest rising and falling noisily . . . continued and continued . . . for what seemed like a fucking eternity.

I'll always remember, as one does in moments of extremis, the tiny, innocuous details – the blank expressions on the children's faces, the total lack of affect. They were farm kids who'd seen this before many times. They were used to the ebb and flow of life, its at-times-bloody passing. The look on their little faces could barely be described as interest. A passing bus or an ice-cream truck would probably have evoked more reaction. I'll always remember the single dot of blood on the chief assassin's forehead. It remained there for the rest of the day, above a kindly rosy-cheeked face – an eerily incongruous detail on an otherwise-grandfatherly visage. Imagine your Aunt Minnie bringing you a plate of cookies as you sat in front of the TV, a string of human molars strung casually, like pearls, around her neck. I'll remember the atmosphere of business as usual that hung over the whole process as the pig's chest rose and fell, his blood draining noisily into a metal pail. A woman cook came running for the blood, hurrying to the kitchen with it after it stopped draining freely, the death and killing just another chore. More women walked briskly to and from the kitchen with other receptacles. Food was being prepared. And I'll never forget the look of pride on José's face, as if he were saying, This, this is where it all starts. Now you know. This is where food comes from.

He was right, of course. I'm sure that had I just seen a thoroughbred being inseminated, a cow being milked, a steer being castrated, or a calf breeched, I would have been equally ill at ease. I was a pathetic city boy, all too comfortable with my ignorance of the facts, seeing for the first time what was usually handled on the Discovery Channel (just after I changed the channel).

The horse cart, with the now-dead pig aboard, was wheeled around the corner of the barn to a more open area, where his every surface was singed with long bundles of burning straw. All the animal's hair was burned off, a time-consuming process that left black streaks and patches on his thick skin. He was then scrubbed and washed with cork, scrubbed again, and then – another brief but horrible Kodak moment.

I was smoking and trying to look cool, as if what I'd just seen hadn't bothered me at all. The pig was positioned head away, hind legs and butt pointed in my direction. Global Alan, one of the shooters for the TV crew, was standing next to me, shooting from a crouch as the men washed and rinsed the pig's upper body. Suddenly and without warning, one of the men stepped around and, with the beast's nether regions regrettably all too apparent, plunged his bare hand up to the elbow in the pig's rectum, then removed it, holding a fistful of steaming pig shit – which he flung, unceremoniously, to the ground with a loud *splat* before repeating the process.

Global Alan, professional that he is, veteran of countless emergency-room documentaries, never flinched. He kept shooting. You never know, I guess, what footage you might just be required to have during the editing process, but I had a hard time imagining the 'Pig-fisting' scene on the Food Network.

Alan just kept shooting as the man quickly cut a perianal moat, yanked out about a foot of intestine, and tied it into a dainty knot. Under his breath, Alan's only comment was, 'Oh yeah . . . that's in the show.' When I looked over at him, he tapped the side of his camera and added, 'Video gold, baby, video gold . . . I smell Emmy!'

'This is on cable,' I pointed out.

'An Ace, then,' said Alan. 'I want to thank the Academy . . .'

The pig was wheeled into the barn, his legs tied in a spread-eagle position, and the carcass was hung from an overhead crossbeam, to much grunting and exertion from the butchers. The animal's belly was now split open from crotch to throat, his back, on both sides of the spine, cut and allowed to bleed out, and his still-steaming entrails pulled gently out of his abdomen and placed on a wide plywood board to be sorted. God help me, I assisted, stepping right in and putting my hands inside the warm cavity, pulling away heart, lungs, tripe, intestines, liver, and kidneys and letting them slide wetly onto the board.

Have you ever seen *Night of the Living Dead*, the black-and-white original version? Remember the ghouls playing with freshly removed organs, dragging them eagerly into their mouths in a hideous orgy of slurping and moaning? That scene came very much to mind as we all sifted quickly through the animal's guts, putting heart, liver, and the tenderloin aside for immediate use, reserving the large and small intestines for washing, separating out the tripe, kidneys, lungs – and bladder. Just as Armando had promised, the bladder was indeed inflated, tied at one end, and hung in the smokehouse to toughen up a bit.

The intestines were taken to a large trough, where for the next few hours a woman in an apron washed them inside and out. Later, they'd be used for sausages. The now-clean, white body cavity was washed with red wine to inhibit bacterial growth and my victim left to hang there in the cold barn overnight, a pail below.

It was time to eat.

A tablecloth was laid over a small table in the barn, only a few feet from the recently departed, and men and women brought a snack for the hardworking butchers and their helpers. The chief assassin whipped out a battered squeeze box and began to play, singing in Portuguese. *Vino verde* was poured. A frittata-like creation of egg, chorizo, and onions appeared. There was a bowl of cooked beans – like favas, but garbanzo-colored – which you had to slip out of their skins before popping them into your mouth. This was accompanied by a little grilled liver, olives, and sheep's milk cheese. A select group of pig killers and relatives gathered round to eat, a slight rain falling outside the barn doors. The old man with the squeeze box, that drop of blood still on his forehead, began a melodic address, what could only be described as Portuguese barnyard rap, an homage to the pig. On such occasions, the words change to reflect the individual circumstances of each particular pig, celebrating its transformation from livestock to lunch, and challenging others present to join in with their own verses.

While I can't remember the exact lyrics – as translated by José – I can tell you with some assurance that the words of the first verses went something like this:

> *This pig was a strong one*
> *He didn't want to die*
> *He kicked and he struggled*
> *Sprayed blood in my eye*

Looking around the barn, the old man continued playing, throwing it out to the crowd:

> *I'm needing some help here*
> *I can't do it again*
> *Will one of you bastards*
> *Step right on in*

At which point, one of his helpers indeed chimed right in with:

> *This beast was a pisser*
> *A pig with some guts*
> *When Luis stabbed him*
> *He kicked me right in the nuts*

This went on for quite a while, accompanied by much eating and drinking. I tried to eat lightly – a difficult thing to do in Portugal.

A few hours later, we gathered around two large tables in the farmhouse for a hearty lunch of *caldo verde*, kale soup. Very different from the chunky soup studded with potatoes, kale, beans, and sausage that I remember from my early days on Cape Cod. 'That's Azores people's food,' said José. This was a smoother concoction of chorizo-flavored kale, potato, and stock, the potatoes cooked to the point of near emulsification with the finely chiffonaded kale. No discernible chunks and a subtler flavor.

There must have been thirty assorted family members, friends, farmhands, and neighbors crowded into the stone-walled room. Every few minutes, as if summoned by some telepathic signal, others arrived: the family priest, the mayor of the town, children, many bearing more food – pastries, *aguardiente* (brandy), loaves of mealy, heavy, brown, delicious Portuguese bread. We ate slices of grilled heart and liver, a gratin of potato and *bacalao*, the grilled and sliced tenderloin of our victim, and sautéed *grelos* (a broccoli rabe-like green vegetable), all accompanied by wine, wine, and more wine, José's father's red joining the weaker *vino verde* and a local *aguardiente* so powerful, it was like drinking rocket fuel. This was followed by an incredibly tasty flan made with sugar, egg yolks, and rendered pork fat, and a spongy orange cake. I lurched away from the table after a few hours feeling like Elvis in Vegas – fat, drugged, and completely out of it.

At the tables, the locals, having yet to finish this meal, were already planning the next one. The Portuguese, if you haven't gathered this already, like to eat. They like it a lot. 'You can see why we don't really eat breakfast in Portugal,' joked José. The word *svelte* does not come to mind a lot when in Portugal, either as a description or as a desirable goal. One is not shy about second helpings.

A few hours later, at José's parents' house, I was already well into dinner, the other guests yet more members of the Meirelles's extended family. We started off with freshly toasted almonds from the farm, pickled pearl onions, fried baby sardines, marinated olives and pickles, then moved quickly on to *rojoes papas de sarabuhlo* – an amazing soup of bread, stock, fresh cumin, bits of pork, and blood. The blood had been simmered earlier at the farm, until it formed a congealed cake, somewhat like *boudin*, grainy and pudding-textured. Whisked into the soup, it was fabulous. I knew now why José had always insisted on thickening coq au vin with fresh pork blood. We had pork confit with potatoes. We ate *alheiras* (a lightly smoked pork sausage) followed by *bucho recheado*. I was loving this, although hoping for the assistance of a gurney to get me back to my bed when it was all over.

We got together again the next day for lunch back at the farm. But first, there was work to be done. The pig was cut down, the legs put aside for cured hams. We rubbed them with sea salt, pepper, and garlic, then packed them into a crate in the larder, buried in more salt. The center-cut *poitrine* was laid on top of the salt for a lighter cure. The hams would be removed in a month, then hung, smoked, and dried. Meat was cut large for one kind of chorizo, small for another, then left to hang in the smokehouse. As we broke down the pig, José's mother hovered, selecting the cuts she'd need for lunch.

Lunch was *cozido*, a sort of Portuguese version of pot-au-feu: boiled cabbage, carrots, turnips, and confited head, snout, and feet. José made sure I got a hefty portion of each part – and I've got to say, pork fat never tasted so good. As is customary, the double-starch rule was disregarded. Both rice and potatoes appeared as sides. Dessert was something called 'bacon from heaven,' made, unsurprisingly, of yet more egg yolks, along with sugar and ground almonds. I felt as if I were going to explode. When I was invited to kick around the old bladder ball by the farmhand's kids, they scored off me at will. I could barely move.

Dinner was a casserole of tripe and beans. Ordinarily, I don't like tripe much. I think it smells like wet sheepdog. But José's mother's version, spicy, heavily jacked with fresh cumin, was delicious. I mopped up every bite, José demonstrating the

Portuguese way to crumble that thick country bread onto the plate, add a little olive oil, and smash every vestige of remaining sauce and scrap into a tasty, greasy, wonderful paste before shoveling it into your mouth.

I learned a lot about my boss in Portugal, and I had some really good meals. I learned, for the first time, that I could indeed look my food in the eyes before eating it – and I came away from the experience, I hope, with considerably more respect for what we call 'the ingredient.' I am more confirmed than ever in my love for pork, pork fat, and cured pork. And I am less likely to waste it. That's something I owe the pig for. I know now what a pork chop costs in terms of the living, breathing thing that was killed to supply it. I learned to really enjoy tripe – and that there is no part of the animal's anatomy with which I'm uncomfortable – though I don't think I'll be kicking bladder around Riverside Park anytime in the near future. I learned that in José's Portugal, they never stray far from what they've always known to be good. It's been over a century since anyone needed to cure codfish in salt, for instance, but they still love it. Because it's good. If you joke with José, and say, 'José! It's all pork, *bacalao*, pork, *bacalao*, egg yolks, pork – and more *bacalao*,' he'll probably raise an eyebrow, smile, and say, 'Yes? So? What's wrong with that?'.

Portugal was the beginning, where I began to notice the things that were missing from the average American dining experience. The large groups of people who ate together. The family element. The seemingly casual cruelty that comes with living close to your food. The fierce resistance to change – if change comes at the expense of traditionally valued dishes. I'd see this again and again, in other countries far from Portugal.

And I'd seen an animal die. It changed me. I didn't feel good about it. It was, in fact, unpleasant in the extreme. I felt guilty, a little bit ashamed. I felt bad for that pig, imagining his panic, pain, and fear. But he'd tasted delicious. We'd wasted maybe eight ounces of his total weight.

It would be easier next time.

BACK TO THE BEACH

MY YOUNGER BROTHER, CHRIS, is about as different from me as anyone can be. While I've spent my whole life living a hand-to-mouth existence, paycheck to paycheck, letting the good times roll, not giving a fuck, a rapidly aging, now-aged hipster, Chris has always been the responsible one, the good son. He never smoked weed. He certainly never did drugs. His hair was never, ever too long or too short for the times. He graduated from an Ivy League school – probably (if I know him) with distinction. I've never seen him roaring or staggering drunk. He saved, and continues to save, his money, never having wasted it on a fast car or a loose woman or (as in my case) some cool-looking high-tech surveillance equipment, which looked good in the catalog when under the influence. He owns a house in Westchester, has a beautiful wife and two adorable, bright, and well-behaved children. If he doesn't drive a Volvo, he probably should. His job, as best as I can understand it, is as a currency specialist for a bank; I think what he does is fly around and advise various South American, European, and Asian investors when to drop dollars and buy yen, when to trade deutsche marks for baht or dong or drachmas. If there's an evil streak in there, I have yet to find it. And I've been looking my entire life.

Chris has no particular reason to love me. I bullied him without mercy as a child, tried, in a fit of jealous rage, to bludgeon him to death as an infant (fortunately for us both, my chosen instrument was a balloon), blamed him constantly for crimes of which I was invariably the true perpetrator, then stood by and listened gleefully as he was spanked and interrogated. He was forced to watch the endlessly unfolding psychodrama at the dinner table when I'd show up late, stoned, belligerent, a miserable, sullen, angry older brother with shoulder-length hair and a bad attitude, who thought Abbie Hoffman and Eldridge Cleaver had it about right – that my parents were fascist tools, instruments of the imperialist jackboot, that their love was what was holding me back from all those psychedelic drugs, free love, and hippie-chick pussy I should have been getting had I not been twelve years old and living at home. The fights, the screaming matches, the loud torments of my painful and pain-inducing early adolescence – he saw it all. And it probably screwed him up good. On the plus side, however, I had taught the little bastard to read by the time he was in kindergarten. And I did keep my mouth shut when he finally decided he'd had enough and coshed me over the head with a pig-iron window counterweight.

There were, I guess, at least some good memories of growing up with Tony, and I think our summers in France as kids might have provided some of them. Each of us had been, for most of those times, the only English-speaking company the other had had. We hung out together, explored the little town of La Teste, spent hours playing army with little green plastic men in the back garden of my aunt's house there. We traded *bandes dessinées*, Tintins, Lucky Lukes, and Asterixes, played with firecrackers, and, when really bored, ganged up on my poor mother. Surprisingly or not, over the years we've become very close. When I suggested a trip together down memory lane, Chris didn't hesitate.

'Let's do it,' he said. It was probably the most madcap thing he's ever done.

The idea was to leave our loved ones behind and, just the two of us, reexperience the France of our youth. We'd visit the house in La Teste. We'd eat in all the same places in town, and in neighboring Arcachon. We'd go out at the crack of dawn to the oyster parks in the *bassin* where I'd enjoyed my first all-important oyster and had my first real food-related epiphany. (Chris actually ate and liked the tasty bivalves now.) We'd climb the dune of Pyla again, gorge on sugary pastries (without having to ask permission), drink as much Bordeaux as we pleased, buy lots and lots of firecrackers and throw them into the German blockhouses we'd played in as kids at the beach. Who could hinder our good time now? Who could stop us?

We'd gorge on *saucisson à l'ail, soupe de poisson*, big bowls of hot chocolate with buttery baguettes – and we'd drink as many Kronenbourgs and La Belles and Stellas as we damned well pleased. I was forty-four; Chris was forty-one. We were grown-ups now: a respected currency analyst and a best-selling author. Our mother was in New York and had decades ago given up trying to correct our behavior. Our father, though never really a disciplinarian, had died back in the eighties. We could do whatever we wanted. We were free to act like children again. It was the perfect way and the perfect place, I thought, to look for the perfect meal, in our old stomping grounds near the beaches of southwest France.

We met in Saint-Jean-de-Luz, Chris coming from Switzerland, I from Portugal. Together, we drove in a rented car to Arcachon, stopping only for *gaufres*, the hot waffles covered with powdered sugar, which we'd gotten as a postbeach treat as kids. We could eat as many as we wanted now. It's mostly flatland in the southwest – mile after mile of pine trees, planted over a century ago to dry up the mosquito-infested marshes and to keep the long strip of seaside dunes from burying the interior in sand. There's not a lot to look at, but we were happy enough recognizing the familiar names on the signs, smelling French diesel fuel again, getting closer and closer to a place we hadn't been to together in over twenty-eight years.

It was night when we arrived in Arcachon, the summer resort town next door to the tiny oyster village of La Teste-de-Buch. It was January, about as off-season as off-season can be: cold, windy, with a constant drizzle of penetrating, bone-chilling rain. When considering the heady, sentimental, exciting implications of recapturing the past, I'd overlooked such earthly matters as temperature and precipitation – and the fact that we'd very likely be freezing our asses off in a boarded-up ghost town. We checked into a dark, drafty clapboard and chintz House of Horrors hotel on the water, an insane tchotchke-filled barn, decorated with Art Deco stained glass, fake Tiffany lamps, Austro-Hungarian figurines, moldy carpets, rococo furniture, and absolutely no other guests. Picture Norman Bates operating a 'romantic getaway' in the Catskills, off an old, no-longer-used highway, and you'll get the idea. *Depressing* is not sufficient to describe it. Outside my window, beyond a concrete patio and a pool filled with floating clumps of dead leaves, the Bay of Biscay lay flat and gray, a few fishing boats scudding along its surface, the beach empty except for a few gulls, the lights of Cap Ferret winking in the black distance across the water.

The first night, I slept badly, dreaming of my aunt, Tante Jeanne, yelling at me for throwing firecrackers into the out-house: '*Défendu! Prison!*' she shrieked. Even my dreams seemed penetrated by the smell of dank, musty upholstered chairs and the peeling pink wallpaper.

Chris woke up looking cheerful and excited. Not me. I declined breakfast in the hotel, wondering when they'd seen their last guest – and if he'd survived the experience. My brother and I hurried to the station and took the short ride to La Teste. It may not have been summer, and we may well have been two silly old farts bundled up to our chins, but for a few moments of anticipation, after stepping off the train, we might have been kids again. Neither of us had said a word the whole way, only smiled, a giddy inability to put into words what we both were feeling. Just standing there on the platform, I felt for a· brief moment as if it really were 1966 again. The bare telephone pole that I'd shimmied up as a kid to win a chocolate bar during the Fête du Port was still there in the square in front of the station. The port, with its sagging moorings and old-style *pinasses* (flat-bottomed fishing boats), the oyster boats, the two-story cinder-block and stucco homes with their red tile roofs – all looked exactly the same.

Shoulder to shoulder, we strolled down empty streets under a cold gray sky, doing our best to ignore a quiet mist of rain. 'It's this way,' said Chris in a hushed voice. 'Past the fire station and the gendarmerie.'

'I can't believe I'm here,' I said. 'I can't believe it.'

We found rue Jules Favre just where we'd left it, and after one block, then two: our house. Or what used to be our house. The driveway had changed. It being winter, there were no roses blooming in the front garden beyond the hedges. The wooden shed to the right, where my father had posed for a photograph as a little boy – in beret and short shorts – where my brother and I later posed (in the same much-hated outfits), was still there. But the swinging gate we'd leaned upon, trying desperately to look cool, or at least less ridiculous, was gone. The house where our neighbor, the oyster fisherman, Monsieur Saint-Jour, had lived had been torn down and a new home erected in its place. The house my uncle Gustave had begun before his death (I remembered clearing bricks with him) was much the same. Beyond a new white picket fence and well-trimmed hedges stood our old summer home. There were a few seconds of stillness as Chris and I peered over the gate.

'That was my room,' said Chris, pointing to a window on the second floor.

'Mine was across the hall,' I whispered.

'Yeah. You got the better one.'

'I'm bigger.'

'Tante Jeanne and Oncle Gustave were downstairs there.'

'Why are we whispering?' I muttered.

'Should we knock on the door?'

'You go. Your French is better. I want to see the back garden.'

My brother hesitantly approached the house and rang the bell. Soon, the current owner emerged, a short older man, completely unfazed by the appearance of two tall, goofy-looking Americans and a camera-toting TV crew in the middle of winter. After a brief chat with Chris, he agreed to let us look over the old place, leading us around the side, through an old gate, to the rear patio and garden area, where Chris and I had played as kids: trapping lizards, exterminating snails, re-creating D-Day with our little army men. Beyond a low wall was a table where Tante Jeanne had served us *salade de tomate*, potato omelettes, steamed mussels, sautéed sole, buttery *haricots verts*, those big bowls of hot chocolate, and Bananya. The hand-cranked water pump was gone, and the old well from which it drew long plugged. The chipped ceramic pitcher we'd had to fill before visiting the outhouse was, of course, no longer there, but the outhouse still stood, and the compost heap behind it. Next to it, the lone American-style bathroom in southwest France, which my mother had insisted on building. Next to that, the outdoor fish kitchen and shed, where I'd stashed my Kronenbourgs and cigarettes as a twelve-year-old. The stone archway and heavy wooden door were still there, leading to a back alley. And around front, the garage, where my uncle had kept a 1930s Citroën sedan up on blocks, and his wine cellar – much the same. The garden was all grass now.

'Think there are still little plastic army men buried in there?' I asked.

'Unquestionably,' said Chris. 'Probably still raise a company at least.'

We didn't go inside. It would have been too . . . weird. I often have nightmares about returning to our old house in New Jersey and finding strangers sleeping in my bed. I didn't want to experience that for real.

'I'm kinda excited . . . and kinda bummed out,' I confessed to Chris as we walked slowly out.

'Yeah. Me, too,' said Chris. 'Let's get some *pain raisin* around the corner at the *boulangerie*. It's gotta still be there.'

We had one bit of unfinished business on the property. Assuming the position, we posed for a photograph, roughly where we'd stood as children so many summers ago. We had on no berets this time, thank God. And we were both, without any possibility of argument, finally old enough for long pants.

Le stade muncipal (the stadium), where we'd watched the young men from the town chase and be chased by bulls, and *la forêt* (the forest), where the menacing hermit had lived, appeared to be housing developments now. The vacation homes with their summery names like Le Week-end and La Folie were shuttered and forlorn-looking in their emptiness.

We walked down the middle of rue Jules Favre, turned a

corner, and found the *boulangerie* still open. Entering with the customary '*Bonjour, madame*,' we were greeted with a warm, sweet-smelling waft – brioches, and baguettes baking. We bought a bag of *pain raisin* – the sticky raisin Danishes we'd had so often as kids – a baguette, a croissant, and a brioche, eager to try it all, to see if it tasted the same.

'The same,' said Chris, exuberant.

I was not so thrilled. Something was holding me back. The baked goods, after all this time, were identical in taste and appearance. The shop smelled just as it had twenty-eight years ago. But something was missing.

There was once a little café around the corner called Café Central. It had become our default dinner of choice on those nights when my mother had not felt like cooking or when we'd been unable to agree on where to go or what to eat. It had been a simple neighborhood joint with chipped plaster and white-washed walls, football posters, a few local fishermen drinking *vin ordinaire* in the small dining room. I had fond, maybe overly fond, memories of their dark brown *soupe de poisson*, their clumsy but delicious *crudités variées*, their *bavette à l'échalote* (flank steak with shallots) with limp but tasty *frites*.

It was called Le Bistro now, and it had been decidedly gussied up. There were candles on the tables, tablecloths, framed paintings of oyster boats on the pastel-colored walls, furniture that didn't wobble. But the fish soup was the same: dark brown, flecked with shreds of fish, milled bone, redolent of saffron, garlic, and anise; it was accompanied, just as I'd remembered, by little fried croutons, grated Gruyère cheese, and a little crock of rouille, the garlic and pepper mayonnaise. It was delicious. My first taste in almost thirty years of a soup that had seriously inspired me in my professional life. As a young chef, I had toiled mightily to re-create it, again and again, chasing the recipe, fooling with ingredients and amounts and procedures, until I'd finally gotten it right. Fact is, however wonderful the soup might have been, mine is better now. I use lobster. I roast the shells. I garnish mine with hunks of claw meat, making, finally, a heartier, more luxurious version. It may have tasted the same, but, like visiting an old girlfriend and wondering, What the hell did I ever see in her? I guess things had moved on.

Desperately seeking epiphany, I ordered oysters – which couldn't have been better – a plate of rouget, the tiny, bony but delicious fish from the Med, fried sardines, a pan-roasted *magret de canard* (duck breast) in green pepper sauce, and a *bavette* for good measure.

But it still wasn't happening for me. It's not that I wasn't happy. It was great to sit at a table in France again, to look up from my food and see my brother again, to watch him unrestrainedly enjoying himself, bathing in the normalcy, the niceness of it all. Compared to most of my adventures, this was laudable. Gentle. Sentimental. No one to get hurt. Waste, disappointment, excess, the usual earmarks of most of my previous enterprises, were, for once, totally missing from the picture. Why was I not having the time of my life? I began to feel damaged. Broken. As if some essential organ – my heart perhaps – had shriveled and died along with all those dead clumps of brain cells and lung, my body and soul like some big white elephant of an Atlantic City hotel, closed down wing by wing until only the lobby and facade remained.

We walked off dinner by the port. 'See that dock over there?' I said to Chris, pointing out a sad-looking wooden structure collapsing slowly into the water. 'I remember sitting on that dock when I was fifteen. Sam and Jeffrey and Nancy – all my friends – were in Provincetown that summer. And I was stuck here. Jesus! I was miserable here then! I was a lonely, bitter kid. I never got so much as a hand-job in this fucking town . . .'

'That was later. That was the last year we were here. When we were kids, it was fun, wasn't it?'

'I guess so. I don't know. I'm still pissed about those shorts. Those berets. Jesus! What a thing to do to a kid.'

Chris started to look worried. 'Calm down. It's over. No more shorts. Put it behind you. Let it go.'

'If you see a phone booth, let me know. I'm thinking about calling Mom. I got a few scores to settle. Those shorts . . . And maybe I should settle the Pucci incident while I'm at it. Did Pucci really have to be put down? I have my suspicions, let me tell you! And what kind of a name is that for a puppy? Puccini? There should be a law against pet names that cute . . . And no Cocoa Puffs! Remember that? All my friends were eatin' Cocoa Puffs, Trix, all the Lucky Charms they wanted! What did I get? "Too sweet. Bad for your teeth." '

His big brother appearing to be on the verge of some sort of psychotic break, Chris did his best to pull me out from under whatever dark cloud was gathering. 'Relax! You need a drink or something? Jesus, Tony. You can have all the Lucky Charms you want now! I saw a *supermarché* in Arcachon. We can go buy a box right now.'

'It's okay,' I said, jolted back into the present. 'I don't know. I think I miss Dad.'

'Me too,' said Chris.

We set off for the dune of Pyla, Europe's largest sand dune, a favorite outing long ago. Where once my brother and I scampered up its steep face on young legs, we now slogged, wheezing in boots in the loose sand, pausing every few yards to catch our breath in the wind and cold. Pyla is a gargantuan pile of sand, skyscraper high and miles long, rising over the Bay of Biscay on one side and spilling slowly into pine forest on the other. There used to be blockhouses, pillboxes, and gun emplacements on top, but when we finally reached the summit, they appeared to have long ago been buried in the sand. We stood there, Chris and I, with a thin spindrift of sand hissing along the dune's surface, grit catching in our teeth, looking out at the gray-blue water, the seemingly endless pines and scrub, yearning for . . . something.

Our father had come here as a child, too. Back in the hotel, my brother had shown me an old hand-tinted stereoscopic slide my uncle must have taken back in the thirties. In it, young Pierre Bourdain, age eight or nine, skin browned by sun, stands triumphantly at the dune top, no doubt anticipating the best part of a child's day trip to Pyla: the run down the dune face, leaping faster and faster, momentum and gravity pulling his legs out from under him, until he would topple over onto his face, to finish the trip in a whirl of sand, rolling dizzily, ecstatically to the bottom. His worried parents would have been waiting for him at the bottom – as ours were years ago – ready to treat him to a *gaufre* at the stand a few yards away. That's how I imagined it anyway.

'C'mon, Chris,' I said, running straight at the precipice. 'Race you to the bottom.' Doing the best I could to imagine myself ten years old, I hurled myself into space, dropped, then ran as hard as I could, finally falling and rolling, Chris right behind me.

There was no waffle stand at the bottom. No *gaufres*. Two confused-looking backpackers in comfortable Scandinavian hiking boots watched bemused as two overaged American knuckleheads rolled to a stop near their feet. The souvenir stands were closed. Not a Pschitt, an Orangina, a Bananya, or a *citron pressé* to be had. Cold silence but for a few rustling pines.

What is an oyster if not the perfect food? It requires no preparation or cooking. Cooking would be an affront. It provides its own sauce. It's a living thing until seconds before disappearing down your throat, so you know – or should know – that it's fresh. It appears on your plate as God created it: raw, unadorned. A squeeze of lemon, or maybe a little mignonette sauce (red wine vinegar, cracked black pepper, some finely chopped shallot), about as much of an insult as you might care to tender against this magnificent creature. It is food at its most primeval and glorious, untouched by time or man. A living thing, eaten for sustenance and pleasure, the same way our knuckle-dragging forefathers ate them. And they have, for me anyway, the added mystical attraction of all that sense memory – the significance of being the first food to change my life. I blame my first oyster for everything I did after: my decision to become a chef, my thrill-seeking, all my hideous screwups in pursuit of pleasure. I blame it all on that oyster. In a nice way, of course.

At 5:30 A.M., Chris and I set out on an oyster boat with Dominique and Jerome, two local *pêcheur des huîtres*. Their vessel was not the quaint *pinasse* of my childhood. Those days, Dominique explained, were long gone. What *pinasses* remained were used principally as pleasure boats, or to ferry tourists around on day trips and picnics. This craft was a long, flat beast without gunwales – more suitable for loading sacks of oysters – a winch, and an aft wheelhouse.

It was pitch-black on the bay when we set out, Chris and I clinging to the edges of the wheelhouse, Dominique piloting, Jérôme navigating. We putt-putted cautiously out to the middle of the bay, the sun slowly beginning to announce itself, the sky turning purple and black, shot through with hues of gold.

Things had changed on the bay since we'd last floated out with our neighbor Monsieur Saint-Jour to visit his tiny oyster park in 1966. Back then, we'd waited until the tide ran out and the boat came to rest on the bay floor, surrounded by a crude hand-constructed stockade that delineated his property. Oysters then were strewn directly on the bottom, raked, picked over, and sorted on site.

A few years ago, said Dominique, the oysters died – all of them. The bay was reseeded with 'Japanese' seedlings, which took to the water well. This was not the first time this had happened. Originally, oysters had naturally occurred on the region's beds. When they'd gone, 'Portuguese' oysters spilled during a wreck had been encouraged, successfully, to proliferate. In 1970, those had mysteriously died off. Things were better now. In fact, young oysters from here were now exported to Brittany and elsewhere, as conditions were particularly favorable for them here. The number of independent oyster fishermen like my old neighbor had shrunk considerably, though, with only a few larger outfits working in much more spread-out areas. The dreaded European Union regulations – which have been wiping out artisans and independents across the Continent – make it much more difficult for small one- or two-boat partnerships to survive.

The oyster parks looked different, too. It is no longer necessary to allow the tide to completely recede. Oysters are kept sorted by size and age in mesh sacks of varying gauge, on raised platforms, just beneath the water's surface. The sacks allow water and nutrients to flow through the oysters, while keeping most predators out. Raised from the seabed and restrained in bags, the oysters are less likely to experience breakage or damage, though an astonishing 25 to 30 per cent will be eventually discarded as unsuitable.

Dominique pulled the boat alongside a few hundred feet of racks, and immediately the two men suited up in hip waders and dropped into the frigid water. They worked in shirtsleeves and rubber gloves (which filled with water right away), seemingly impervious to the cold. While they loaded heavy, dripping sacks of jagged shellfish onto the deck, they smoked and chatted casually, in no apparent hurry to finish their work and leave the water. The oysters they were loading were still young. They'd be taken back to their shack on shore, sorted again, rebagged, and returned to the water the next day.

Chris and I huddled under thick waterproofs, two layers of sweaters, scarves, and long underwear while the two fishermen prattled on happily about food: lamprey bordelaise (not in season), entrecôte bordelaise (always in season – though the bone marrow for the sauce was increasingly difficult to get and had to be purchased in Holland because of mad cow disease). They talked also of foie gras, and their preferences in oysters. Jérôme had a relative in San Francisco and had tried West Coast oysters there, but he hadn't thought much of them.

They hauled wet bags on deck for about an hour, stacked them neatly, then showed us where the seedlings were raised nearby. This process had not changed at all. Oyster larvae, before their shells fully develop, are at their most vulnerable. Ages ago, fishermen found that the oyster larvae would cling comfortably to the curved surfaces of terra-cotta roof tiles (after a process of whitewashing and sanding them), adhering themselves to the insides. The tiles could be stacked and restacked easily, and then, at the appropriate time, scraped free.

Oysters, by the way, are bisexual in ways undreamed of by career-minded actors. They actually change sex from year to year. If you were to tell an oyster 'Go fuck yourself,' it would probably not be offended. The males of a particular year spew their reproductive juices into the water in a generalized, omni-

directional way – a ubiquitously impregnating cloud that ferti-
lizes whatever's female that year. Picture the swimming pool at
Plato's Retreat back in the 1970s. That fat guy at the other end
of the pool with the gold chains and the back hair? He's getting
you pregnant. Or maybe it's the Guccione look-alike by the
diving board. No way of knowing.

Loaded up with about two thousand pounds of young oysters,
we headed back to port, Dominique and Jérôme smoking roll-
ups and still talking about food. Back at their shack, the two men
demonstrated their oyster-scrubbing apparatus, which blasted
off the outer silt and dirt, the automated sorting equipment – a
multilayered array of large-gauge strainers that bounced back
and forth over a conveyor belt, accompanied by unbelievable
noise and vibration, as it shook the oysters through. There was a
storage and cleaning pool, where the oysters were soaked in
clean, strained bay water – nutrients still intact but dirt and silt
strained away – useful for leeching out internal impurities. The
day's work done, we retired to their shack for a tasting of their
wares, a few dozen fresh Arcachon oysters and a bottle of dry
white Bordeaux. It was eight o'clock in the morning.

In a previous book, I have described my first oyster on
Monsieur Saint-Jour's *pinasse* as a seminal experience. I've never
forgotten that moment: that big, scary, ugly shell in my neighbor's knobby hand, the way he popped it open for me, still-
dripping from the bay, the way its pale blue-gray flesh caught the
light, pulsated, the mother-of-pearl-like interior of the shell like a
jewel box – promising adventure, freedom, sex, as-yet-unen-
countered joys.

I'd hoped that all that would come rushing back when I
slurped down one of Dominique and Jérôme's finest. I knew I
was trying too hard. I knew I was forcing things. It was as
ludicrous as buying your girlfriend not only flowers, jewelry,
perfume, and candy but also the bathing suit Ursula Andress
wore in *Dr. No*, then plainly stating you expect the best sex of
your life. Doubtful in the extreme that events will live up to your
expectations. I don't know whether I really expected to swoon,
fall to the floor, start weeping with joy, or what. No, I do know. I

expected the perfect damn meal. I'd thought for sure that this would be it. But did my first oyster fresh from the *bassin* in thirty-four years do it for me? Did it transport me immediately to some culinary version of Elysian Fields, as I'd hoped? Was it the perfect meal I'd so hoped to find?

Nope. Not really. It's no reflection on the oysters, which tasted much as I remembered them, briny, not too cold (oysters should not, by the way – contrary to conventional wisdom in the States – be buried in ice for hours and served chilled to frigid temperatures; it may make opening them easier for the shucker, but it diminishes the flavor). They were very fine oysters. Maybe even the best. My brother, just as before, was by my side. I'd re-created, as best I could, all the factors present in my youth. But once again, I felt restrained from pure enjoyment. Something was still missing. This was not what I was there for, I realized. This whole enterprise was a sham – the search for 'the perfect meal.' That's not what I'd been looking for at the water's edge in Arcachon, in La Teste's empty streets, in the overgrown garden at number 5, rue Jules Favre, or atop a windy sand dune in January.

My father was, to me, a man of mystery. He probably would have been pleased to hear that, as he considered himself, I think, a simple, uncomplicated sort of a guy. Though warm, sentimental, and passionate about things like literature, art, movies, and especially music, his appreciations ran deep, so deep that what I always suspected was his true nature, that of a secretly disappointed romantic, was nearly out of sight. A shy man with few friends, uncomfortable with confrontation and with large groups, a man who dreaded tie and jacket, unpretentious, amused by hypocrisy, affectation, with a sharp sense for the absurd and ironic, he took a childlike joy in simple things. He was a sucker for films about French schoolkids – the films *The 400 Blows* and *Zéro de Conduite* resonate particularly in my memory. The mischievous, borderline-delinquent children in both films were as close as I ever got to imagining my father as a kid. Despite the fact that he was raised by his widowed French mother in the very neighborhood where I now live, I know almost nothing about his life there. I can't picture him playing with friends in Riverside Park, just outside my window, as he surely must have. I can't picture him emerging from the apartment on Claremont with a stack of schoolbooks under one arm. I can't see him at private school in jacket and tie. I do have one of his old schoolbooks from the time: *Émil et les Détectives*, in French, with his doodlings of goofy Nazis and Stuka dive-bombers in the margins. He used to read to me from that book – the English version – as he read from *The Wind in the Willows, Dr. Dolittle*, and *Winnie the Pooh*. And I remember how he'd do the voices of Toad, Eeyore, and Piglet.

He was in the army as a young man, as a supply sergeant in postwar Germany – about which I also know nothing, only that it seems to have left him with a lifelong appreciation of 'funny' German accents and a suspicion that behind every German accent lurks a terrible wartime secret. He found Mel Brooks's take on Germans entirely in keeping with his own, but his laughter masked, I always suspected, some deeper bitterness and cynicism. He saw something ugly yet fascinating there, I'm sure. He loved, in later years, bleak, multilayered espionage thrillers like those of John Le Carré and Len Deighton, adored films like *The Man Inside*, *The Third Man*, *Funeral in Berlin*, and thought *Dr. Strangelove* was the funniest movie ever made.

I guess I knew him best from what seemed to make him happiest: lying on the couch on his days off, reading Jean Larteguy in French, endless John D. MacDonald novels – adventure stories, usually romantic, a little bit sad, set in faraway climes; watching a new Kubrick film; listening to a new record on his giant JBL studio monitors; fiddling with the dials on his old Marantz radio; or sitting on the beach at Cap Ferret during the two or three weeks he could get away from his job at Columbia Records and join us in France. Eating *saucisson à l'ail* between crusty French bread, sipping *vin ordinaire* in his white terry-cloth shirt and boxer-style swimming trunks, wiggling his toes in the sand, he always looked most completely at ease. He'd charge into the rough surf with me or Chris on his shoulders and try to scare us about the incoming breakers.

Back then, when we'd become bored with the beach blanket and our Tintins and our sandy sandwiches and Vittel, Chris and I would rush off to explore the dunes of Cap Ferret. We'd build forts out of the plentiful driftwood on the wild, usually deserted stretch of beach, play in the massive poured-concrete block-houses the Germans had left behind, exploring the spider holes, the tunnels that often extended underground from the central gun emplacements. We'd play army – on a real battlefield – hunting the dead Nazis rumored to be still decomposing under the sand, and hurl firecrackers down ventilation pipes and into crumbling, sand-filled stairwells. It was a paradise for kids; scores of ominous gray piles loomed up out of the sand in the vast, barren dunes, set back from the water's edge to provide interlocking fields of fire, overlooking that wild and magnificent surf and a beach that seemed to extend forever.

I had the brilliant idea that Chris and I should rent motor scooters and retrace the long drive from Arcachon, through La Teste and Gujan-Mestras, all the way around the bay to Cap Ferret. We'd made the trek many times as a family, first in the old Rover sedan, later in rented Simcas and Renaults. It would be, I thought, more tactile and immediate on scooters. We would be able to smell the air, get a better view of the towns as we passed through, unobstructed by dashboards or windows. That it was freezing cold and drizzling made no impression on me, caught up as I was in reverie. We dressed for the weather as best we could, packed the traditional Bourdain family lunch of *saucissons*, stinky cheese, baguettes from the La Teste *boulangerie*, Vittel, and a bottle of Bordeaux red, and set out for the beach. Chris crashed his scooter straight out of the hotel parking lot, smacking a street sign and falling over, skinning a significant portion of his shoulder and back. But he clambered gamely back on his bike and soldiered on – good sense having long ago been dispensed with by both of us.

It was cold – extremity-numbing cold. My bike could speed along at a good clip (I'm bigger – I got the good one), but Chris's bike putted along at twenty-five miles an hour, slowing our progress considerably. Our helmets were too tight. In our zeal to recapture the past, we hadn't really checked them for fit beyond a cursory look. My head soon felt like I had a drill bit lodged behind my right eye. The rain whipped and lashed our faces, even at our reduced speed, and soaked us to an ambient, dispiriting damp.

But we were cruising past the boarded-up villas, shuttered restaurants, and businesses we'd so often passed in our youth. This was a bold and heroic venture, wasn't it? A noble attempt to reconnect with our past, to bond, however foolhardy it was to be trying this in January. The trip took about two hours, maybe a bit more, given the frequent pit stops to unhelmet and allow our aching brainpans some relief. We finally arrived at a sandy turnoff, drove slowly down a scrub pine-lined road, parked, dismounted by a dune fence, and began the half-mile walk to the beach. There was nothing but wind, the sound of our heavy hiking boots in the sand, the distant thudding of surf.

'I recognize that one, I think,' said Chris, pointing out a graffiti-covered blockhouse in the distance, midway between beach and pine forest, just visible in the rolling dunes.

'Picnic site?' I suggested.

'Plan!'

We trudged over dunes, berms, hillocks, slow going in the sand, then finally clambered up a thick, sloping concrete wall and sat atop the thing, exactly where we'd played as kids. I laid out a blanket and our little picnic lunch and we chewed silently, our fingers stiff in the cold wind coming off the sea. The *saucisson* tasted the same, the cheese was good, and the wine proved serviceable.

I produced a package of firecrackers, and soon two men in their forties were playing army, as they'd done three decades or more ago: dropping explosives down rusted vents, jamming them into discarded bleach bottles, the dull *bang* of the explosions whipped immediately away by the wind, to disappear into the sand. We chased each other around the blockhouse for a while, and when we got tired of blowing stuff up – or, more accurately, when the firecrackers ran out – we nosed around inside, exploring the stairwells and doorways where we'd played Combat and Rat Patrol those many summers ago.

We ambled awkwardly down to the beach, stepped over drift-wood and debris that once, as children, had promised untold possibilities for construction projects and play but now appeared sad and dreary. My brother and I stood by the water's edge looking out at a violent surf, neither of us saying anything for a long while.

'Dad would have loved this,' I said.

'What?' asked Chris, snapping back from his own thoughts.

'The whole idea of this. That we came back. That we came back here again – just the two of us. He would have liked it. He would have liked hearing about it.'

'Yeah,' said my little brother, no longer littler, taller than me now. The mature one.

'Fuck . . . I miss the guy.'

'Me too,' said Chris.

I'd been looking to hook into the main vein on this stretch of my around-the-world adventure. I'd thought everything would be instant magic. That the food would taste better because of all my memories. That I'd be happier. That I would change, or some-how be as I once was. But you can never be ten years old again – or even truly feel like ten years old. Not for an hour, not for a minute. This trip, so far, had been bittersweet at best.

I hadn't, I realized, returned to France, to this beach, my old town, for the oysters. It wasn't the fish soup, or the *saucisson*, or the *pain raisin*. It wasn't to see a house in which strangers now lived, or to climb a dune, or to find a perfect meal. I'd come to find my father. And he wasn't there.

Reasons Why You Don't Want to Be on Television: Number One in a Series

'While you're in the area, let's see where foie gras is made,' said the creative masterminds of Televisionland. 'We're making a food show, remember? All this trip down memory lane is nice and all – but where's the food? C'mon! You like foie gras! You said so!'

'Sure,' I said. Why not? Sounds educational. Sounds interesting. I do like foie gras – love it, even. The swollen fresh livers of goose or duck, lightly cooked *en terrine* in Sauternes, or seared in a pan with a few caramelized apples or quince, maybe a little balsamic reduction, a nice fat slice off a torchon with some toasted brioche. It's one of the best things on earth.

We were right near Gascony, the epicenter of foie gras territory, so sure . . . let's do it! Let's make riveting, informative television, and scarf up some free foie while we're at it. How could we go wrong?

The previous night, I'd sat for the cameras and choked down an absolutely gruesome, clumsily prepared, three-day-old dino-sized portion of *tête de veau* – a terrifying prospect in the best of circumstances. Usually (the way I make it anyway), it's a slice of rolled-up boneless calf's face, peeled right off the skull, tied up – with a stuffing of sweetbreads – and served boiled in a little broth with a few nicely shaped root vegetables and a slice of tongue. It's an acquired taste, or, more accurately, an acquired texture: the translucent fat, the blue calf's skin, and the bits of cheek and thymus gland take some getting past before you can actually enjoy the flavor. The squiggly, glistening, rubbery-looking gleet is – or should be – pretty tender and flavorful. Accompanied by a dab of *sauce ravigote*, or *gribiche*, the dish can be a triumphant celebration of old-school French country food, a conquering of one's fears and prejudices. It's one of my favorite things to cook. The few (mostly French) customers who order it at Les Halles, when I run it as a special, adore it. 'Ahhh! *Tête de veau!*' they'll exclaim. 'I haven't had this in years!' I make it well. And I have always gotten a very good reaction from those I inflict it on. I eat my own, now and again, and I like it.

This stuff was different. First of all, I had ignored all my own advice. Sucked into some romantic dream state of willful ignorance, I'd overlooked the fact that for three days I'd been passing by that specials board with *TÊTE DE VEAU* proudly written in block letters in white chalk. Meaning that it was, without question – particularly considering this was off-season Arcachon – the same unsold *tête* on day three as they'd been offering on day one. Business was hardly so good, and they'd certainly not been so swamped with orders for this (even in France) esoteric specialty, that they'd have been making a fresh batch every day. How many veal heads were they getting in the whole town per week? Or per month? Even worse, I'd broken another personal rule, ordering a not-too-popular, potentially nasty meat and offal special in a restaurant that proudly specialized in seafood – a very slow restaurant specializing in seafood.

My brother, who is usually pretty daring in his tastes these days when it comes to food, had ordered the sole. I'd ignored his good example. During the meal, he'd looked at me as if I were gnawing the flesh off a dead man's fingers and washing it down with urine. By any parameters, it had been disgusting; under-cooked, tough, seemingly devoid of cheek, tasting of some dark refrigerator and, worst of all, absolutely slathered with a thick, vile-tasting *sauce gribiche* – a kind of mayonnaise/tartar sauce variation made from cooked egg yolks. I'd swallowed as much as I could for the benefit of the cameras, trying to look cheerful about it, and, far too late, simply said, 'Fuck it!' then tried sneaking away half my food into a napkin concealed below the table (as I had not wanted to offend the chef).

So the next morning, at eight o' clock, feeling none too fine from what had easily been the worst head I'd ever had, I found myself standing in a cold barn, watching my genial host, foie gras farmer and producer Monsieur Cabenass, jam a pipe from a long, long funnel down the throat of a less-than-thrilled-looking duck and begin grinding what looked like a food mill until a fistful of cornmeal disappeared down the creature's gullet. All this before breakfast.

The funnel seemed to reach the very bottom of the duck's stomach. Monsieur Cabenass would give the ducks a stroke, nudge them not too forcefully between his legs, tilt their heads back, and then give them the business. Seeing such a thing with an undigested wad of veal head still roiling in your stomach tends to inspire the gag reflex. Global Alan, the shooter who'd been standing next to Monsieur Cabenass, certainly seemed to think so: He suddenly turned an awful hue of green and went running for the door, disappearing for the rest of the morning.

Though not feeling too good myself, I endured a learned discourse and demonstration of the entire process of raising and feeding ducks and geese for foie gras. It was not as cruel as I'd imagined. The animal's feet are not nailed to a board, as some have said. They are not permanently rigged up to a feeding tube, endlessly pumped with food like some cartoon cat while they struggle and choke in vain. They are, in fact, fed twice a day – and each time a considerably lesser amount comparative to body weight than, say, a Denny's Grand Slam Breakfast. Monsieur Cabenass did not strike me as a cruel or unfeeling man, he appeared to have genuine affection for his flock, and, more often than not, the ducks would actually come to him when it was funnel time. He'd simply reach out an arm and they'd come, no more reluctantly than a child having his nose wiped by his mother.

He held up one particularly plump duck and let me run my hand over its swollen belly, its warm, protruding liver. He was not yet 'harvesting,' though he showed me some photos – a display akin to a highway safety film, and about as appetizing. Ordinarily, I like blood and guts, but rarely do I like them first thing in the morning. And never with the sound of a violently heaving and coughing cameraman in the distance. By the time we retired next door to the little shop where the Cabenass clan sell their products, I was not feeling well at all.

For my tasting pleasure, Madame Cabenass had assembled a spread of conserve de foie gras, mousse de foie gras, *rillettes de canard*, and confit, along with some sliced croutons of baguette and a bottle of Sauternes. The Cabenass product was top-drawer – it regularly takes the prize at competitions and tastings – but I like my foie gras fresh: not canned, not preserved, not in mousse, and not '*en souvide*.' In fairness, it had been a while since harvesting, and the fresh stuff was long sold. Any other culinary adventurer would no doubt have been thrilled. And while I do like Sauternes with my foie, not at nine o'clock in the morning. Foie gras should be enjoyed at one's leisure, not choked down in front of a camera in the cold, cruel morning after a nauseating *tête de veau* experience the night before.

There was a lot of food there. Once again, fearful of giving offense to my very kind hosts, I scarfed everything in front of me, smiling and nodding appreciatively, conversing (with the help of my not noticeably disturbed brother) in my tortured French. The drive back to the Norman Bates Passion Pit in Arcachon was the longest journey in memory. Global Alan, in the car ahead, had his head hanging out the window at a crazy angle, periodically drooling as we passed through quaint country villages, by Crusade-era churches and lovely old farmhouses. Alberto, the assistant producer, at the wheel of the lead car, was soon feeling bad, as well. My brother drove our car, feeling fine, taking the turns way too hard for my taste – my stomach beginning to flip and gurgle like some incipient Krakatoa. I held on for dear life, hoping to make it back to the privacy of my hotel bathroom before erupting. I just made it.

Five hours of rib-cracking agony later, I was lying, near delirious, in my ugly hotel room, trash bucket to my right, alternately sweating and shivering under a pink poly-blend blanket, the television remote control out of reach on the floor. I'd just been considering the possibility – however slight – that I might someday feel better, when suddenly, the TV show I'd not really been watching ended and the highlights of what was next flickered across my screen. The true horror of France revealed itself in all its terrible quirkiness. This has to be a joke, I thought. It can't be! It's a punch line, for Chrissakes! No! But it was happening. A ninety-minute biography – with clips – of the glorious career of that great French hero, the recipient of France's highest honors, Jerry Lewis. The great man's entire oeuvre coming *tout de suite* to my television screen, promising to bombard my already-toxin-riddled brain with a lifetime of mugging, simpering, whining shtick.

It was too much. I tried, in my desperately weakened condition, to reach the remote control, felt the blood drain from my head and the bile rise in my throat, and had to fall back into the pillows, inspiring a whole new bout of dry heaves. I couldn't turn the damn TV off, couldn't change the station. Already, scenes from *The Disorderly Orderly* were searing their way into my softened brain, causing me whole new dimensions of pain and discomfort. I picked up the phone and called Matthew, the one member of our crew who was as yet unafflicted, and begged for him to come over and change the station.

'Is it *The Day the Clown Cried*?' he asked. 'That's a vastly underrated classic, I'm told. Never seen by American audiences. Jerry plays a prisoner in a concentration camp. That Italian guy won an Oscar for the same idea! What was it? *Life Is Beautiful*? Jerry was *way* ahead of his time.'

'Please, you gotta help me,' I gasped. 'I'm dying here. I can't take it. You don't do something fast, I'm a dead man. They're gonna have to fly Bobby Flay in to shoot the Cambodia stuff. You wanna see Bobby Flay in a sarong?'

Matthew thought about that. 'I'll be right over.'

He showed up a few moments later – with his camera running. He stood over my bed, getting a 'white balance' off my bloodless face. He filmed and filmed, while the room tilted and whirled around me, panning back and forth between me, moaning in my sodden sheets, and Jerry, in *Cinderfella*. He shot close-ups as I heaved and pleaded. Cutaways of the out-of-reach remote control, slow pullbacks to reveal the source of my torment, the distance between me and the remote as I groaned, promised, threatened. Just before he finally reached down and tossed me the remote, allowing me to put a merciful end to a scene from Jerry's masterpiece, *The Nutty Professor*, I heard Matt say, 'This is gold, baby! Comedy gold!'

Don't make television. Ever.

THE BURN

BACK TO NEW YORK, Christmas dinner, wake up, exchange a few presents, and it's back on the infernal machine: New York to Frankfurt, Frankfurt to Singapore, Singapore to Ho Chi Minh City, another marathon of smoke-free flights, my personal circle of hell, sitting next to the smelliest man on earth, the engines droning on and on without variation, making me yearn for turbulence – anything to break the boredom, the gnawing, terrible sense that I'm in some gruesome state of suspended animation. Is there anything so expensive and yet so demeaning as tourist class on a long flight? Look at us! Stacked ten across, staring bleary-eyed straight ahead, legs and knees contorted, necks at unnatural angles, eagerly – yes, eagerly – waiting for the slop gurney finally to make its way down to us. That all-too-familiar brackish waft of burned coffee, the little plastic trays of steamed food, which would cause a riot in a federal penitentiary. Oh God, another Sandra Bullock film, another Willis. If I see Helen Hunt squinting at me from a hazy airline screen one more time, I'm opening the emergency door. Being sucked into thin air has got to be preferable to that. I find myself looking for any diversion, anything to take my mind off the nicotine yen: Focus on the snoring human compost heap across the narrow aisle, pretend that if I stare hard enough, he'll explode.

By now, I've come to know the smoking areas of airports all over the world. I find similarly afflicted passengers speed-smoking about twenty feet from the gate in Frankfurt. In Singapore, you have a choice of two – count 'em, *two* – smoking lounges: a

52

foul-smelling glass fishtank inside the mammoth shopping arcade, and an al fresco area where there's always an interesting bunch of Asian adventurers. They sit on benches in the roaring heat and humidity, nursing Tiger beers, happily sucking up cigarettes and jet fumes in the blinding dawn light. The accents of those talking are Aussie, Kiwi, Brit, French, Dutch – all drunk and red-faced, exhausted. Each carry-on bag tells a story of a long time away from home.

Tan Son Nhut airport. Ho Chi Minh City. Everybody still calls it Saigon. You can light up a smoke the second you're off the plane. The customs inspector has a butt in his mouth. I like Vietnam already. The last pitched battle of the Vietnam War (what they call the American War here) was fought on these tarmac strips, in these lounges. Crumbling American-built Quonset huts still line the runways. You've seen the movies. You've read the books. Do I have to tell you about the blast of heat that hits you in the stomach when you make it past the baggage claim and through the glass doors? The wall of humanity waiting outside? Saigon. A place I never thought I'd live to see.

I wake up at 3:00 A.M., chest pounding in the cold, damp room. I'm on the tenth floor of the New World Hotel. I've sweated through the blankets after yet another violent and very disturbing dream. It must be the antimalarial pills. There's no other explanation for the vivid, full-color nightmares I've been having since I arrived. I can smell blood and motor oil still – the dreams seem to be in Sensurround, fully textured affairs, where I can actually feel vibrations, physical exertion. This time, I was rolling and rolling in an out-of-control car, spinning off the asphalt of a dream highway and down a steep decline. I could feel myself bouncing off the door frames, the seats, the crumpling dash. I could hear the glass on the instrument panel shattering, the windshield safety glass cracking in starburst patterns.

I wake up, my arms sore from bracing myself against the collision. Absentmindedly, I run a hand through my hair to brush away nonexistent shards of safety glass.

Maybe it was the snake wine.

Earlier in the evening, I'd gone to see Madame Dai in her tiny law office-turned-café/salon, and after the spring rolls and the rice-noodle cakes and the beef wrapped in mint leaves dipped in *nuoc mam*, she'd asked in her perfect, elegantly inflected French if I'd care for a '*digestif*.' I'd said yes, of course, utterly charmed by the diminutive but stately Vietnamese woman in her black dress – a former man-killer if there ever was one. She'd disappeared for a moment into the kitchen while I'd looked idly at the photographs of old friends on the wall: Pierre Trudeau, the Pope, the head of the Central Committee, François Mitterand, various war correspondents, former lovers, a portrait of herself as a young woman in the 1940s, looking absolutely Dragon Lady in a slinky *ao dai*. When Madame Dai returned, she held a large glass jar filled with snakes – a single full-beaked bird still in plumage, entangled by serpents deep in the clear rice wine.

I can still taste it.

When am I awake? When am I asleep? All Saigon has a dreamlike quality for me. Wandering down Dong Khoi Street, the former rue Catinat, headed away from the river, past the Majestic, I turn the corner and there's the Continental Hotel, the Caravelle, the gaudy Rex; I wade through a sea of scooters and cyclos and motorbikes to a narrow side street where, among the dusty pillboxes, broken timepieces, foreign coins, used shoes, cigarette holders, and dented dog tags, there peek out stained Zippos (both real and fake) inscribed with the poignant personal mottoes of their original owners:

VIETNAM
Chu Lai 69–70
Always ripped or always stoned
I made a year. I'm going Home.

I find one by the compasses, feeling absolutely ghoulish as I read another plaintive commemoration of one young man's long-ago year abroad:

HUE
DA NANG
QUI NHON
BIEN HOA
SAIGON

On the other side of the lighter, the sentiment:

When I die, bury me face down
So the whole world can kiss my ass.

This is a city named after a cook. Maybe you didn't know
that. Ho Chi Minh was a very fine, classically trained culinarian.
Prior to helping found the Vietnamese Communist party, he
worked at the Carlton Hotel in Paris, for no less a chef than the
great man himself, Auguste Escoffier. It is said he was a favorite
of the old man. He worked as a saucier there, later as a cook on a
transatlantic liner, then as a pâtissier at the Parker House in
Boston. He was – the Commie thing aside – one of us, like it or
not: a guy who spent a lot of hours standing on his feet in busy
hotel and restaurant kitchens, a guy who came up through the
ranks the old-school way – a professional. And yet he still found
time to travel under about a zillion aliases, write manifestos, play
footsie with the Chinese and the Russians, dodge the French,
fight the Japanese (with U.S. help, by the way), beat the French,
help create a nation, lose that nation, and organize an ultimately
successful guerilla war against America. Communism may suck,
but old Uncle Ho was one interesting guy.

And this is where his dream ends: on the tenth floor of the
New World Hotel, an overchilled high-rise mausoleum in the
city center; with a swimming pool elevated from the noise and
exhaust of the city's streets, where one can look up from one's
blender drink at poolside (though the developers have done their
best to mask the view with foliage) through trellised flowers and
see the ramshackle apartment blocks of the Workers' Paradise,
where barefoot old women live on less than a dollar a day.

At the New World, one can walk directly from the maddening

heat of the streets into the gigantic, sweeping lobby, past the gingerbread house display for the holidays ('Festive Table!'), past the cocktail lounge, where a Vietnamese cover band, the Outrageous Three, are playing note-perfect Barry Manilow tunes, ride the silent elevators up to the Executive Floor, or to the health club, the driving range, or tennis court. One can sit on the enclosed tenth-floor terrace, sipping 333 beer (pronounced *bababa*), or enjoying a little port wine and Stilton from the complimentary buffet while rubbing one's fingers over a dead soldier's Zippo.

Is it the antimalarials I've been taking in preparation for the Mekong Delta and Cambodia that are curdling my dreams? Was it the snake wine? Or is it the fact that I'm in the Vietnam of my dreams – all of our dreams. Was it Tricky Dick, all those years ago, who called everything we did here – all the waste, death, folly, the legacy of still-permeating cynicism we inflicted on ourselves – 'our long national nightmare'? In Saigon, walking the streets, it's hard to separate the real from the fantasy, the nightmare from the wish, a collection of film and video images that have long ago been burned into so many of our cortices. The ceiling fan in *Apocalypse Now*, the choppers coming in slow with a *Whuppwhupppwhupppwhuppp* . . . the running girl, flesh hanging off her arms from a napalm strike . . . burning bonzes toppling over . . . the point-blank bullet to the head . . . that lush longed-for green that drove generations of mystics, madmen, technocrats, and strategists insane. The French, the Americans, ruined for decades by tiny little farmers in black pajamas, slogging through those beautiful rice paddies behind water buffalo. Yet it always looked so beautiful, so . . . unknowable.

I wake from yet another nightmare. This one was even worse. I was a witness at an execution. I can almost still smell the smoke and cordite from the guns. Feeling nauseated and guilty, I read for a while, afraid to go back to sleep. I'm rereading Graham Greene's *The Quiet American* for about the fifth time. It's his Vietnam novel, set in the early days of the French adventure here. He wrote much of it – it is said – at the Continental Hotel, just down the street. It's a beautiful, heartbreakingly sad book. But it's not helping my state of mind, which is becoming increasingly deranged. I've got to get out of this room. Even with the air conditioner on, everything's wet. Condensation has built up on the windows. The carpet feels moist and smells stale. My sheets have been sweat through. My clothes are soggy. Even the currency is wet; a pile of near-worthless dong sits limp and moist on the nightstand. I head out for the Ben Thanh market, about twelve blocks away.

I stroll past quaking rabbits, squawking chickens, trembling deer mice, past meat counters where vendors squat barefoot on their cutting boards, calmly eating from chipped bowls. The smell is heavy, narcotic: durian, jackfruit, seafood, *nuoc mam* – the ubiquitous fish sauce condiment of choice all over Southeast Asia. At the center of the enclosed market, past the vegetables, meat, fish, live poultry, nostrums, jewelry, and groceries for sale, is a large area of food stalls selling a psychedelic rainbow of good-looking, good-smelling, unbelievably fresh stuff. My mood begins to improve immediately. Everything is brightly colored, crunchy, exotic, unrecognizable, and attractive. I suddenly want everything. Without warning, I'm happy, exhilarated, delirious with hunger and curiosity. A manic-depressive on a happy jag, I'm on top of the world.

I sit down at a clean white counter with a crowd of Vietnamese and order a bowl of *pho*, a spicy noodle soup that comes with a variety of ingredients. I'm not sure exactly which *pho* I'm ordering, but it all looks good, so I simply point at what the lady next to me is eating. Is there anything better to eat on this planet than a properly made bowl of *pho*? I don't know. Precious few things can approach it. It's got it all. A bowl of clear hot liquid, loaded with shreds of fresh, white and pink crabmeat, and noodles is handed to me, garnished with bean sprouts and chopped fresh cilantro. A little plate of condiments comes next: a few wedges of lime, some ground black pepper – which, judging from my neighbors at the counter, one makes into a paste, adding lime juice to pepper and stirring with chopsticks – a dish of *nuoc mam*, a dish of chili fish oil, some chopped red chili peppers. The proprietor hands me a cold plastic-wrapped towel, which, once again emulating my neighbors, I squeeze – until the air is forced to one end – and then pop loudly between my hands. Everyone claps encouragingly. This sound, the *pop pop pop* of plastic-wrapped hand towels exploding, is the backbeat to Saigon. You hear it everywhere. Inside the wrapper is a cold, fresh, clean towel to wash and refresh with. The *pho* is fantastic – spicy, hot, complex, refined, yet unbelievably simple. The astounding freshness of the ingredients, the brightly contrasting textures and colors, the surprising sophistication of the presentation – the whole experience is overwhelmingly perfect. The proprietor beams at me before I even take a mouthful. He knows it's good. I wipe my bowl out, wash it down with a little clear plastic sandwich bag of lychee juice, and hand over a few moist dong.

At the beginning of a fierce compulsion to eat everything in sight, I bounce around like a hungry pinball from stall to stall. A woman crouches by a doorway with a wok of oil sizzling over a few coals. Crisping on the surface are a few tiny little birds, head, feet, wings intact, their entrails bursting yellow, billowing out through golden fried bellies. They look good. They smell good. I buy one, pick it up by the feet, the smiling woman urging me on, letting me know I'm doing it right. I wolf the thing down, gnawing it right up to its feet, beak, brain, tiny crunchy bones and all. Delicious. And again, so fresh. Everything, everywhere, is fresh, astoundingly fresh. And not a refrigerator in sight.

Another woman beckons me over and offers me a slice of jackfruit. I accept and offer her money. She declines, simply watches, smiling as I eat. I am loving this. I am really, really loving it. I order a spring roll at another stall, watch as the owner wraps freshly hacked cooked prawn, mint, basil, lotus root, and sprouts in rice paper, then eat that and order a shrimp kebab, a sort of shrimp cake wrapped around a stick of sugarcane and grilled. It's a wonderland of food here. Tiny intricately wrapped and shaped *banh* – triangular bundles of rice cake and pork inside carefully tied banana leaves – dangle from stalls, like the hanging salami and cheese you see in Italian markets. I try some.

Smashing. There's food everywhere, inside the market, outside on the street; anyone not selling or cooking food seems to be eating, kneeling or squatting against walls, on the floor, in the street, tucking into something that looks wonderful.

I leave the market and head toward one of the many little coffee joints, picking my way through the stream of motorbikes and cyclos, past more food vendors, men and women carrying yokes, a pot of *pho* hanging from one end, utensils and garnishes from the other. Everything I see, I want to put in my mouth. Every pot of soup or noodles over a few sticks of burning wood is fresher and better-looking than any stuff in a New York market.

Sitting down on a tiny plastic stool, maybe a foot off the ground, I order coffee. I feel short of breath from the rapidly building heat, the humidity, all those delicious, intoxicating smells pulling me in every direction at once. An empty coffee cup and a banged-up strainer over a tin receptacle hits my wobbly little table. The grounds strain slowly, drip by drip, into the lower container. When it's all gone through, I pour my coffee into my cup and take a sip. It's simply the best coffee I've ever had: thick, rich, strong, and syrupy, like the dregs at the bottom of a glass of chocolate milk. I'm instantly hooked. The proprietor, a toothless old woman, has a suggestion. She brings out another coffee, this time with a tall glass of ice and a can of condensed milk. When the coffee has filtered through, it's poured over the ice. Mingling with the milk below, it's a slow, strangely mesmerizing process, delightful to watch and even better to drink. As the black coffee dribbles slowly through and around the ice cubes, swirling gently in dark-on-white wisps through the milk, I feel Vietnam doing the same thing to my brain. I'm in love. I am absolutely over-the top gonzo for this country and everything in it. I want to stay forever.

Are there any more beautiful women? They drive by on their motorbikes in tight white silk *ao dais*, slit to the tops of their thighs, black silk pants underneath, driving gloves that reach beyond their elbows, white surgical masks covering their faces, bug-eyed dark sunglasses, and conical straw hats. Not an inch of flesh is visible, and I'm totally enamored with them. Sitting on my stool drinking iced coffee and watching them, I feel a twinge of pain for Greene's hero in *The Quiet American*, so hopelessly in love with a young Vietnamese girl who can never and will never return his affections in kind. It's a paradigm for the whole American experience here in some ways. Poor LBJ, shaking his head, unable to understand that that little Uncle Ho fella over there, offered a badly needed dam and hydroelectric system for the Red River Delta – in return for selling out his dream of a united country – turned him down flat. All those well-meaning Green Beanies in the early days of the war, the would-be Lord Jims, warrior priests, idealistic CIA officers, AID specialists, medics and mercenaries, hurt, wounded, confused that these people just wouldn't love them back the way they thought they deserved to be. We took out our lover's pique later, by sending in the marines.

I sit there for a long time, sipping iced coffee, smelling motorbike exhaust, freshly baked baguettes (they're really good here), burning joss, the occasional waft from the Saigon River, thinking back to Madame Dai and my first night in town.

'*Les Français*,' she began, listing all the regimes she's lived through, '*les Japonais, les Français – encore! – puis les Américains, le Président Diem, les Américains, Thieu, les communistes.*' She smiled, shrugged, casting a skeptical glance at my translator, Linh, who, as Madame Dai was well aware, would later have to report this conversation to the ominously named People's Committee.

'Le Président Thieu wanted to put me in jail,' she said, 'but he . . . could not. I was too . . . *populaire*. His cabal said I would become a hero in jail.' The first female lawyer in Vietnam under the South Vietnamese government (now referred to as the 'Puppet Regime'), she saw her law practice shut down when the North Vietnamese rolled into town. Eventually, she was allowed to reopen – as a café, still operating, as she does today, out of her musty law offices, the walls lined with law books, memorabilia, and photographs of better days. She's on some kind of governmental advisory committee, she explained, which was perhaps why it was okay for me to visit. She still entertains visiting dignitaries from the West.

'I love to flirt with communism,' she said, giggling and goosing Linh. 'The "Government of National Reconciliation," ' she scoffed. 'Reconcile what? I was never angry!'

She served a choice of two menus to guests – most of them visiting Westerners: French or Vietnamese. I hadn't come here to eat escargots bourguignonne, so I chose Vietnamese. Madame Dai floated back into a rear kitchen, where a few loyal retainers were preparing a spread of *ban phong tom* (shrimp crackers), *goi sen* (lotus salad with chicken and shrimp), *cha goi zoua* (fried spring rolls), *ba la lop* (beef wrapped in mint leaves), *com duoung chau* (Saigonese rice with pork, egg, and green beans), *mang cua* (asparagus soup), a mint, pineapple and cucumber salad, and pork grilled over charcoal. The meal ended with crème caramel, an innocuous but delicious reminder of colonial days. Madame Dai was educated in France, and she led the conversation toward fond memories of cassoulets, *choucroutes, confit de canard*, clearly enjoying simply pronouncing the words after so long. Occasionally, she paused to put a finger to her lips, then delivered a tap on the table. '*Les meecrophones,*' she stage-whispered, making sure that poor squirming Linh – who does not speak French and was not enjoying when we did – heard every word. 'I am CIA?' she asked sarcastically. '*Non*, I tell zem. I am KGB!' Both acronyms made Linh sit upright with barely concealed alarm. If there's anyone the Vietnamese hate, it's the Russians. Apparently, after the war, a lot of their 'advisers' and technicians walked around the country like conquering heroes, pretending they'd won the war for the Vietnamese. They were rude. They were loud. They were – it is said – lousy tippers. 'I love to flirt with ze communism,' said Madame Dai for the second time. She involved me in a well-known Vietnamese joke, very popular in the seventies, during the period of 'reeducation.'

'What religion are you?' she asked.

'Uh . . . no religion,' I said – clearly the right answer for the punch line.

'Oh!' she exclaimed with mock horror. 'You are VC!'

Even Linh laughed along with this. He'd heard it, too. At last, we left Madame Dai out in front of her café, a tiny figure in a black dress and stockings, sweeping away a few bits of litter with a straw whisk broom.

When I finally leave the market, the streets are dark, and I pass a few blocks where not a single electric light appears – only dark open storefronts and *coms* (fast-food eateries), broom closet-sized restaurants serving fish, meat, and rice for under a dollar, flickering candles barely revealing the silhouettes of seated figures. The tide of cyclists, motorbikes, and scooters has increased to an uninterrupted flow, a river that, given the slightest opportunity, diverts through automobile traffic, stopping it cold, spreads into tributaries that spill out over sidewalks, across lots, through filling stations. They pour through narrow openings in front of cars: young men, their girlfriends hanging on the back; families of four: mom, dad, baby, and grandma, all on a fragile, wobbly, underpowered motorbike; three people, the day's shopping piled on a rear fender; women carrying bouquets of flapping chickens, gathered by their feet while youngest son drives and baby rests on the handlebars; motorbikes carrying furniture, spare tires, wooden crates, lumber, cinder blocks, boxes of shoes. Nothing is too large to pile onto or strap to a bike. Lone men in ragged clothes stand or sit by the roadsides, selling petrol from small soda bottles, servicing punctures with little patch kits and old bicycle pumps.

The next morning, I'm right back at the market, where I have a healthy breakfast of *hot vin lon*, essentially a soft-boiled duck embryo, still in the shell, a half-formed beak and bits of dark crunchy matter buried in the partially cooked yolk and transluscent albumen. I eat it – but don't exactly love it. It will not be replacing bialys on my breakfast table. I hear for the first time what will become a regular refrain in Vietnam, particularly when eating something that only a few days ago one would never have imagined putting in one's mouth. While running my spoon around inside the eggshell, scraping out the last bits of goop and feather, a man sitting next to me sees what I'm eating.

He smiles and says, 'Make you strong!' While he doesn't make any rude accompanying gestures, I gather that *hot vin lon* is supposed to ensure an imminent erection and many, many sons. Not feeling too great from my embryonic breakfast, I soothe my stomach with a bowl of *chao muk*, a hearty soup made with ginger, sprouts, cilantro, shrimp, squid, chives, and pork-blood cake, garnished with fried croutons. This goes down well, and after a morning 333, I start across the street, until I'm stopped short.

I'm already used to the amputees, the Agent Orange victims, the hungry, the poor, the six-year-old street kids who you see at 3:00 A.M. and cry, 'Happy New Year! Hello! Bye-bye!' in English, then point at their mouths and go 'Boom boom?' I am almost inured to the near-starving Dondis, the legless, armless, scarred, and desperate, sleeping in cyclos, on the ground, by the riverbanks. I am not, however, prepared for the shirtless man with the pudding-bowl haircut who approaches me outside the market, his hand out.

He has been burned at some time in the past and is now a nearly unrecognizable man-shaped figure of uninterrupted scar tissue beneath the little crown of black hair. Every inch from the waist up (and who knows how far below) is scar tissue. He has no lips, no eyebrows, no nose. His ears are like putty, as if he's been dipped and melted in a blast furnace, then yanked out just before dissolving completely. He moves his jack-o'-lantern teeth, but no noise emanates from what used to be a mouth.

I feel gut-shot. My exuberant mood of the last few days and hours comes crashing down. I just stand there, blinking, the word *napalm* hanging inevitably over me, squeezing every beat of my heart. Suddenly, this is not fun anymore. I'm ashamed. How could I come to this city, to this country, filled with enthusiasm for something so . . . so . . . meaningless as flavor, texture, cuisine? This man's family has very possibly been vaporized, the man himself transformed into a ruined figurine like some Madame Tussaud's exhibit, his skin dripping like molten wax. What am I doing here? Writing a fucking book? About food? Making a petty, useless, lighter-than-air television fucking show? The pendulum swings all the way over and I am suddenly filled with self-loathing. I hate myself and my whole purpose here. I blink through a cold sweat, paralyzed, certain that everyone on the street must be watching. Radiating discomfort and guilt, I'm sure that any casual observer must surely associate me and my country with this man's injuries. I spy a few other Western tourists across the street in Banana Republic shorts and Lands' End polo shirts, comfortably shod in Weejuns and Birkenstocks, and I want suddenly and irrationally to kill them. They look evil, like carrion-eaters. The inscribed Zippo in my pocket burns, no longer amusing – suddenly about as funny as the shrunken head of a close friend. Everything I eat will taste like ashes now. Fuck writing books. Fuck making television.

I'm unable even to give the man money. I stand there useless, hands trembling, consumed by paranoia. I hurry back to my refrigerated room at the New World Hotel and sag back onto the still-unmade bed, stare at the ceiling in tears, unable to grasp or to process what I've seen – or to do anything about it. I go nowhere and eat nothing for the next twenty-four hours. The TV crew thinks I'm having a breakdown.

Saigon . . . Still only in Saigon.

What am I doing in Vietnam?

WHERE THE BOYS ARE/WHERE
THE GIRLS ARE

THERE WAS BARELY A sound to be heard in the empty streets of San Sebastián's *parte vieja*, just the clip-clopping of my boots on wet cobblestones echoing against four-hundred-year-old buildings. It was late at night, and Luis Irizar and I carried food through the dark.

Luis was the main man at the Escuela de Cocina Luis Irizar, the cooking school that bears his name, a capo, maybe even a consigliere, in the city's vast culinary subculture. Had it not been so late, and the streets so empty, there would have been passersby waving at him, shopkeepers calling out his name, former students coming out to give him a hug, a handshake, and a hearty hello. Everybody who has anything to do with food in San Sebastián knows Luis. Where we were headed at this late hour was an institution particular to this food-crazy city, the Gaztelubide, an exclusive all-male clubhouse for one of San Sebastián's many gastronomic societies. If you love food, San Sebastián's got it all: an unwavering faith in its own traditions and regional products, a near-religious certainty that it's got the best cuisine in Spain, a language and culture that go back – literally – to the Stone Age. And more Michelin stars per capita than anywhere else in the world.

If you listen to the locals, San Sebastián isn't even really Spain. It's Basque country, that vaguely defined, famously independent area of southwest France and northern Spain where the street signs are in Basque (lots of names with *t*'s and *x*'s and few

vowels) and woe to anyone who too obnoxiously asserts obei-
sance to another culture. There's a bunch of good ol' boys here
who call themselves ETA – and they make the IRA look like
Mouseketeers. Screw with them at your peril. While the great
majority of Basques look disapprovingly on car bombs and
assassinations, their interest in independence and self-determi-
nation is right under the surface. Scratch lightly and it's in your
face.

I wasn't worried about bombs or kidnappings. I've long ago
found that nationalism bordering on militancy is often accompanied by large numbers of proud cooks and lots of good stuff to
eat. San Sebastián is just about the best example of this state of
mind. Good food, good restaurants, lots to drink – and 'Leave
me alone!' Not a bad place for a hungry, globe-trotting chef,
early in his quest for the perfect meal.

Luis and I entered Gaztelubide with our supplies. We passed a
wide, oblong-shaped dining area lined with wooden tables and
benches, then walked into a nice-sized, professionally equipped
kitchen, crowded with men in aprons. The men were working
earnestly on various individual cooking projects, the stovetops
fully occupied with simmering pots and sizzling pans, while a
few onlookers drank red wine and hard cider in the dining area
and rear cloakroom. I was out of my element. First, I was at least
fifteen years younger than anyone there. This society hadn't
opened the books to new membership in many years. Second, all
these cooks were amateur – as opposed to professional – cooks
(save Luis), guys who cooked for love, for the pure pleasure and
appreciation of food. Third was the 'all-male' thing, an expression which, in my experience, is most often accompanied by
signs reading PEEP-O-RAMA and BUDDY BOOTHS – or, worse,
FOOTBALL ON THE BIG SCREEN! For me, a night out 'with the
guys' – unless we're talking chefs, of course – usually veers into
the territory of bar fights, Jäger shots, public urination, and
vomiting into inappropriate vessels. Without the civilizing per-
spectives of women, too many guys in one room will almost
always, it seems, lead the conversation, as if by some ugly,
gravitational pull, to sports stats, cars, pussy, and whose dick is

bigger – subjects I've already heard way too much about in twenty-eight years in kitchens.

Virginia, Luis's daughter and the director of the cooking school, had put my mind somewhat at ease earlier, assuring me that I'd have a good time. 'Go,' she said. 'You'll have fun . . . Tomorrow night,' she added ominously, 'you come out with the girls.'

Now I was in the inner sanctum putting on an apron and preparing to assist Luis in the preparation of a traditional Basque meal – a tall glass of hard cider in one hand, a bucket of soaking *bacalao* (salt cod) in the other. 'You dry the *bacalao* on the towel, like this,' said Luis, demonstrating for me exactly how he wanted it done. He blotted a thick filet of cod on both sides, ready to make his move to an open burner on the crowded stovetop.

'Next you go like this – '

There was no argument about who was boss here. I happily complied as Luis slapped down a heavy skillet, added some olive oil, and began to bring it up to heat. When the oil was hot enough, I seared the pieces of fish lightly on both sides.

We were making *bacalao al pilpil*, about as old-school Basque a dish as you are likely to find. After setting the seared fish aside, I covered the half-cooked filets in more hot olive oil. Then, moving over to a countertop and using a thick earthenware casserole, I followed Luis's example and carefully swirled in a gentle clockwise motion until the natural albumen in the fish bound with the oil, creating a thick, cloudy emulsion. At the very end, Luis spooned in some *piperade*, an all-purpose mixture of tomato, peppers, and onions, which gave the sauce a dark pink-and-red-flecked finish and an inviting spicy aroma.

'Keep it warm here,' said Luis, balancing the casserole dish between two simmering stockpots.

Next: *cocoches*, the salt-cured cheeks of hake, soaked in milk, then seasoned, floured, dipped in egg, and fried until crispy and golden brown. Luis walked me through the process while frying serrano ham – wrapped langoustines on skewers on the flattop next to me, charring them lightly on both sides. People kept refilling my cider glass and handing me glasses of *txakaoli*, a sort of greenish white wine similar to *vino verde*. I was beginning to feel that warm buzz, an artificial sense of well-being and inflated self-image so conducive to enjoying a fine meal. We were joined by a brawny and gregarious former student of Luis's, who explained the society's drinking policy: Drink as much as you like – on the honor system. At the end of the night, count up your bottles, fill out a ticket totaling the damage, and leave the money in a hanging covered pot by the untended bar.

The food almost ready, Luis showed me to a table, set down some glasses and high-poured me a big drink of *patxaran*, the deadly local brandy made from berries and anise. With the bottle held about two feet over the glass, he did the same for himself, winked, and gave me the Basque toast of '*Osassuna!*' before draining his glass in one go. I was beginning to understand what went on here. Soon, we were well into the *patxaran* and happily tearing at our food. The cheeks were terrific, the pilpil, served at blood-warm temperature, surprisingly sweet and subtly flavored, the *piperade*/oil emulsion a nice counterpoint to the salt cod and much more delicate than I'd expected. The langoustines were great, and a surprise addition of wild mushroom *salpicon* in a sort of rice-paper vol-au-vent – another cook's contribution, I think – was wonderful.

All the other cooks' food seemed to be coming up at the same time, and the tables were soon crowded with burly, barrel-chested men animatedly devouring their creations in food-spattered aprons, the clatter and roar of conversation punctuated by exclamations of '*Osassuna!*'

We were having a jolly time at my table, and visitors from other tables frequently swung by to say hello to me, Luis, and his former student. Conversation ranged from the exact frontiers of Basque territory (Luis's friend claimed everything from Bordeaux to Madrid – wherever there was good stuff to eat) to the incomprehensible aversion to mushrooms shared by most non-Basque Spaniards. Luis was quick to point out that the Basques, not Columbus, had discovered America. When I mentioned that some Portuguese friends had just made the same claim, Luis waved a hand and explained everything. 'The Basque are fishermen. We were always fishermen. But we were also always a small country. When we found cod, we didn't tell people about it. And we found a lot of cod off America. Who should we have told? The Portuguese? They'd have stolen it all. Then we'd have had nothing.' Things seemed normal in the large room, a big crowd of happy eaters, speaking in a mixture of Spanish and Basque, glasses clinking, more toasts.

Then things got weird.

An old, old man, referred to as 'el Niño' ('the Baby'), on account of his advanced age, sat down at an old upright piano and began pounding out what was clearly the introduction to the evening's entertainment. I broke out in a cold sweat. My most terrifying nightmare scenario is that I might someday be trapped on a desert island with only a troupe of cabaret performers for diversion – and menthol cigarettes to smoke – doomed to an eternity of Andrew Lloyd Webber and medleys from *South Pacific*. A guy in a dirty apron stood up and launched into song, his tenor voice impressive. Okay, I thought, opera, I can handle this. I had to hear this at home when I was a kid. I should be able to handle it now.

What I was not prepared for was the chorus. Suddenly, everyone in the room began pounding their fists on their tables, rising, then sitting down in unison to provide alternating verses of chorus. This was the wackiest thing I'd seen in quite awhile. It was a little frightening. Then, one after the other, every man in the room – tenors, baritones – got up to sing, belting out arias and other solos in heartfelt, heart-wringing renditions. Then came a really creepy – but funny – duet between two lumberjack-sized fellows, one doing what was clearly the male part, the other doing the female in a scary but good falsetto, accompanied by appropriate gestures and expressions. You have never seen such sincere, evocative grimacing, agonizing, chest pounding and garment rending, such earnest cries of feigned torment, pain, and bold challenge. These men could cook. They could drink like heroes. And every damn one of them could sing like a professional. I gathered they practiced – a lot.

Just when I was beginning to fear that soon we'd all be stripping down to our Skivvies for a little towel snapping in the steam room, the mood became decidedly nationalistic. No more opera. Instead, lusty anthems of Basque independence, marching songs, songs about battles won and lost, loud homages to dead patriots, nonspecific vows to take to the streets in the future. The men were all lined up together now, two rows of raised fists, swinging in time, feet stomping, shouting triumphantly. A few more glasses of *patxaran* and I'd be storming the barricades myself. It got only louder and more festive (and my table wetter, from all the high pouring) as the evening progressed. The ranks of empty bottles near me grew from platoon to company strength, threatening to become a division.

'We don't do this in New York,' I told Luis.

I don't remember much after that.

I woke up in the Hotel Londres y Angleterre, one of the many Victorian piles built on San Sebastián's English seaside-style strand, which curves around a beautiful scallop-shaped bay. Should I tell you about castles and forts and Crusade-era churches, the unique and lovely facades on the buildings, the intricate wrought iron, the old carousel, the museums? Nah, I'll leave that to Lonely Planet or Fodor's. Just believe me when I tell you that the city is beautiful – and not in the oppressive way of, say, Florence, where you're almost afraid to leave your room because you might break something. It may be beautiful, but it's a modern city, sophisticated, urbane, with all the modern conveniences artfully sandwiched into old buildings. The French vacation there in large numbers, so there are all the fashionable shops, brasserie-type lunch joints, patisseries, nightclubs, bars, Internet cafés, and cash machines you'd expect of a major hub – along with the homegrown cider joints, tapas bars, small shops selling indigenous products, and open-air markets you hope for. As San Sebastián is still Spain, there is the added benefit of being part of a society that has only recently emerged from a repressive dictatorship. If you're looking for hard-living, fun-loving folks, Spain is the place. During the days of Franco's dictatorship, the

Basque language was illegal – writing or speaking it could lead to imprisonment – but now it's everywhere, taught in schools, spoken in the streets. The supporters of ETA, as in any good independence movement, are profligate with the use of graffiti, so there's an element of Belfast to the walls and parks and playgrounds – except they're serving two-star food across the street.

With a crippling hangover, I limped out of the hotel and back to the *parte vieja* in search of a cure, noticing a few surfers getting some nice rides off the long, steady curls in the bay.

Chocolate and *churros*. A thick, dark, creamy cup – almost a bowl, really – of hot chocolate, served with a plate of deep-fried strips of batter. *Churros* are kind of like flippers: sweet dough forced through a large star-tipped pastry bag into hot oil and cooked until golden brown, then piled onto a plate, powdered with sugar, and dipped into chocolate. The combination of sugar, chocolate, hot dough, and grease is the perfect breakfast for a borderline alcoholic. By the time I was halfway through my cup, my headache had disappeared and my worldview had improved dramatically. And I needed to get well fast. I had, I suspected, a big night ahead of me. I'd seen that look on Virginia's face before, when she'd told me that I'd be going 'out with the girls'. It was a look that made my blood run cold as the memories came rushing back. Vassar, 1973. I was part of a tiny minority of men, living in a little green world run by and for women. I'd fallen in – as I always do – with a bad crowd, a loosely knit bunch of carnivorous, brainy, gun-toting, coke-sniffing, pill-popping manic-depressives, most of them slightly older and much more experienced than I was at seventeen. Sitting each morning in the college dining facility and later the neighborhood bar with eight or ten of these women at a time, I'd learned, painfully at times, that women have nothing to learn from men in the bad behavior department, particularly when they travel in packs. They drank more than I did. They talked about stuff that made even me blush. They rated the sexual performance of the previous night's conquests on a scale of one to ten, and carved up the class of incoming freshmen ahead of time – drawing circles around their faces in the *Welcome to Vassar* pamphlet introducing the new fish – like gangsters dividing up building contracts.

I was afraid. Very afraid.

When I showed up at the cooking school, a whole posse of women was waiting for me: Luis's daughters Virginia and Visi (also a chef), and three friends, their faces brimming with mischief. I'd compounded the danger factor by bringing along my wife, Nancy, a woman with her own limitless potential for causing mayhem, and I knew, just knew, that the all-male adventure the night before was a trip to Disneyland compared to what was in store for me now. There's an expression in Spain that translates as 'a little bit – often,' a phrase usually invoked before setting out on a *poteo* – what we might call a 'bar crawl.' Essentially, the way a *poteo* works is this: You bounce around from one tapas joint to another, eating what they call *pinchos* (the local term for tapas) and drinking *txacoli*, red wine, in measured amounts. Drop in, eat what's great – and only what's great – at each particular bar, then move on.

We had the TV crew lurking ahead and behind us as we set out through the streets of the *parte vieja*, and I was keeping a sharp, worried eye on Nancy, who hated the idea of making a television show, hated being near a camera, and had already taken a serious dislike to the producer for keeping me busy most of the day shooting 'B-roll,' meaning scenery, shots of me walking around and pretending I was thinking deep thoughts, while she stewed, neglected, in a hotel room. If the producer elbowed her out of a wide shot one more time, I knew, she was going to sock him in the neck. I'd seen her use that punch before – on a too-friendly woman at a sailors' bar in the Caribbean. She'd leaned behind me, drawn back, and walloped a much larger woman two stools down, straight in the carotid. The woman went down like a sack of lentils. I didn't want to see that again. I made out Matthew, the producer, walking backward in the darkness and decided there would be no contest. Nancy could take him with one arm behind her back. Besides, she already had allies. She was now commiserating with Virginia and Visi and their friends behind me. I could hear them all laughing, the other women immediately sympathizing. If things degenerated into senseless violence, I'd just walk away and leave Matthew to his fate. Besides, I was still pissed about the Jerry Lewis incident.

The girls – that's how they referred to themselves – were all sharp, attractive, fiercely independent women in their mid to late thirties, happily single and totally unneurotic about sex. When a camera guy, making casual conversation, asked one of the friends if she liked to dance, she shrugged and said, 'I like to fuck' – not an invitation, by the way, just a casual statement of fact. I felt, in spite of the lingering potential for violence, reasonably comfortable and among friends. These women acted like . . . well, cooks.

It takes experience to navigate the tapas bars of San Sebastián the way we did that night. Temptation is everywhere. It's hard not to gorge too early, fill up too soon, miss the really good stuff later in a haze of alcohol. The first place was a good example: Ganbara, a small semicircular bar with no seats and room for about twenty people standing shoulder-to-shoulder. Laid out in a breathtaking display on clean white marble was the most maddeningly enticing spread of bounty: snow-white anchovies glistening in olive oil, grilled baby octopus salad, roasted red and yellow peppers, codfish fritters, marinated olives, langoustines, pink-red fat-rippled serrano, *pata negra* and Bayonne ham, stuffed chilis, squid, tarts, empanadas, brochettes, salads – and the most awesome, intimidatingly beautiful mountain range of fresh wild mushrooms: gorgeous custard-yellow chanterelles and hedge-hogs, earth-toned cèpes, morels, black trumpets. Cooks seared them to order in black pressed-steel pans and the room was filled with the smell of them. Visi cut me off before I started blindly eating everything in sight; she conferred with the cooks for a moment while a bartender poured us small glasses of red wine. A few moments later, I had a pungent mound of searingly hot sautéed wild mushrooms in front of me, crispy, golden brown, black and yellow, with a single raw egg yolk slowly losing its shape in the center. After a toast of red wine, I ran my fork around the plate, mingling yolk and fungi, then put a big forkful in my mouth. I can only describe the experience as 'ready to die' – one of those times when if suddenly and unexpectedly shot, at that precise moment you would, in your last moments of consciousness, know that you had had a full and satisfying life, that in your final moments, at least you had eaten well, truly well, that you could hardly have eaten better. You'd be ready to die. This state of gustatory rapture was interrupted by more wine, a tiny plate of tantalizing baby octopus, and a few sexy-looking anchovies. I was at first confused by an offer of what looked to be a plate of fried zucchini sticks, but when I bit inside and found tender white asparagus, I nearly swooned.

'Let's go,' said one of the girls, tearing me away from a long, lingering look at all that ham. 'Next place is famous for fish cakes.' We walked six abreast down the cobblestone streets, the girls laughing and joking – already best pals with my wife – who speaks no Spanish and certainly no Basque. I felt like part of the James/Younger gang. At the next joint, Luis's former student recognized me from the street, entered, took one look at the female desperadoes I was keeping company with, and bolted immediately from the premises, badly outnumbered.

'This place is famous for hot food – especially the fish cakes. You see? Nothing on the bar. Everything here is made to order in the kitchen,' said Visi. We drank more red wine while we waited for the food. I was soon digging into a hot, fluffy fish cake of *bacalao*, onions, and peppers, smeared onto a crust of bread, followed by the even better *morro*, a braised beef cheek in a dark expertly reduced demiglace. Yes, yes, I was thinking. This is the way to live, perfect for my short attention span. I could easily imagine doing this with chef friends in New York, ricocheting from tapas bar to tapas bar, drinking and eating and eating and drinking, terrorizing one place after another. If only New York had an entire neighborhood of tapas bars. The whole idea of the *poteo* wouldn't work if you had to take a cab from place to place. And the idea of sitting down at a table for *pinchos*, having to endure a waiter, napkins, a prolonged experience, seems all wrong.

Another joint, then another, the red wine flowing, the girls getting looser and louder. I don't know how one would translate 'Uh-oh, here comes trouble,' but I'm sure we heard it in our rounds as our crew swept into one tiny bar after another. I remember anchovies marinated in olive oil, tomato, onion, and parsley, cured anchovies, grilled anchovies, fried sardines, a festival of small tasty fish. More wine, more toasts. I recall stumbling through an old square that had once been a city bullring, apartments now overlooking the empty space. Past old churches, up cobblestone steps, down others, lost in a whirlwind of food.

At San Telino, a modern, more upscale place (inside an old, old building), I found a more nouvelle take on *pinchos*. Wine was poured as soon as we entered. I had, I recall, a spectacular slab of pan-seared foie gras with mushrooms – and, glory of glories, a single squid stuffed with *boudin noir*. I hunched protectively over my little plate, not wanting to share.

More wine. Then more.

The women still looked fresh. I felt like I'd awakened under a collapsed building, the room beginning to tilt slightly. I was speaking Mexican-inflected kitchen Spanish, which is always a bad sign when wondering if I'm drunk or not – and the girls had only begun.

After a few more places, I finally called it a night. Somehow, we'd gotten into the tequila by now. I'd seen a chunk of hash cross the bar, there was a fresh row of shot glasses being lined up, and Nancy was looking at one of the crew's idle cameras like she was going to use it as a blunt object. It was time to go. One seldom leaves a good impression on one's hosts by suddenly sagging to the floor unconscious.

It's great, sometimes, to be a chef. It's even great, sometimes, to be a well-known chef – even if one is well known for things completely unrelated to one's skill in the kitchen. There are perks. It's even better when you're with a better-known chef, a longtime resident of the community in which you're eating, and you're looking to get treated well in a really fine restaurant. No one gets fed better in good restaurants than other chefs. And when you're really, really lucky, you get to sit at the chef's table, right in the kitchen, attacking a three-star Michelin tasting menu in the best restaurant in Spain.

Which is where I was, sipping from a magnum of Krug in the kitchen of Arzak, a family-run temple of Nouvelle Basque on the outskirts of San Sebastián, the best restaurant in town, I was assured by just about everyone I'd met – which, of course, meant it was also the best restaurant in Spain, and therefore the world. I'm not going to weigh in on the 'who's best' issue, but I will tell you that it was a flawless, remarkable, and uniquely Basque experience. Yes, yes, there is that other place, where they serve the seawater foam and the desserts look like Fabergé eggs, but I wasn't going there, so I can't offer an informed opinion, though I'm happy to sneer at it in principle.

Chef/owner Juan Mari Arzak was one of the fabled 'Group of Ten,' back in the heady, early days of French nouvelle cuisine. Inspired by the pioneering efforts of French chefs like Troisgros, Bocuse, Vergé, Guérard, et al., Arzak and a few others had determined to move the traditional elements and preparations of Basque cuisine up and forward, refining it, eliminating any heaviness, redundancy, silliness, and excess. He took a much-loved, straightforward family restaurant and turned it into a cutting-edge three-star destination for serious gourmets from all over Europe, a must-see whistle-stop on every self-respecting chef's world tour. And he did it without compromising, without ever turning his back on his roots or on Basque culinary traditions.

Luis and Juan Mari greeted one another like two old lions. The chef showed us around his immaculate white-tiled kitchen as if we were guests in his home, sitting down at the table with us while the chef de cuisine, his daughter, Elena, took charge of the cooking. Apologies to Elena – and Juan Mari – but I have to tell you, just to set the scene properly, that later, back in New York, when I raved about the meal I had at Arzak to a tableful of multistarred New York chefs (all of whom had already eaten there), they wanted to know only one thing: 'Was Elena there?

. . . Ohhhh God.' There is nothing sexier to many male chefs than a good-looking, brilliantly talented young woman in chef whites, with grill marks and grease burns on her hands and wrists. So Elena, if you ever read this, know that thousands of miles away, a tableful of *New York Times* stars were moved to spontaneous expressions of puppy love by the mere mention of your name.

Elena walked us through each item of food in near-perfect English, apologizing (needlessly) for her accent. The kickoff was pumpkin ravioli with a squid-ink sauce infused with red pepper. Next, little toast points with a puree of Basque sausage and honey, a tiny cup of sheep's-milk yogurt with foie gras – almost obscenely good. Like all my favorite haute chefs, the Arzaks don't mess about with the extraneous or nonsensical. Presentations represented the food to best effect and never distracted from the ingredients. The Basque elements were always front and center; you knew, at all times, where you were. There was crayfish with eggplant caviar, olive oil, and parsley, and then an alarmingly shrewd yet deceptively simple creation I'd never seen nor even heard of before: a fresh duck egg, whole, yolk and white undisturbed, which had been removed carefully from the shell, wrapped in plastic with truffle oil and duck fat, then lightly, delicately poached before being unwrapped and presented, topped with wild-mushroom duxelles and a dusting of dried sausage. It was one of those dishes that, while absolutely eye-opening and delicious, inevitably makes me feel small, wondering why I could never have come up with such a concept. Eating it was bittersweet, the experience tinged as it was with the certain knowledge of my own bad choices and shortcomings. How did they come up with this? Did the idea appear like the theory of relativity appeared to Einstein – in dreams? What came first? The egg? The duck fat? It was so good. It hurt to eat it.

The menu kept coming. A vegetable tart with chestnuts, white asparagus, baby bok choy, and wild mushrooms; sea bass with a sauce of leek ash, a green sauce of fresh herbs, and garnish of one flawless diver's scallop; wild duck, roasted in its own juices, the defiantly fat-flecked jus allowed to run unmolested around the plate; a duck consommé with roasted tomato. It was one of the best meals I'd ever had. In one of those 'It can't get any better than this' moments, an ashtray appeared, allowing me to enjoy a postmeal cigarette inside a three-star kitchen. Life was good.

Listening to Luis Irizar and Juan Mari Arzak discuss cuisine, the things they'd accomplished, was like listening to two old Bolsheviks reminisce about storming the Winter Palace. I envied them that they were so good at what they did, that they were so firmly grounded in a culture, a place, an ethnoculinary tradition, that they were surrounded by such limitless supplies of good stuff – and the clientele to appreciate it fully. Would such advantages have, in my time, changed my own trajectory? Made me a better chef? A better cook?

As another American writing about Spain famously said, 'Isn't it pretty to think so?'

HOW TO DRINK VODKA

WRAPPED UP AGAINST THE cold in the small outer entryway of the midnight train from Moscow to Saint Petersburg, I watched the faint shaking of the silver samovar of hot tea and hand-wrought silver cup holders and glasses at the end of the first-class carriage. Snow collected in narrow drifts on the floor and around the window glass as I smoked.

It was February of the coldest, snowiest winter in Russia for a hundred years. Out there in the hinterlands of snowed-over farms and disused factories, people were dying in droves, heating oil was short, and President Putin was talking of arresting and indicting a few provincial governors who'd mishandled supply. In the news, an American graduate student had been detained for marijuana possession, the charges suddenly – and ominously – upgraded to espionage. A Russian colonel, charged with rape and murder, implicated directly by forensic evidence and the testimony of his fellow officers, was arguing for acquittal and garnering considerable support from the remnants of Commie hard-liners.

Outside the window of my snug sleeping compartment with its triple locks, mile after mile of birch forest, snow-covered farmland, and frozen lakes swept by, glimpsed for a second and then gone. So far, Russia had been everything I'd wanted it to be.

It was the Russia of my dreams and adolescent fantasies that I was looking for: dark, snowy, cold, a moody and romantic place of beauty, sadness, melancholy, and absurdity. In Moscow, the white-topped minarets and onion domes, the tall redbrick battlements of the Kremlin, the imperious, gloomy facades of GUM department store, the snow-smeared cobblestones of Red Square – they all looked exactly as I'd hoped they'd look. The Lubyanka – KGB headquarters and the site of the notorious prison where a countless number of Stalin's victims had been tortured, coerced, interrogated, and finally dispatched with a single gunshot to the neck – looked strangely neutered now that Dzerzhinsky's statue no longer gazed down on its square. There may have been slot machines on the subway, casinos everywhere, prowling hookers, and street signs sponsored by Western brand names – GORKY STREET – BROUGHT TO YOU BY THE FINE FOLKS AT PHILIP MORRIS! – but this still looked like the Russia of my fevered imaginings: dead drops, brush contacts, burst transmissions, betrayals. It was where Kim Philby, Donald MacLean, and Guy Burgess had spent their days in pampered limbo. This had been the epicenter, ground zero for all the evil in the world (according to my kindergarten teacher and most right-thinking Americans) back when I was a little kid, crouching under my desk during duck-and-cover drills, the cause of or justification for all sorts of dimly remembered madness: the Cuban missile crisis, my neighbors' backyard bomb shelter, Vietnam, JFK, CIA, LBJ, Nixon – all the purported saints and boogeymen of my youth. I grew up thinking the Big One could come at any moment, and this country – or fear of it, the way my country reacted to the threat – radicalized, marginalized, and alienated me in ways that still affect me.

And there was 'Dimitri,' my first and most important mentor and partner in the restaurant business. The first professional I knew who was actually passionate about the craft of cooking, a guy who cooked on his day off. Romantic, curious, literate, maudlin, gregarious, mercurial, he had been my first glimpse of Russia's beating heart and dark, tormented soul. As the train chugged through the snow, I wanted a closer look at that soul. I wanted borscht, *zakuski*, caviar, black bread, and vodka. I wanted a big furry hat and snow on my boots.

A lightly padded fist crashed into the nose of an overweight lug with a crew cut, flattening it with a sickening, wet *Whapp* sound.

The larger of the two men in the cage dropped back onto the canvas; blood spread across his face, running off his chin onto his chest. His opponent, a ripplingly muscled young fellow in clapped-out tube socks and faded athletic shorts, didn't hesitate – he drove his knee twice into the fallen man's liver and began pounding mercilessly at the side of his skull with both fists.

The mood in the room was controlled but festive, kind of like a company cocktail party. Well-dressed women in short short skirts and backless dresses looked on from their tables, expressionless behind carefully applied makeup. Next to them, their male friends, most of a type and appearance described in Russia as 'flathead' – big, bordering on huge, with monster muscles bulging through elegant dark suits, low brows, brush cuts, and the eyes of underwater predators – sipped drinks and talked among themselves, the women largely ignored. The venue? I'll call it 'Club Malibu.' (I still have friends who live there.) It was a modern black and chrome nightclub/disco/restaurant complex built inside an older building, sort of goombah chic, circa 1985 (like the China Club), with recessed lighting, glitter balls, big noise, and nice clothes. I was sitting ringside on a high leather-backed stool with an older guy with shoulder-length hair and one of those denim brim caps that Freddie Prinze might have worn. He spoke not a word of English and I spoke no Russian. An apparently well-known singer/songwriter, he shared the VIP table with me, close enough to the ring to catch the blood spray. I was at the VIP table because that's what it took for me to get a glimpse of what my Russian friends sarcastically call the 'new Russians,' the mad, bad, and very dangerous to know successors of old Russians. In the new Russia, everything is possible. And nothing is for certain.

It had taken some arranging to pull this evening off, and a lot of very diplomatic and circumspect negotiation. After a late-night meeting with a rough-looking but willing intermediary, and a lot of talking around the issue with middlemen, finally 'Gregor' showed up at a midnight rendezvous with a photo album. After a few shots of vodka and some *zakuski*, he proudly walked me through a collection of photographs depicting him with various thick-necked gentlemen holding automatic weapons; in some shots, they were stripped to the waist, their bare chests and backs decorated with tattoos of cathedrals, minarets, and Cyrillic lettering. Hearing that my associates would like to shoot video of whatever ensued, he became excited, assuring me that should we want to shoot a major Hollywood production in Saint Petersburg or Moscow, he could 'provide security,' make sure there were no 'difficulties or red tape.' He'd done it before, he boasted, naming two recent film productions. I looked closely at the photographs, determined never to make any of these guys mad at me.

Club Malibu was set back from Nevsky Prospekt in Saint Petersburg, easy to find by the rows of gleaming Jaguars, BMWs, Porsches, and Mercedes parked illegally out front. After passing through a metal detector and undergoing a thorough, somewhat intrusive pat-down and frisk – as well as a few gruff questions in Russian – followed by a hushed phone conversation, I was led up thickly carpeted steps, vibrating from loud techno music. At the foyer to the main ballroom, where tonight's event, No-Holds-Barred Caged Extreme Fighting and Senseless Brutality, would soon be under way, Gregor approached me like an old friend, giving me a big warm for-show hug and kisses on both cheeks before deferentially showing me to my reserved table. This demonstration of closeness and friendship, I'd been told, was very important to how welcome I'd be there. I'd worn my best Crazy Joe Gallo outfit for the occasion: black fingertip-length leather jacket, black silk shirt, black silk tie, black pants, pointy black shoes, my hair gelled into what can best be described as late Frankie Avalon, doing the best I could to look like a person who could realistically be introduced as 'a friend of ours from New York.'

For two hours, I sat and drank and nibbled caviar with blini, watching the most outrageously ugly and pointless violence I'd ever witnessed. The well-dressed audience, some of whom seemed in mute collusion with some of the contestants (I saw at least two blatant dives taken), consisted of a mix of flatheads and older, more distinguished fellows, most accompanied by

tall, high-cheekboned, long-legged, and invariably blond women
with spectacular breasts and cold, cold eyes. When one of the
contenders in the ring caught an elbow to the face, foamy red
sputum bubbling from his lips, I was reminded of the farm kids
in Portugal at the pig slaughter as I glanced around the room.
The women stared blankly at the sickening carnage.

One poor brute after another stepped into the ring and was
quickly pounded into submission. Choking, kicking, kneeing,
flying elbows, head butts – almost every bout ended with one
man on the mat, the other's arm around his throat, choking off
his air supply and simultaneously stomping his abdomen with
both knees. I counted, at the end of the evening, two KOs, two
fixed fights, and ten TKOs – all concluded by near asphyxia. It
was nauseating. It was ugly. It was kinda cool.

My local contact, translator and fixer in Russia was the amazing
Zamir, a genial, funny, well-informed guy with a dark mustache,
a three-day-old growth of beard much of the time, and a fur-
lined hat with earflaps. Worldly, experienced, fatalistic about
the way things were going in his country, Zamir, on this subzero
afternoon, was taking me out to experience a much-beloved
Russian institution, a traditional *banya*, or sauna, the place
Russians of all ages have relaxed with family or friends on
weekends for ages. In this case, it was a small sweatbox in the
middle of the snow-covered countryside, next to a frozen lake in
the woodsy community of Shuvalovo, about thirty miles outside
of Saint Petersburg. Zamir's friend, Alexej, a musician, drove,
while Zamir sat in the passenger seat. We weren't even out of
town yet, taking the corner by the Hermitage onto the road that
runs alongside the Neva River, when we were pulled over by a
traffic cop.

'Where are your papers?' went the routine. Apparently, there
never are the appropriate papers in these instances. The cop
didn't even wait for Zamir or Alexej to search. 'Fifty rubles,' he
announced. Grumbling, Alexej gave him a few notes, and the
cop simply wrote down the amount in a small lined notebook
before putting the money in his pocket and waving us along.

We stopped at a market on the outskirts of town for some traditional *banya* treats to take along. Soon, we were driving past apartment blocks of worker flats, looking like inner-city projects of the 1950s and 1960s, and then empty spaces appeared, punctuated by swatches of birch forests, the country dachas of old apparatchiks, run-down gingerbread houses, set back from the road on untended plots of woodland behind peeling picket fences.

The wheels of our car crunched over thick hard-packed snow as we left paved road and wound slowly through forest, finally arriving at the edge of a vast frozen lake. A worse-for-wear wooden house sat next to a small log-and-shingle cabin, smoke rising from a chimney. A rickety ice-encrusted walkway with a shaky-looking railing extended out over the lake, then descended down thickly glazed steps to an eight-by-four-foot hole in the ice, a black oblong of water one degree above freezing, already hardening at the surface.

We were met by a red-cheeked woman in sweater and overalls. She ushered us inside and showed us into one of three tiny wood-planked rooms, each with its own inner sauna, where Zamir and I quickly stripped, wrapped ourselves in towels, and broke out the drinks and snacks: beer, vodka, dried, salty sprats, a few smoked sable fish, stiff, pungent, and still on the bone, a little dried sausage, and a loaf of dark bread. After a beer, Zamir and I stepped into the closet-sized sauna, took our places on the higher, hotter of the two wooden benches, and started to sweat. Coals glowed in the corner of the tiny room. A battered pitcher of water stood by, a thick bundle of birch branches protruding, their leaves submerged and soaking. We sat in there for a long time, sheets tucked under us, groaning and breathing loudly, and when it seemed that any second I'd pass out, we retired to the outer chamber to devour the food. The deliciously oily, salty fish and a few beers renewed us enough to venture inside again.

Twenty minutes later, Zamir asked me if I was 'ready for my interrogation.' I warily assented, having a pretty good idea what was coming. Our thick-wristed hostess entered the sauna, motioned for me to lie naked on my stomach, and began savagely flogging me with the foliage ends of the birch branches. WHACK! ... WHACK! ... WHACKWHACKWHACK! I started with each blow – not too painful in and of themselves – because my bare chest was being scalded through the thin sheet on the skillet-hot upper bench. But it is one of my many failings that I don't want to look like a wuss, even when medical imperative and good sense dictate otherwise, so I gritted my teeth and endured without complaint. Dead leaves flew every-where, clinging to my flesh as she whipped and whipped, the blows coming more frequently now, more forcefully, as she informed me in fractured English of the many health benefits this treatment provided. When my whole body was a glowing, irritated red and my chest covered with angry, soon-to-blister burns, every pore on my body open to the elements, she stepped back, opened the door, and pointed to where I'd known from the beginning I'd eventually have to go.

I paused long enough to throw on a bathing suit. While the prospect of exhibiting my genitals to Food Network viewers, under ordinary circumstances, had a perverse appeal, I preferred that they not be pignoli-sized when I did. I hurled open the outer door, jogged carefully in bare feet out onto the slippery walkway to the lake, lowered myself down two icy steps, and dropped into the frozen lake.

To say that the experience was shocking, that it knocked the wind out of me, that it was cold would all be grievous under-statements. It was like getting hit by a phantom freight train – every cell, every atom of my body went into mad panic. My balls scrambled north, headed somewhere around my collarbone, my brain screamed, my eyeballs did the best they could to pop out of my skull, and every pore, wide open only a few seconds earlier, slammed closed like a plugged steam pipe. It was a punch to the chest from God's fist. I sank to the bottom, bent my knees deeply, and pushed up, breaking the surface with an involuntary high-pitched shriek that must have sounded to residents across the lake like someone had just hooked their cat up to a car battery. I struggled for purchase on a guide rope completely glazed over with an inch of ice, my hands unable to grab hold,

85

and floundered, slipped, and finally managed to clamber up a few steps and flop onto the snow-covered ice.

Strangely, once out of the water, I felt fine. In fact, I felt incredible. I wasn't cold at all. With a confident, even jaunty, spring in my step, I walked along the surface of the frozen lake, ankle-deep in snow, feeling as toasty and comfortable as if I'd been sitting in front of a fire in a big woolly sweater. I walked around the cabin for a bit, pausing to chat with a barrel-chested naked Russian hockey coach, who informed me that he didn't even bother to use the sauna before jumping in the lake. He came only to swim. Every few seconds, there was another splash as a naked Russian flopped into the water. The coach wanted to talk about American hockey, but as my bare feet were beginning to stick to the ground, I stepped back inside. I sat with Zamir and gratefully slugged back a mouthful of vodka. I felt good. Really good. So good that after a bit more of the black bread and sausage, a few nibbles of fish, and lots more beer and vodka, I was ready to go again.

I was drunk. I was happy. If not *the* perfect meal, this was, in many ways, a perfect one. Good food, good company, exotic ambience, and an element of adventure.

Back in Saint Petersburg, we turned the corner by the Hermitage, only to get pulled over once again by a traffic cop. 'Aw, this isn't fair,' complained Alexej. 'We just got shaken down in the same place a few hours ago. We paid already!'

The cop considered this for a moment, peered into the car, and agreed. 'You're right,' he said. 'It's not fair.' He closed his little pad, withdrew his hand, and waved us along.

In a well-worn rabbit-fur coat, Sonya pushed her wide shoulders through the crowded entryway of the Kupchina market. This was a working-class district, and the other customers around her, also in ratty furs, bore the same resigned expressions and stooped postures you see on the IRT train bearing passengers in from Queens for morning shifts at city restaurants – the look of hardworking people going to and coming from unglamorous jobs. Given her dark mascara and rough Slavic features, her less-than-diminutive size, and the seriousness of her intent, the others got out of Sonya's way as she approached the long row of butcher counters. She was a woman on a mission, a heat-seeking missile, a professional at shopping. 'What's this?' Sonya inquired of a leathery-looking man in an apron as she disdainfully fingered a perfectly fine-looking pork shoulder draped over his countertop.

'Beautiful pork shoulder,' said the butcher, already wary. He knew what was coming.

'It looks older than I am,' sneered Sonya, easily in her late thirties. 'How much?'

After getting an answer, she spun away without a backward glance, her eye already on another piece a few yards down. The butcher called her back, the pork suddenly cheaper by a few rubles. I traveled slipstream in Sonya's considerable wake, doing my best to keep up as she barreled from vendor to vendor in the hangar-sized unheated space, keeping my eyes constantly on the massive rabbit coat and the mop of red hair as she careened purposefully down the crowded aisles, collecting meat, root vegetables, herbs, and *mise-en-place* for our lunch. Few running backs ever had it so good. People saw Sonya coming and moved quickly aside. I didn't know what she was saying to these people, but I had a pretty good idea. Sonya examined a bunch of beets, hefted a couple of them, then launched into a gruff interrogation of the merchant. Unsatisfied with the response, she headed for another neatly arranged pile, muttering something over her shoulder that was certainly not a compliment.

I had been led to believe that Russia was all bread lines, shortages, empty shelves, produce rotting in the train yards, oranges only a rumor. And surely that must have been the case elsewhere. The country, as we are constantly reminded by panicky anchormen, is in financial shambles. The army hasn't been paid. Most people live on about a dollar a day. Gangsters roam at will, bombing, assassinating. Saint Petersburg itself is the contract-killing capital of Russia – which is perhaps why so many flatheads are able to find steady employment as bodyguards. Mail arrives – or it doesn't. Farms lie fallow, factories molder. So why, in a not at all well-to-do neighborhood, is there a public market that could give Dean & Deluca or Zabar's a run for their money? In front of me lay counter after counter of pristine-looking vegetables: yellow peppers, melons, fresh herbs, bananas, pineapples, tubers, root veggies, lettuces. Butchers broke down on site whole sides of beef, lamb, pork, whacking away with heavy cleavers against deeply bowed and scarred chopping blocks. Beautiful free-range chickens, head and feet still attached, were arranged in orderly and attractive rows over deli counters. Little of it was refrigerated – but it was cold in there and the stuff was moving fast. There was a customer for every steak, hoof, scrap, bone, foot, and jowl. Women in heavy coats and babushkas considered single squares of pork fat as if shopping for a new car. People didn't so much haggle as argue, delivering impassioned rants about the virtues and deficiencies of a slab of bacon, which almost always ended in a sale.

What the Kupchina market lacks in foreign specialties and produce, it makes up for in homegrown exotica: yard after yard of brightly colored homemade pickled vegetables; every variety of absolutely gorgeous-looking smoked fish – sturgeon, sable, salmon, sprats, chubs, sterlet (a cousin to the sturgeon), herring – heaped one on top of the other inside glass display cases; tubs of caviar and fish roe; a dairy section where white-uniformed, white-kerchiefed women offer varieties of fresh and aged farmer cheese, yogurt, sour cream, hand-churned butter, curds, and sweet condensed milk.

Sonya, however, was not impressed. She did not look around. She knew what she wanted. She finally found some potatoes she liked and loaded them into the growing cargo of plastic shopping bags under her arms, then clomped across a few feet of concrete floor to lift a bunch of carrots with a skeptical pinkie finger.

'You call this a carrot?' she challenged. A few moments later, she was bullying an old woman over a bunch of fresh dill. Having given another butcher a few moments to reflect on her requirements, she veered back in his direction, settling – after more bitterly fought negotiations – on a slab of pork belly, some lightly cured bacon, and a fat beef shank. She counted out each ruble as if giving away nuclear codes.

I was in love. If I could ever fall for a woman who reminded me of Broderick Crawford, it would be Sonya. She's a fabulously imposing, nonstop talker, a great cook, a survivor, an artist, a hard drinker – a force of nature. There's a whiff of Janis Joplin about her. Unflappable, been around the block, she's a woman of surprising dimension and abilities. Her shopping list nearly complete, she stepped out into the cold, picked her way across a thick layer of soot-covered ice, and bought half a handful of fresh garlic from one of the impoverished-looking babushkas lined up outside.

'I live this way,' she barked, in heavily accented English, beckoning with her head.

I followed obediently.

Sonya lives with a roommate in a walk-up apartment, which she reaches by climbing up a flight of unlit concrete stairs. The kitchen is cramped but homey, with cracked linoleum floors and a *Sputnik*-era TV set, small gas stove, sink, refrigerator, and a little round table that doubles as a prep bench and serving area. The common areas are filled with the accumulated possessions of many years: shoes, boots, knickknacks, photographs, weathered furniture, a Commie-period poster of a kerchiefed female factory worker with her finger to her lips, the Cyrillic admonition clearly stating something like 'Loose lips sink ships.' One thing you get plenty of in Russia, no matter what your economic circumstances, is irony.

Sonya takes photographs in her spare time. The walls are decorated with her work – severe yet strangely beautiful studies of a now nearly invisible feature of Russian urban landscape: the air vents and entryways to Cold War bomb shelters. They sprout like toadstools from vacant lots, poke up through the weeds of public parks, and in the crumbling corners of Stalin-age housing developments. She has self-published a calendar, each month represented by a mushroom-shaped cylinder of concrete and metal grillwork.

'I like Texas,' she said as we stood in her kitchen. 'You like Texas?' She had recently traveled across America on a Greyhound bus, visiting friends. 'Also I like Salt Lake City, Cincinnati, and Miami. Miami is very nice.' She had seen far more of my country than I had, I told her.

'This is a lot of work,' she said. She'd been rolling out dough for *pelmeni*, meat-filled dumplings – a distant relative of the wonton, a legacy of one of the long-ago Mongol incursions – and would like it very much if Mr. Famous Traveling Chef Author Guy – or somebody, *anybody* – would pitch in. I stepped in, helping her to spoon dots of the meat into the dough on an octagonal cutter. Sonya laid on a top layer of dough, clamped down on the cutter, and about sixteen *pelmeni* at a time dropped through the other side. I tamped them closed, pinched and shaped, then placed them on cookie sheets in neat rows. She kept up a steady stream of patter in Russian and English, bopping back and forth between the two languages, making use of whichever was most comfortable at the time. Zamir sat next to me, filling in the blanks in her English, offering explanations when needed. Alexej sat across from me, looking morose. Outside the kitchen door, Igor, a hired cameraman from Moscow, hovered, filming – or not – according to his own mysterious agenda.

When the *pelmeni* were assembled, Sonya swung her attention over to the borscht simmering on her stovetop. I had been looking forward to this. In Russia, as my old friend Dimitri memorably pointed out to me, borscht is barely a soup; it's damn near an entrée: a chunky hot stew of meat, onions, carrot, cabbage, beets, and potatoes, a rib-sticking dark red concoction perfect for filling the belly cheaply on an icy winter night. The cold, watery bright pink puree you might have seen in the States is barely related. Sonya had made a stock from selected cuts of meat in a pressure cooker, a piece of kitchen equipment, by the way, that, while rarely seen in America, is viewed as a godsend by much of the rest of the world. Then she began sautéeing onions, carrots, and bay leaf, added the stock, threw in the meat and potatoes, then the cabbage, and finally, so as not to discolor or overcook it, grated in the peeled beet at the last minute. I saw some caraway seeds and a few other herbs go in, but when I asked her what they were, she pretended not to understand me. Cooks. The same everywhere.

'A drink,' Sonya said pointedly, 'for the workers,' casting a skeptical eye at the inactive Russian contingent in her kitchen. Soon we were all toasting with tall shot glasses of her homemade cranberry vodka, and readying ourselves to eat. Sonya dropped table settings and condiments around the wiped-down table as if she were dealing a hand of blackjack. A heaping bowl of fresh sour cream appeared at the center of the table, along with bowls of fresh chopped dill, chopped scallions and parsley, and some bottled condiments for the *pelmeni*: horseradish, mustard, and, unexpectedly, a bottle of catsupy stuff that tasted like Heinz chili sauce.

We wiped out the cranberry vodka as Sonya ladled big chunky portions of hot borscht into chipped bowls; she demonstrated how to complete it by heaping a huge spoon of sour cream into mine, topped by a fistful of dill and scallion. Just before sitting down to eat, she reached into the freezer and extracted a full bottle of Russian Standard vodka, plunking it down without comment.

'No one drinks water in this country,' I said to Zamir.

'Not advisable,' he replied. 'The tap water here is very bad for you. You don't drink the water in Russia. Not that we would . . .'

Another toast to hands across the water, another to the spirit of international cooperation, a toast to the chef, a toast to the guests – and we were off.

The borscht was sensational. I worked my way through two bowls, noticing that the wiry Alexej finished three. The *pelmeni* were up next. Sonya cooked them in boiling water until tender, fished them out with a strainer, and deposited a pile on each of our plates. One dresses one's own, according to preference, from ingredients at the table. I selected a little sour cream, dill, mustard, and horseradish. To my surprise, the Russians all went for the catsup.

I ate my way around Saint Petersburg for a week, with Zamir, Alexej, and Igor coming along. Alexej had loosened up considerably around me. One night, he invited me back to his flat, where his wife had made blintzes. It was in an uninviting-looking workers' block, with thick graffitied concrete walls, and dark hallways. But behind the multiple door locks, Alexej lived like a New York City nightclub owner: raised carpeted floors, recessed lighting, an enormous bathroom with hot tub, Jacuzzi, and full sauna, a wet bar, home recording studio, wide-screen TV, and entertainment center. My Russian driver lived far better than I do! I was introduced to his lovely wife, and his young son, who, along with his father, treated me to some Stevie Ray Vaughn covers on a brand-new drum kit and Stratocaster guitar.

On another night, we ate braised reindeer in juniper at the Povorodye restaurant, a steeply gabled log structure on the outskirts of Pushkin Park, where Catherine the Great's gaudy summer palace still stands. Gaping at the gigantic gold and pastel-colored behemoth set in a wooded estate and surrounded by the stately former homes of nobles and retainers, one could easily understand the rage of the peasantry in pre-Revolution days. The palace must have been a grotesque affront to a largely starving, uneducated, downtrodden peasantry, people who were struggling even for bread. Looking at this gorgeous Italian-designed abomination, where maybe ten people and their servants lived, one could understand the blind exultation they must have felt when the Romanovs were brought down.

At Povorodye, while a Georgian folk band played, Zamir showed me, step by step, how to drink vodka while we waited for our reindeer to be served. First, if at all possible, make sure you have food present. Even a simple crust of bread will do. We had an enticing selection of traditional appetizers in front of us: pickled garlic, cucumbers, mushrooms, some smoked eel, a little sturgeon, some salted salmon roe, and a loaf of heavy country bread.

Step one, demonstrated Zamir, is the toast. To others present, to your parents, to your country – anything will do. Hold a full shot of vodka in one hand and food – bread is easiest – in the other hand. Exhale. Inhale slowly. Knock back your entire shot in one gulp, immediately inverting your glass over the table to allow the microscopic last drop to fall out, proving you're not a wuss or a reactionary revanchist Trotskyite provocateur.

Then take a bite of food. If you don't have any food, a long, lingering sniff of your wrist or cuff will do. (I know it sounds strange, but trust me.) Repeat the procedure up to three times every twenty minutes throughout the drinking period. This is about as fast as your system can absorb all that alcohol. If you follow this regimen carefully, you can and will retain a state of verticality throughout the entire meal and into the postmeal drinking.

In all likelihood, you will make it away from the table without disgracing yourself. You will probably make it home without help. After that, however, you're on your own. Remember: They're professionals at this in Russia, so no matter how many Jell-O shots or Jäger shooters you might have downed at college mixers, no matter how good a drinker you might think you are, don't forget that the Russians – any Russian – can drink you under the table.

Be prepared, by the way, no matter how bad you might feel when you wake up, to do it again – with breakfast.

Zamir and I finished our reindeer (which tasted like slightly gamier venison) and strolled outside in the knee-deep snow. Near the restaurant, an area had been cleared and iced for skating. Kids played around a straw figure representing winter; it would be burned in effigy that night at the Farewell to Winter festivities. Families with children and toboggans and sleds slogged in heavy overcoats and fur hats from nearby homes, looking cheerful and excited, red-faced in the cold.

'I should put reindeer on our Christmas menu,' I mused out loud. 'Can you picture it? All those crying kids, wondering if that's a chunk of Rudolph or Blitzen lying on their plate?'

'I take it you don't have children,' observed Zamir.

We ate piroshki in town, at a Russian fast-food joint. Adorable-looking women in white-peaked caps and spotless red-and-white uniforms with low décolletage dished up pastries filled with meat, fish, cabbage, and sausages. Put out of your mind, by the

way, any idea that Russian women are all wide-bodied babushkas with faces like potatoes. They're not. I'd never seen so many
tall, beautiful, well-dressed women in one place in my life. That
they seem about as soft and cuddly as a fistful of quarters is
beside the point – they're gorgeous. At a blintz place, My
Mother-in-Law's Blintzes, more creamy-white-breasted girls
behind a spotless counter efficiently prepared and served
made-to-order crepes wrapped around various sweet and savory
fillings.

We ate *ukha*, a clear fish soup, and wood-roasted trout on
Krestovsky Island, a two-story structure by a frozen pond. The
cooks were out back, dressed in paratrooper camos in the snow,
feeding fish into wood-burning ovens in a windblown lean-to.
We drank tequila in a cellar bar filled with Russian kids, a band
playing phonetic English versions of ska, country-western, and
blues standards. I bought the obligatory fur hat, then went ice
fishing on the frozen Neva River, my two companions factory
workers who came a few times a week to get away from their
families. When I saw their catch – tiny whitebait-sized fish,
which they said they gave to their cats – I got the idea that these
guys weren't there to catch the big one. When one of them
cracked open a lunch box at eight o'clock in the morning and
offered me a slug of vodka, I got the full picture.

'Zamir,' I said, 'you've been dunking me in frozen lakes,
involving me in reindeer killing, poisoning me with vodka. Let's
go someplace nice and eat some high-end stuff. Some fish eggs.
Let's dress up and go out for one last blowout.'

That night, we trudged through the snow and a vicious wind
on Vasilevski Island (Saint Petersburg is made up of about 120
islands). It was dark and extremely cold.

Zamir and I stepped into the Russkya restaurant, a cavernous
but cozy, rustically elegant space with wide wood floorboards, a
plain plaster interior, dramatic ceilings, and a big brick and
mortar oven in the dining room. A relaxed flathead in a tight
jacket sat by the coat check, providing security, a suspicious-
looking bulge under his left shoulder. We were greeted right
away by a friendly host, who helped us peel off our layers and

then showed us to two large glass jars of homemade vodka and another jar of cloudy greenish liquid.

'Homemade mustard seed and horseradish vodka,' I was informed. The greenish liquid was 'cucumber juice,' essentially pickle brine. The idea was to down a shot of the spicy, throat-burning vodka, then chase it immediately with a glass of brine. Sounds pretty loathsome, right? And either element alone would indeed have been troublesome. But in correct order, the searing neutral spirits followed by cooling and oddly mellowing brine was delicious, sort of like my earlier experience at the *banya*: sweating and burning, followed by dunking and freezing. To-gether, somehow, it works.

We sat down and had a few more of these 'one-two punch' concoctions and some bread. Our waitress, a cute but unusually assertive young woman, seemed to materialize regularly with more of the stuff. 'Don't vorry,' she said, 'I am strong. If you get drunk, I can carry you home.' She was fairly petite, but I believed her.

Now, I famously hate salad bars. I don't like buffets (unless I'm standing on the serving side: buffets are like free money for cost-conscious chefs). When I see food sitting out, exposed to the elements, I see food dying. I see a big open petri dish that every passing serial sneezer can feel free to drool on and fondle with spittle-flecked fingers. I see food not held at ideal temperature, food rotated (or not) by person or persons unknown, left to fester in the open air unprotected from the passing fancies of the general public. Those New York delis with the giant salad bars where all the health-conscious office workers go for their light, sensible lunches? You're eating more bacteria than the guy standing outside eating mystery meat on a stick. I remember my own words when designing buffets at a large club: 'Fill 'em up on free salads and bread, so they go light on the shrimp.'

Russkya's first-course salad bar, however, was not bad. It helped that the restaurant was empty and the food looked fresh. A long white table was covered with goodies: *pashket* (a liver pâté), *grechnevaya kasha* (buckwheat groats with mushrooms and onions), pickled beets, smoked fish, pickled herring, potato salad, potato latkes, and shaved paper-thin slices of chilled, uncooked pork fat. It was the perfect accompaniment to the early stages of what I was beginning to understand would be a marathon vodka-drinking session. A full bottle of Russian Standard had already hit our table when Zamir and I returned from the buffet, and our waitress, watching us like a severe schoolmarm, seemed hell-bent on seeing us both carried out on stretchers.

Two huge plates loaded with osetra caviar and the traditional garnishes arrived at our table. We eyed the big mound of gray-black fish eggs, lemon wedges, separated hard-cooked egg yolks and whites, finely chopped onion, sour cream and chives, and a warm stack of fluffy, perfectly cooked buckwheat blinis. Then I dug in, not messing about with garnishes, shoveling about half an ounce into my mouth in one bite. The blinis were perfect, the little eggs bursting between my teeth.

'She says there is a problem with our table,' said Zamir, our waitress standing at his shoulder with a grave expression on her face. 'Our waitress says we are not drinking enough vodka. She is concerned.'

I searched my waitress's face, trying to find a hint of a smile. Was she kidding? I didn't know.

Try to imagine this happening in an American restaurant or bar. Your waiter comes to your table and says he doesn't think you are consuming enough booze, that you need more alcohol, and you need to consume it quickly. Our highways would be demolition derbies of colliding muscle cars overloaded with drunken frat boys, senseless Yuppies, and out-of-control secretaries stoked on spritzers and woo-woos. In Russia, though, this is apparently normal. At the time of their deaths, three out of five Russian men, I am told, are found to have a blood-alcohol level exceeding what one needs to qualify for a DWI. That doesn't mean the booze killed them, just that the majority of Russian men happen to be drunk when they die. Hundreds, if not thousands, do die every year directly from the effects of drinking cheap rotgut – bathtub brews sold as vodka but more like lighter fluid or paint remover. I shudder to think what the threshold for 'intoxicated' is if pulled over by a cop in Russia. I'm guessing about fifty rubles.

After we'd knocked off maybe four ounces of caviar and a half bottle of vodka, our entrée arrived, a whole roasted sterlet. Already smashed, Zamir and I were not off the hook. Even though we were well past the 'I love you, man' stage, exchanging slurred toasts every few minutes, our waitress returned to our table to admonish us.

'You will both be considered traitors to your countries and your people if you do not drink more!'

When we finally staggered out into the street, it was snowing hard, the wind howling off the river, a half bottle of Russian Standard sloshing around in our stuffed bellies. Zamir and I exchanged loud expressions of friendship and devotion, our coats flapping open in the frigid wind.

Reasons Why You Don't Want to Be on Television: Number Two in a Series

'We forgot to do the entrance scene,' said Chris, the producer, bundled up like some sub-Arctic smurf in Gore-Tex and stocking cap. 'We need to get you entering the restaurant. You know: "Where are we, why are we here, and what do we expect to find?" '

That all-important establishing shot had yet to be made, the part where Zamir and I, presumably sober, yet to eat that fine meal, are seen approaching the restaurant's door, opening it, and stepping inside. This sort of shot is necessary – as has been explained to me repeatedly by one frustrated producer after another – for purposes of continuity and edification for the viewing audience. 'We don't want 'em getting confused, thinking they're watching Emeril's Christmas Luau.'

This meant that while Igor and Chris shot, Zamir and I were to do our best to pretend that we had not just gorged ourselves on a large and luxurious meal, that we had not been forced into drinking about fifteen shots of vodka by a maniacal waitress.

Needless to say, it took a lot of takes. Most were scratched from the get-go by obvious slurring and stumbling, Zamir and I practically holding each other up as we lurched through the snow toward the increasingly blurry front door of the Russkya restaurant. By the second or third take, I was fully convinced there were, in fact, two doors.

'Shooo, Zhamir, ol' buddy, where we goin' now?' I'd burble in a hideous, inebriated parody of witless TV preamble, before staggering into a wall.

Finally, after many false starts, our lips freezing to our teeth, we had a near-flawless take: a few carefully enunciated remarks, some softball questions to my Russian friend and guide, the two of us picking our way down the street, Igor walking backward, with his camera facing us, Chris shooting from the side. Shoulder-to-shoulder we went, coats flapping, scarves blowing, two hungry, happy men about town, on their way to dinner.

In the finished shot, we appear to be doing everything right. I'm saying the right things, Zamir is responding appropriately; there are no obvious indicators of our total inebriation – other than the fact that we both seem curiously oblivious to the cold and wind and snow.

And we were doing fine until the last second, when, mid-sentence, I disappeared out of the frame in a sudden exit stage left. Zamir shot out an arm, reached off-camera, and pulled me back into the frame, rescuing me from what was very nearly a headlong tumble off the curb.

'Let's do it again,' said Chris.

'Lesh fix it later . . . In the editing room,' I said. I was learning.

SOMETHING VERY SPECIAL

'HERE, THIS PLACE . . . They have something very special,' said Abdul, a short, stocky Moroccan with a mustache, thick gold watch, and an alarmingly orange-and-green tweed sport jacket over a dress shirt. 'Very special' in Abdulspeak – as I had quickly come to learn – meant one of three things when talking about what to eat in Morocco: couscous, tagine, brochette. Morocco, while known for its excellent food and its many good cooks, is not renowned for its infinite variety of dishes. Or for its restaurants.

We were approaching the town of Moulay Idriss, an important spot in Morocco's introduction to Islam, a town named after a relative of the Prophet. It's a crowded but picturesque hill town, studded with box-shaped houses built at kitty-cornered angles, with narrow streets, high walls, and hidden markets. Until recently, nonbelievers like me were forbidden entrance. These days, as long as you're out by dark, it's okay to visit.

I'd frozen in Portugal and Russia, and been cold in Spain. I'd been cold *and wet* in France, so I'd been looking forward to Morocco. I figured desert, right? Burning sands, a relentless sun, me in full mufti. I'd read about the Long Range Desert Group, a collection of British academics, cartographers, geologists, ethnographers, and Arabists who, during World War II, had put aside their Poindexter glasses and their public school mores and spent a few years doing behind-the-lines raids with the SAS, cheerfully slitting throats, poisoning wells, committing acts of sabotage and reconnaissance. In the photos, they looked tan, for God's sake! OK, that had been Libya. Or Egypt. I wasn't even in the Middle East. But the desert – the sun, the heat – I'd got that right, right? Morocco, I'd been sure, would be a place where I could warm my bones, brown my skin.

So far, I could not have been more wrong. It was cold. The best hotel in neighboring Volubilis was yet another damp, chilly, crummy hovel. On the fuzzy television, a male Arab translator did all the voices on *Baywatch* – from Hasselhoff's to Anderson's – the original sound recording still there in English, the Arabic just laid over – and louder. An electric heater across the room from the bed threw off enough heat to toast a hand or a foot at a time.

But no matter. I had not set out to eat my way around the world expecting nothing but 340-thread-count sheets. I knew it wouldn't all be blender drinks by the pool and chocolates on the pillow. I had fully expected to face extremes of temperature, unusual plumbing arrangements, dodgy food, and the occasional insect on the way to what I was seeking.

And what I was looking for here, ultimately, was yet another moment of underinformed fantasy. I wanted to sit in the desert with the Blue Men – Tuaregs – a once-fierce tribe of nomadic Berbers who'd drifted back and forth between Yemen and Morocco for centuries, raiding caravans, disemboweling travelers, and eating whole lamb in their desert camps. I wanted to squat in the desert beneath the stars, with nothing but sand from horizon to horizon, eating the fat of the lamb with my fingers. I wanted to smoke hashish under a brightly swollen moon, leaning against my camel. I wanted a previously unattained sense of calm in the stillness of the desert.

For now, however, I was in a minivan, climbing the hill to Moulay Idriss, with Abdul, a TV crew, and a cluster of very sinister-looking plainclothes detectives in wraparound sunglasses, assigned by the Ministry of Information, in the back. A tall man in a green fez and djellaba was waiting for us in the shabby town square. His name was Sherif. He operated what was as close to an authentic Moroccan restaurant as one is likely to find in Morocco – a country where few natives would even consider eating indigenous cuisine in such an environment. By 'authentic,' I mean no belly dancing (not Moroccan), no tableware, no bar (alcohol forbidden), no 'tagine of monkfish,' and no women in the dining room. If you and your fraternity brothers are looking for a cool new spot to spend spring break, you can cross Moulay Idriss right off your list.

After a few *salaam aleikums*, introductions, and gravely reproduced documents and permits in French, English, and Arabic, we followed Sherif through a forbidding archway, squeezed past heavily laden donkeys and men in djellabas, and proceeded up Moulay Idriss's twisting cobbled streets. Street beggars and urchins began their approach, caught sight of our 'security escort', and quickly shrank away. Why the cops were with us, I don't know. They didn't talk. Abdul didn't talk to them. Sherif ignored them. They were just there.

Halfway up the hill, I smelled something wonderful and paused to take it in. Abdul smiled and ducked into an open doorway. It was a community bakery, dating back to the eleventh century, with a gigantic wood-burning oven, where an old man fed loaves of round, flat Moroccan bread on a long paddle, taking others out, sending them skittering across the bare floor. The smell was fantastic. Hooded, veiled women in long, shapeless robes arrived every few minutes with trays of uncooked dough.

Abdul explained: 'See here?' he said, pointing out three diagonal slashes on the surfaces of one batch waiting for room in the oven. 'These people – everybody here – every family makes their bread. In the house. Maybe two times a day. They bring here to bake. This mark. These marks, they are so baker can tell which family is the bread.'

I examined the shelves of coded dough, a few stacks of cooked loaves, fascinated by the nearly imperceptible but very real differences. Most of the loaves I saw had no identifiable markings that I could see.

'Many many no markings,' said Abdul, smiling. 'This baker . . . he work many years here. Very long time. For same families coming all the time. He can tell which breads for which families from the shape. He can tell.'

The setup was medieval: a dark room of bare stone, brick, fire, and wood. Not an electric bulb or a refrigerator in sight.

'Come see,' said Abdul. He showed me through another opening next door. We stepped down a few crumbling stone steps into near blackness, with only a bright orange flame winking from below. At the bottom of the steps, surrounded on all sides by a deep trench of firewood, a skinny, toothless old man poked long iron tongs into a pit of flame.

'This fire for bakery,' said Abdul. 'And for other place. There.' He indicated beyond a far wall. 'The *hamam*. Sauna. Where peoples go to wash. For to sweat. Very healthy. We go later. This *hamam* very old. Maybe one thousands of years.'

Sherif's place, near the top of the hill, operated for the benefit of 'enlightened' tourists, was in what had once been a private home, built – like most of Moulay Idriss – in the eleventh century. It was a three-story structure rising around a small courtyard. The walls were covered with ornate mosaics of blue-and-white tile, lined by low couches covered with pillows and fabrics, a few low tables, and embroidered tuffeted stools. As soon as we entered, we were invited to sit and immediately brought sweet, very hot mint tea.

The kitchen was on roof level, where a team of white-clad women was at work preparing our meal: *kefta* (a Moulay Idriss specialty), tagine of mutton, and a selection of salads and cold dishes. *Kefta* refers to spicy meatballs of lamb and beef served en brochette (skewered), or, as for that day's meal, cooked in sauce and finished with beaten egg so it resembles a saucy open-faced meatball-studded omelette. The women cooked tagine, sauce, and meatballs in pressure cookers over an open flame fed by roaring propane tanks. Laid out around the large white-tiled space, open on one side to the sky, the elements of basic Moroccan *mise-en-place* were arranged in seeming disarray: garlic, onion, cilantro, mint, cumin, cinnamon, tomato, salt, and pepper. There were no stoves, only hissing tanks of volatile-looking gas. Food was chopped using the old thumb against blade method, just like grandma used to. There were no cutting boards. There were only paring knives. The restaurant, I was informed, was quite comfortable serving up to three hundred meals out of this kitchen. That day, we were the only guests.

From the mosque next door came the muezzin's call to prayer – a haunting chant, beginning with '*Allahhh akbarrrrr*' (God is great), which occurs five times a day all over the Islamic world. The first time you hear it, it's electrifying – beautiful, non-melodic, both chilling and strangely comforting. Upon hearing it, you understand – on a cellular level – that you are now 'somewhere else.' You are far from home and all the ambient noises of American life. Here it was roosters and the muezzin's call, the ululating sound of women talking on rooftops.

Sitting in a tiled dining area on comfortable cushions with Abdul and Sherif, the three silent coppers propped up in a row against a far wall, we were brought a silver tray and water pitcher with which to wash. One at a time, our waiter poured water over our hands, allowed us to scrub with a cake of green soap, then poured water again to rinse.

Bread arrived in a big cloth-covered basket – the same flat bread I'd seen earlier at the bakery – and Abdul broke off sections and placed them around the table. One does not simply reach for bread here; one waits to be served.

'*Bismillah*,' said Abdul.

'*Bismillah*,' said Sherif.

'*Bismallah*,' I said, quickly corrected by my hosts.

A large selection of salads was placed in a circle: potato salad, marinated carrots, beets, olives of many kinds, mashed okra, tomato and onion. One eats without knife or fork, or any other utensils, using one's right hand, always. There are no southpaws in Islam. You don't use your left at the table. You never extend it in greeting. You don't reach with it. You never, ever use it to grab food off the family-style platters of food. You don't eat with it. I was really worried about this. It's enough, one would think, learning to eat hot, often liquidy food with one's fingers – but only one hand?

Practice was clearly required. I had to learn to use bits of bread, pinching the food between two – and only two – fingers and the thumb of the right hand, the digits protected by a layer of folded bread. Fortunately, I soon noticed that a lot of cheating goes on. Both Abdul and Sherif used quick moves with the bent fingers or knuckles of the left hand to push or position recalcitrant bits into the right.

Individual styles varied. I caught Abdul tearing the white centers from each little triangle of bread, creating an ersatz pita pocket of the crust, making it easier to scoop food. I called him on it, accused him playfully of cheating while I struggled with thick, not easily folded hunks. 'No, no,' protested Abdul. 'I do like this so I do not get fat. I am on . . . diet.' A little pile of white bread centers formed beside him.

After a peek at Sherif's technique, I decided to stick with the more traditional approach, forcing my fingers to learn. It was messy at first, and one does not lick one's fingers here – as you are constantly revisiting the same communal platters as the others at the table. Napkins are rare. The bread, issued periodically throughout the meal, serves double duty as both utensil and napkin. It took me a while, but I got better over time.

The waiter brought a big tagine of bubbling-hot *kefta*, set it down on the table and removed the top. A tagine – I should explain to avoid confusion – refers to the cooking vessel of the same name. Nowadays, since the introduction of the pressure cooker, it is used largely as a serving platter. The tagine is a large, shallow, glazed bowl, with a sloping, conical top like a minaret's peak. Nomadic peoples used to carry them from camp to camp, preparing slow-cooked meal-in-one fare over open fires, using the tagine as an all-purpose stewpot. It was a low-maintenance way for women to cook: Simply put the food on the fire, then move on to other pressing chores, like tending to livestock, gathering wood, nursing kids, making bread – all this while the stew (also referred to as tagine) cooked. In Morocco, if you didn't know already, like the James Brown classic, it's a man's, man's world. The women cook. The men often eat their meals separately. Should you be invited to the home of a Moroccan for dinner, the lady of the house will cook, hidden from view in the kitchen, with maybe a sister or mother to assist her, while you and any other male guests are entertained in the dining area. The women of the host's family will eat in the kitchen. The tagine was both boon and curse to women, in that the basic foods of the region – lamb, mutton, fowl, couscous – take a long time to cook. The pressure cooker cut serious cooking time out of the average workday, freeing the cook at least to dream of other activities.

I was getting pretty good at the pinch with my fingers. And just in time, as the next course was a searingly hot tagine of mutton and onion with green pea sauce. It tasted terrific – dark, spicy, hearty, with big hunks of now-tender mutton shoulder nearly falling off the bone into screaming hot sauce. I managed to avoid scalding my fingertips, careful to eat a lot. Portions are large, as a good Muslim always prepares more than is required for immediate use, anticipating that most important figure of lore – the hungry traveler in need – who might unexpectedly appear. It is considered an ennobling act, a sacred duty, to provide hospitality to the needy. To waste even bread is a sin. A dropped piece of bread found on the street is often retrieved by a devout Muslim and left by the entryway to a mosque, as to leave food lying about like trash would be an offense to God. So I made sure to eat as much as I possibly could.

The three plainclothesmen sat impassively against the wall while the platters were cleared and a few plates of dates and figs were served with more of the sweet mint tea. At the end of the meal, the hand-washing procedure was repeated, followed by a presentation of burning incense. Sherif held his fez over the smoke from the burning sticks. Abdul wafted the fumes around his neck. A silver container was brought around and the three of us shook rosewater on our hands and clothes. The cops smiled, showing off their gold-capped teeth.

Abdul pulled the van to a halt just outside the walls of Fez el-Bali, the old city of Fez, an enclosed medina of ten thousand or so narrow, indecipherably arranged, completely unmappable streets, alleys, cul-de-sacs, pass-throughs, corridors, homes, businesses, markets, mosques, souks, and *hamams*. Over thirty thousand residents live densely packed together in a labyrinth that a lifetime of exploration would never fully explain or reveal – even to a native. Cars, motorbikes, and any other kind of vehicle are not permitted inside the city's walls, as they would be useless. It's too crowded, the streets too narrow, a busy rabbit warren of crumbling walls, sudden drops, steeply inclined steps, switchbacks, turn-offs and dead ends. A thin old man in a djellaba was waiting for us by the outer wall and promptly loaded our luggage into a primitive wooden cart, then headed to a slim break in the wall of what remains – in form, if not in function – a fortress city.

The old city dates back to A.D. 800 and many of its standing structures were built as far back as the fourteenth century. It has been the center of power and intrigue for many of Morocco's ruling dynasties. The fortress architecture is not just a style statement. The buildings, the layout, the walls, the location, as well as the city's agricultural and culinary traditions, all reflect an ancient siege mentality. As the Portuguese and Spanish have adopted *bacalao* – a method of preserving fish for long periods – as a way to ensure naval power, the citizens of Fez have a culinary repertoire developed around survival, food hoarding, preservation, and self-sufficiency. Back in the old days, marauding armies from other regions were common, and the standard medieval strategy for taking down a walled city was simply to surround it with superior force, choke off its supply routes, and starve the opponents out. Fez's mazelike walls within walls structure, surrounded by exterior fortifying walls, were constructed as defense against that tactic. Neither infantry nor cavalry would have had an easy time of it even once inside the outer walls, for troops would have had to divert constantly into narrow columns, vulnerable to attack from ahead, behind, and above.

A building's exterior reveals nothing of what's inside. A simple outer door might open onto a palatial residence or a simple private home. Furthermore, between the floors of a building, many homes have hollowed-out areas suitable for stashing food and hiding fugitives. An early hub for the spice routes from south and east, Fez made use of the spices and ingredients from other cultures, particularly when it came to the practical necessities of repelling potential invaders. Air-dried meat, pickled vegetables, preserved fruit, cured food, a protein diet consisting largely of animals easily raised and contained behind high walls – all remain features of Fez's cuisine. The preponderance of inaccessible wells and walled gardens are design features one might well find quaint and even luxurious now. Back then, they were shrewd and even vital additions to the neighborhood. Wealthier citizens of the old city still pride themselves on growing their own dates, figs, lemons, oranges, olives, and almonds, and pulling their own water out of the ground. Situated in the middle of a wide valley, surrounded by unforgiving hills and plains, invaders almost always began to go hungry before the residents and were forced to withdraw long before the food ran out inside the walls.

We followed our porter up and down nameless dark alleys, past sleeping beggars, donkeys, soccer-playing kids, merchants selling gum and cigarettes, until we arrived at a dimly lighted doorway in a featureless outer wall. A few sharp knocks echoed through an inner chamber, and an eager young man appeared to welcome us into a deceptively plain passageway large enough to accommodate riders on horseback. Around a corner, I stepped into another world. A spacious antechamber opened up onto a quiet enclosed patio, with a round breakfast table situated beneath a lemon tree. The air smelled of oleander and fresh flowers. Looming up in the center of a vast open space of terraced patios with tiled floors rose what can only be described as a palace, a gargantuan high-ceilinged structure surrounded by outbuildings, a large garden with fruit trees, a small pond, and a well – the residence, it appeared, of a medieval merchant prince, all within the impenetrable walls of the crowded medina.

My host was Abdelfettah, a native of the old city of Fez. Educated in Britain, he spoke with the unmistakable accent of the British upper classes – but is, as they say there, quite the other thing. A few years ago, with his English wife, Naomi, and two children, he'd returned to his beloved hometown and begun work restoring this magnificent estate tile by tile, brick by brick, doing much of the work himself. He now wore only traditional garb, djellaba and *babouches* (pointed yellow slippers), having turned his back on the world outside his walls. Abdelfettah and Naomi have dedicated themselves to preserving the ancient culture and traditions of Fez – and their own luxurious piece of that tradition. No television and no radio were on the premises. Outside the main house and kitchen annex, Abdelfettah maintained a studio, where he spent hours each day creating indescribably intricate reliefs in white plaster, hand-carving endlessly repetitious non-representational designs and patterns into its surface. At the far end of the garden, construction was under way for a center for Moroccan music, where local musicians and aficionados will assemble and work.

I was taken through a well-equipped kitchen and breakfast area to the main building. It was a towering square structure, built around a large interior courtyard. The inner walls rose over a hundred feet in a wide, wide shaft to the roof and sky, every inch decorated with precise hand-painted and -assembled mosaics of small white and blue tile. The cedar doors to my room on the ground floor, which opened onto the courtyard and a gurgling fountain, were at least six times my height, and carved with the same kind of skillfully executed patterns as Abdelfettah's plaster reliefs, many of which occupied spaces over entryways and interior windows. I could easily imagine two big bald guys, shirtless and wearing silk pantaloons and fezzes, flanking each side of the almost ridiculously tall doors, opening them to the accompaniment of a hammered gong.

My residence contained a sitting room and a bedroom, with elaborately handcrafted bookshelves, couches covered in embroidered cushions, and Berber rugs on the floors. Upstairs, beyond the top of the estate's walls, no windows opened onto the outer world. Those peeking in from a vantage point on the hills outside the city would see only a bare white surface. As I unpacked my belongings, the muezzin's call from the mosque next door resonated through the hard-tiled courtyard. It was easily the most fantastic residence I had ever seen, much less stayed in, a building many times older than my whole country.

My host was a serious man, although he possessed a well-hidden whimsical streak. His former life revealed itself only in flashes – a spark of interest in the mention of a Western film, a sudden yen for an American cigarette. Other than that, he was concerned only with his home, his lifestyle, and the preservation of Fez's traditions. He was resolute in his determination to restore the property fully to its former glory, and, if possible, to influence others to do the same. Fez is now under siege of a different sort, as hundreds of thousands of Moroccans, dispossessed from their rural homes by drought or poverty, have flooded the old city in recent decades. The buildings are filled with squatters; the infrastructure is crumbling. The tendrils of the Great Satan – Internet cafés, housing developments, fast-food joints – lick at the outer walls. The once-proud elite of political thinkers, philosophers, and merchants has largely fled elsewhere.

It was my host's work with plaster that spoke most articulately of his seriousness and dedication. There are no faces in Islamic art, nor any images of animals, plants, historical tableaux, or landscapes. Anything God created is a taboo subject for an artist. The artist must speak in severely constrained fashion, within the framework of centuries-old traditions and practice. Yet despite those constraints, I saw in Abdelfettah's work – and, later, in the works of other Islamic artists – a universe of possibilities for beauty and expression. I was reminded of Moroccan food, where there may be only a few standard dishes but infinite room for subtle variations exists. Abdelfettah showed me how he did the work, allowed me to feel as the metal tools pushed through one section of softly yielding plaster, routing delicately into the pristine white surface. Again and again, I saw those tiny repeating patterns, never varying from God's plan, always within the controlled borders of the design, kept firmly in control yet emanating outward, layer upon layer, ring around ring. It takes a long time to do a single piece – how long, I have no idea. And there were scores of them all over the house. (On occasion, Abdelfettah worked for others. He did, he confided, Mick Jagger's bathroom recently.) The challenge of all that work, all that elaborate detail, and his unwavering faith in what he was doing, his discipline, his certainty that he'd chosen the right path, provoked and disturbed me in new ways. Why couldn't I be that certain – about anything? Why had I never found anything that so commanded my attention and effort, year after year after year? I looked at Abdelfettah, wondered what he was really seeing in all those tiny grooves and repeating patterns, and I envied him. The professional kitchen has always provided me with my own measure of certainty, a thing to believe in, a cause. Cooking, the system, has been my orthodoxy – but never like this. Mine has been a sloppy, dysfunctional life. I yearned for whatever it was he had that I didn't, imagining it could only be peace of mind. My efforts, during a lifetime of cooking, have all been eaten – by the next day, a memory at best. Abdelfettah's work will live on forever. I spent the evening reading the Koran, moved by its seductive, sometimes terrible severity, its unquestioning absolutism, trying to imagine the people within its pages, their very human problems and their extraordinary, often cruel solutions.

I woke up the next day under three layers of blankets, the toaster-sized electric heater on my nightstand warming my left ear and little else. My host had dragooned his mother, sister, a housekeeper, and a servant into preparing two days of meals, a full overview of the classic dishes of Fez. I was in the perfect place to enjoy Moroccan food. Ask just about anyone in the country where the best food is and they'll tell you Fez. Ask where you should eat this food in Fez and they'll invariably tell you to eat in a private home. Certainly, if you want to eat Moroccan food like Moroccans eat it, you're not going to find it in a restaurant.

When I went for coffee in the kitchen, Abdelfettah's mother was already hard at work, rubbing and kneading freshly made pellets of semolina between hands decorated with the reddish purple designs you see on elderly women, making couscous from scratch. His sister was making *waqa*, a crepelike substance used for wrapping *pastilla*, a much-loved pigeon pie. Pigeons were marinating, almonds toasting in the controlled chaos of the crowded kitchen. I had a light breakfast of curds and dates, a few pastries, then decided to explore the medina. To have done so alone would have been madness. I never, and I mean never, would have been able to find my way home. Abdul was not a native of Fez and would have been a bad choice as guide. I relied instead on a friend of Abdelfettah's; let's call him Mohammed.

When you're in Fez's old city, picking your way carefully down steep steps, hunching to scurry through tunnels, squeezing past overloaded donkeys in dark, narrow shafts, ducking beneath strategically placed logs that had been cemented into opposing walls to discourage mounted riders hundreds of years ago, it looks the way they tried but failed to make it look in a hundred movies. You can't stand; you have to keep moving, or you're in somebody's way. In the medina, just to look around is to feel how far you are from everything you know.

The smell of the tanneries is intense. Leather is 'cured,' according to Mohammed, in pigeon shit. If you want to know why that Jerry Garcia hat your old pal from the ashram brought you when he returned from here back in the seventies still smells like shit, now you know. One encounters a tantalizing mixture of fragrances – spices, food cooking, the dyeing pits, freshly cut cedar, mint, bubbling hookahs – and as one approaches the souk, the smells only get stronger. The souk, or market, is laid out according to an ancient guild system. This means that merchants or tradesmen of a particular kind still tend to flock together, grouping their businesses in one area. We passed a whole street of knife sharpeners, grimacing old men pumping foot-cranked stone grinding wheels with one leg, sparks flying. They looked like mad one-legged bicyclists. Carpet merchants were clearly at the top of the hierarchy these days, maintaining whole buildings covered floor to ceiling with mounds of Berber rugs, carpets, runners, and blankets. I submitted to an invitation to take a look. Seated at a low table, I was 'pulled' by the offer of mint tea, 'hooked' by the inevitable offer to show me a few particularly beautiful carpets, and 'closed' when I ended up blowing eight hundred smackers on stuff I had never intended to buy. After ensuring that every inch of my apartment would soon be filled with livestock-scented floor coverings and itchy blankets, I stepped, blinking, onto the streets. As Mohammed had probably had a profitable morning from the referral, I figured he'd be suitably motivated to find me the cannabis products Morocco had once been famous for. He smiled at my request, disappeared for a few moments, and returned with three thumb-sized hunks of hashish and a piece of kif, the sticky pollen cake made from the marijuana plant.

Feeling good about things, I continued exploring the market. Butchers occupied a long thatch-covered strip of street, their hunks of bleeding meat slung over counters or hanging from hooks – much of it cut into segments I could identify from no meat or cookery chart I'd ever seen. Piles of sheep's heads, still woolly and caked with blood, lay in pyramids; carcasses hung in the humid stillness, drawing flies. Meat cutters hacked with cleavers and scimitars. People bullied through the crowds atop their beasts of burden, and pedestrians paused to poke, prod, fondle, haggle, and taste. Baskets of snails and periwinkles gurgled in wicker baskets at the fish vendors. Stalls displayed dried beef and jerky, photogenic piles of spices and herbs, counters of fresh cheese, leaf-wrapped wheels of goat cheese, tubs of curds, olives – every hue and type of olive filling barrel after barrel – dried fruit and produce, preserved lemons, grains, nuts, figs, dates. A woman made *waqa*, peeling the filament-thin crepes off a hot plate with her fingers. Another woman made slightly thicker, larger crepes on a giant cast-iron dome, pouring batter over what looked like an oversized wig stand in a department store window. They blistered and bubbled until solid; then she would peel them off and slather them with a sweet spreadable paste of ground nuts and dates. She folded up one of these great floppy objects and presented it to me. Delicious.

Turbans, fezzes, kepis, keffiyehs, bangles, chadors, and baseball caps bobbed above the shoulders of the crowd, a sea of headgear moving slowly through the confined spaces. It was work just walking a block. Nudged by the tide to the outer margins of the souk, I saw tailor shops with whole families kneeling inside, sewing. Carpenters lathed and sanded pieces of furniture, metalworkers hammered and tapped, and women filled buckets from community fountains. There were shoes, toys, jewelry, pressed tin, gold, wood, leather, and clay handicrafts – much, if not most, of the same stuff you see in dusty storefronts in the East Village. Believe me, you have, or at least have had, most of this stuff. Those groovy little inlaid boxes you used to keep your stash in? The stash pouch your first girlfriend gave you? They still have them in Fez, if you need new ones. I have come to believe, after traveling all over the world, that there's a giant factory complex in Macao or Taiwan where all the world's native handicrafts come from, a vast assembly floor where workers string seashells and beads for sale everywhere from Rio de Janeiro to the Caribbean to Da Nang, thousands of Chinese convicts screwing together Moroccan rifles, carving Mexican chess sets, and slapping paint on novelty ashtrays.

Returning to the walled idyll of Abdelfettah's home, I hurried to the rooftop and rolled a fat spliff of hashish-laced tobacco. I smoked deeply while the muezzin's call echoed through the courtyard. Abdelfettah's children were playing with 'Torty,' their pet turtle, by the fountain. I peered lazily at the rooftops of the medina and gazed at the cemeteries and hills beyond.

Reasons Why You Don't Want to Be on Television: Number Three in a Series

Goofy with hash, I was worthless as a television host. I sat at the table with Abdelfettah and his wife, Naomi, eating a spectacular meal of wonderful thick *harira*, a lamb and lentil soup traditionally served to break the fast of Ramadan. There were salads, brochettes, and an absolutely ethereal couscous served with Fez-style tagine of chicken with raisins and preserved lemon. While we ate, Matthew and Global Alan stood directly across from the table, both their cameras pointed from the hip straight at us, expectantly. Under the unblinking gaze of their lenses, I felt unable to say a single enlightening or interesting thing. Repartee with my kind hosts was beyond me. I shrank from the artificiality of the whole enterprise, the forced nature of turning to Naomi, for instance, and casually inquiring, 'So, Naomi, maybe you'd like to tell me about the entire history and culture of Morocco, its cuisine, and, uh, while you're at it, could you explain Islam for us? Oh, pass the chicken, please. Thanks.' I was enjoying the food, competently snatching fingerfuls of couscous and tagine between the excellent bread. But I couldn't talk.

Next to me, Naomi radiated unease. Abdelfettah looked, understandably, bored. Matthew cleared his throat impatiently, waiting for me to elicit a few recipes, some anecdotes. I liked my hosts, but Naomi, while quick, articulate, and informative off-camera, froze when the cameras turned on. I couldn't do it to her. In my state of neurotic, hash-heightened sensitivity, I just couldn't put her on the spot, knowing the cameras would then move in for a closer shot. *I* certainly had nothing to add to the world's knowledge of Morocco. I was just finding a few – a precious few – things out myself. Who am I, Dan Rather? I'm supposed to face the camera and spit out some facile summary of twelve hundred years of blood, sweat, colonial occupation, faith, custom, and ethnology – as it relates to a chicken stew – all in a nice 120-second sound bite? I'm not even Burt Wolf, I was thinking. And I hate Burt Wolf. Watching him in his flawlessly white chef's coat, with his little notepad, pretending to take notes for the camera while he leans inquisitively over some toiling chef in a French country kitchen, the voice-over giving the viewing audience the short course on the French Belle Epoque. I used to watch those shows and want to leap through the TV screen, grab a fistful of Burt's chef's jacket, and scream, 'Take that off, you useless fuck! Give the man some room, for God's sake! Let him work!' But I was Burt now. Worse than Burt – because I had no idea, no clue, what I was doing. In my madcap lurch around the world, I'd done no preparation. I knew nothing. About any-thing.

I could have pointed out, I guess, that the raisins and preserved lemon were distinctive of Fez-style tagine. I'm sure I could have described for the viewing audience the difference between cous-cous made from scratch and couscous made out of the box, talked about the way it's cooked – in the couscousière – steaming over the simmering sauce from the tagine. I'm sure, if I'd stitched a smile on my face and gathered my thoughts, and had the heart to do it, I could have gotten Abdelfettah to discuss his hopes for his city, his planned music center, his art, knowing full well that that would have ended up on the cutting room floor. As Matthew squirmed and fumed, the clock ticked, each second dropping like molten lead into the vast pool of unusable footage. What was I going to say? Abdelfettah had found something here, but however beautiful, however righteous and unpolluted by the outside world it was, I knew I could never live this way. Maybe, I mused, if the cameras were gone, maybe then I could give myself over more wholeheartedly to the experience. Maybe I'd be more able to relax. But I knew better. Even with the added conve-niences of a high-speed modem, hot tub, bowling alley, regular deliveries of deli food and pizza from New York, and Krispy Kreme doughnuts, I couldn't live like this. Ever. My hosts seemed so content and at home within the context of their city, their family, and their beliefs that I felt it completely inappropri-ate to nudge them into the automatic dumb-down that comes with addressing a lens.

My last meal at Abdelfettah's was *pastilla*, the delicate, flaky pigeon pie, wrapped and baked in *waqa* with toasted almonds and eggs, then garnished with cinnamon. Like everything I'd eaten, it was wonderful. But I felt pulled in twelve directions at once. I was not happy with being the globe-trotting television shill. I had been cold and away from home for far too long. I yearned for the comfort and security of my own walled city, my kitchen back at Les Halles, a belief system I understood and could endorse without reservation. Sitting next to these two nice people and their kids, I felt like some news anchor with a pompadour, one of the many glassy-eyed media people whom I'd flogged my book with around the United States. 'So, An-thony, tell us why we should *never* order fish on Monday.' My spirits were dropping into a deep dark hole.

I was being 'difficult.' I was being 'uncooperative.' I really was. An executive producer was flown out from New York to soothe my troubled conscience, to help me feel better about the enterprise. She showed me some rough cuts of earlier shows, pointed out that I wasn't doing that badly, if I remembered to look at the camera, if I'd only stop cursing and smoking and slagging other Food Network chefs all the time, maybe look at a map before visiting a country. Three minutes into this motivational meeting, the producer mentioned that her boyfriend had been kidnapped by aliens. She said this casually, as if mentioning that she'd seen the Yankees/Red Sox game last week. He'd built an alien landing strip in their apartment, she added, her tone frighteningly devoid of irony or skepticism. I waited for the part where she'd say, 'Oh yeah, I know. He's nuts. Barking mad. But I love the big lug.' That would have been enough for me. I waited, but nothing came. She continued gently pointing out my many deficiencies while urging me on. I think I even jokingly inquired if her boyfriend had mentioned any rectal probing being involved, a suspiciously regular feature of rural alien abductions. She didn't laugh.

I was alone.

I spoke with Naomi before leaving, apologized for myself, thanked her for enduring the crew, and the cameras, expressed regret that I was leaving her beautiful home, and this amazing city, without really having gained any knowledge or real insight. She handed me a small piece of paper on which she'd copied a verse by Longfellow: 'And the night shall be filled with music,/ And the cares, that infest the day,/Shall fold their tents, like the Arabs/And as silently steal away.'

I hoped so. I truly did. I had very high hopes for the desert. I needed it.

It was a nine-hour drive from Fez to the desert. We passed through snowcapped mountains with Swiss-style vacation homes – a remnant of the French occupation – through forests and valleys, across the Moyen-Atlas, and down onto mile after mile of absolutely flat, hard-packed, pebble-strewn dirt. One long, undulating ribbon of asphalt stretched on and on for hundreds of miles. Occasionally, we glimpsed in the distance wadis, mesas, mountains, cliffs, great mounds of packed dirt. Every fifty miles or so, an oasis appeared. Some oases were simply small clusters of the ubiquitous sand and mud castles, while others were vast wedding cake-like Casbahs, groupings of homes and mosques, schools and markets, small plots of green crowded around tall palms, clinging to where water passed, or had once passed, or was likely to pass again. Coming from New York, one tends to take water for granted. Here in the desert, it's life or death. One builds where water flows or trickles. One pulls it from the ground. Some of the larger oases stretched for miles in the wide, deep crevices where the earth, thousands or millions of years ago, had split open, cracked like an overcooked brownie.

I began seeing camels with regularity alongside the road, with blue- or black-clad Berbers holding the reins or riding on top. I saw women with tattooed faces in the same black or blue scarves, the colors and markings denoting tribe. And I saw something else again and again in the middle of the vast, monotonous expanses of hard, waterless desert, where for thirty miles we'd passed nothing – not a house, not a single structure, no stick of wood or blade of grass to distract the eye from horizon to horizon. There, sitting by the side of the road, were lone watchers, people who'd hiked for miles from beyond the curve of the earth to sit and watch the occasional car or truck blow past them at eighty miles an hour, never slowing. These people didn't beg, or wave, or even raise their heads to smile. They sat impassive, watching in silence in their rags as evidence of the modern world roared past, leaving them in a cloud of dust.

Abdul owned only one cassette tape: Judy Collins's *Greatest Hits*. I tried sleeping. I tried shutting it out, but, in the end, the soulless trilling and warbling of 'Both Sides Now' slowly ground me down to a state of near-hysterical desperation. The road to Risani seemed to go on forever – especially with Judy exercising her pipes. The scenery changed gradually from the uninterrupt-edly banal red-pebbled desert to breathtaking Martian landscapes of mountain peaks, flat buttes, deep wadis, and cliff towns. Mostly, however, it was dirt. At times, nothing identified what was out the window as being anywhere on earth. Not a living thing. Occasionally – very occasionally – there would be a mud farm, where deep trenches had been dug for building materials, and a few forlorn-looking goats. Seemingly nonsensical property dividers, irregularly piled baseball-sized stones, indicated boundaries between nothing and nothingness. No water, no trees, no animals, and yet there they were, mile after mile of precariously balanced rocks. Finally, Risani appeared, a sun-bleached, dusty, desultory town of dirty streets and disheveled citizenry. We checked into the 'best' hotel, a faux Casbah of mud and cinder block, the familiar combo of inadequate electric heater, mushy bed springs, and lime-encrusted showerhead. Beer, at least, was available in the lobby – along with a very special menu of tagine, couscous, and brochette.

I had come to Risani to find *meshwi*, the whole roasted lamb so integral to my delusions of desert adventure. It had been arranged in advance over the phone with a group of Tuaregs who guided people around the Merzouga dunes as a business concern. But after a conversation on his battered cell phone, Abdul was telling me that the next night's dinner in the desert would be 'something very special.' I knew what that meant: The bastards were planning a big meal of couscous, brochette, and tagine. I was furious. I had not come all this way to eat couscous again. I could eat that in the lobby with the Japanese and German tourists. I'd come for whole roasted lamb, Berber-style, tearing at fat and testicles with my bare hands around a bonfire with the Blue Dudes, the whole beast, crispy and delicious, laid out in front of me. 'But, but . . .' I stammered, 'I wanted *meshwi*! I was getting *meshwi*!' Abdul shook his head, whipped out his cell phone, made a call, and spoke for a few minutes in Arabic. 'They don't have whole lamb,' said Abdul. 'If you want, we must bring ourselfs.'

'Fine,' I barked, irritated. 'Call them back. Tell them tomorrow morning we'll go to the market, buy a whole lamb, dressed and cleaned, and anything else they'll need. We'll throw it in the back of the car and take it on out. All they've gotta do is the voodoo that they do – cook the damn thing.' The plan was to get up early, swing by the market, buy lamb and supplies, load it all into the back of a hired Land Rover and rush out to the desert before the food began to rot.

Abdul looked dubious.

The next morning, we arrived as planned. The ground meat, vegetables and dry ingredients were no problem. The lamb, however, was proving to be difficult. At a butcher counter down an alleyway to the rear of a flyblown souk, a gold-toothed butcher considered our request and opened his ancient non-functioning stand-up fifties-era Frigidaire, revealing one hapless-looking leg of lamb, cut rudely through the hip and leeching blood.

'He has only the leg,' said Abdul.

'I see that,' I said irritably. 'Tell him I want the whole thing. What do I have to do to get the whole thing?'

'It is bad day,' said Abdul. 'The sheeps, they come to the market Monday. Today is Wednesday. No lamb comes today.'

'Ask him . . . maybe he's got a friend,' I suggested. 'Tell him I'll pay. I'm not looking for a bargain here. I need a whole fucking lamb. Legs, body, neck, and balls. The whole animal.'

Abdul embarked on a long and contentious new tack – one that was of clear interest to the butcher, who raised an eyebrow. I imagine Abdul was saying something like 'You see this stupid American next to me? He has no sense at all! He'll pay a lot of money for his whole lamb. It'll be worth both our whiles, my friend, if you can hook us up.'

The conversation became more animated, with multiple rounds of negotiation. Others joined us, materializing from dusty, trash-strewn alleyways, getting involved in the discussion, offering suggestions and strategies – as well as debating, it appeared, their respective cuts of the action. 'He say one hundred dollars,' said Abdul, uncertain that I'd go for such a figure.

'Done,' I replied without hesitation. Not too terribly far from New York prices, and how often would I get to eat fresh whole lamb in the Sahara?

The butcher abandoned his stall and led us down the sun-streaked streets, deep into a maze of buildings that seemed to go on forever. People came to upstairs windows to look at the strange procession of Americans, Moroccans, and TV cameras below. Children and dogs joined us as we walked, kicking up dust, begging and barking. I looked to my left and noticed a smiling man holding a large, menacing knife. He grinned, gave me the thumbs-up sign. I was beginning to get an idea of what it means when you say you want fresh lamb in Risani.

We arrived at a low-ceilinged manger, surrounded by worried- and unkempt-looking sheep. Our party had shrunk to four people and a TV crew. The butcher, an assistant, Abdul, and I crowded into a tiny mud and straw structure, sheep jostling us as they tried to look inconspicuous. A particularly plump beast was grabbed by the scruff of the neck. Abdul pinched his thigh and then rib sections; a new round of argument and negotiation began. Finally, consensus, and the poor animal was dragged, protesting, out into the sunny street. Another man was waiting for us with a bucket of water and a length of rope. I watched queasily as the intended victim was brusquely pointed toward Mecca. The man with the knife leaned over and without ceremony quickly cut the sheep's throat.

It was a deep, fast, and efficient movement. Were I, for one of many good reasons, condemned to die in the same fashion, I doubt I could have found a more capable executioner. The animal fell on its side, blood gurgling into the alley. There had been no cries of pain. I could readily see the animal's open windpipe; the head appeared to have been damn near cut off. But it continued to breathe, to twitch. While the executioner chatted with his cohorts, he held his victim down with a foot on its head.

I watched the poor sheep's eyes – a look I'd see again and again in the dying – as the animal registered its imminent death, that terrible unforgettable second when, either from exhaustion or disgust, it seemed to decide finally to give up and die. It was a haunting look, a look that says, You were – all of you – a terrible disappointment. The eyes closed slowly, as if the animal were going to sleep, almost willfully.

I had my fresh lamb.

My new pals strung up the body by the ankles, letting the blood drain into a pail. They cut the woolly pelt at one ankle and the butcher pressed his mouth to the opening and blew, inflating the skin away from the meat and muscle. A few more quick cuts and the skin was peeled off like a dancer's leotard. Stray dogs looked on from the rooftops as blood continued to drip, more slowly now. The assistant poured water constantly as the carcass was worked over, the entrails removed and sorted. The head was removed, heart put aside for the butcher, intestines and *crépine* (stomach-membrane) saved for merguez and sausage. Soon, the sheep looked comfortably enough like meat, save for two mango-sized testicles that hung upside down from the inverted carcass in distinctly separate blue-veined scrota. The butcher winked at me – indicating, I gathered, that this part was indeed very good and should be protected during the long ride out to our camp in the dunes – and made two slashes in the animal's belly, tucking a testicle in each.

There was more washing, a fidgety moment during the de rigueur postmortem enema, and then more washing. They were fast. The whole procedure, from 'Baa-baa' to meat, took maybe twenty minutes. I walked back to our Land Rover, retracing my steps with my new buddies in tow. With my hundred-dollar bill in the butcher's pocket, and the eerily bonding experience we'd just shared, they seemed to like me a lot more. The carcass was wrapped in a clear plastic tarpaulin, like a dead wise guy. I got a strangely pleasurable thrill hearing the thump as the body's dead weight flopped into the back of the Rover.

We filled in a few holes in our *mise-en-place* at the souk, gassed up, and headed for the Merzouga dunes. I was looking forward to seeing clean white sand, free of the smells of sheep and fear, far from the sounds of dying animals.

For a while it was more hard-packed lunarscape, until suddenly I felt the tires sink into softer ground, and soon it was sand, sand, and more sand, the vehicle gliding through the frosting of a giant cake. On the horizon were the mammoth red peaks and dips of the Merzouga dunes – the real Sahara of my

Boys' Own adventure fantasies. I felt exhilarated and relieved, considering, for the first time in a while, the possibility of happiness.

A small sandstone hut with blue-clad Berbers sitting on couches awaited us. A camel train had been assembled nearby, the big animals kneeling and ready. We mounted up and set out across the dunes, single file, a lone Tuareg in head-to-toe blue leading on foot, another to the rear. Global Alan rode on the lead camel, just ahead of me, Abdul, still in his orange-and-green tweed jacket, behind me. Matt and the assistant producer rode farther back.

Riding a camel, particularly if you're comfortable on horse-back, is not hard. I was real comfortable, cradled behind the animal's hump on a thick layer of blankets, my beast gently lurching forward. My legs rested in front of me. It was a long ride and I had – in an unusually lucid moment – made proper prior preparations: briefs instead of boxers.

Global Alan, however, had not chosen his undergarments with comfort and security in mind. Already in the awkward position of having to ride half-turned with a camera pointed back at me – for those all-important Tony of the Desert shots – he was not having an easy time of it. Whenever his camel would descend at a steep angle into the deep hollows between dunes, I could hear him grunting and whimpering with pain as his balls were pinched by the saddle. Alan hated Morocco. He'd hated it before we'd arrived, having been there before on assignment. Whenever I'd complained – in France or Spain or Portugal – about crummy bathrooms, uncomfortable rooms, rude waiters, or cold climate, Alan had just smiled, shaken his head, and said, 'Wait till Morocco. You're gonna hate it. Just wait. Buncha guys who look like Saddam Hussein, sitting around holding hands. Drinking tea. You're gonna hate it. Just wait.'

In fact, I was really beginning to enjoy myself. This was exactly the sort of scenario I'd envisioned when I'd dreamed up this scheme. *This* was what I was here for! To ride across desert sands with blue-clad Berbers, to sleep under the stars, surrounded by nothing, to eat lamb testicles in the middle of nowhere. Not to sit stiffly at a dinner table like a pinned moth, yapping at the camera.

After a few hours, we made camp at the foot of a huge dune. The sun was setting and long shadows appeared, growing in the hollows and swells of sand as far as the eye could see. The Blue Men got busy working on a late snack, something to keep us going until we hit the main encampment, where we'd spend the night. One of them built a fire out of a few sticks of wood and dried grass. While the flames burned down to coals and tea was made, the other Berber made bread dough in a small bowl, mixing and working it by hand. He covered it for a while, allowing it to rise under a cloth, then wrapped it around a filling of meat, onion, garlic, cumin, and herbs. Judging the fire to be ready, he brushed aside the coals, dug into the hot sand beneath, and dropped the fat disk of meat directly into the hole, covering it back up immediately. Time to wait, said Abdul.

Warm enough for the moment to remove shoes and socks, to strip down to a single layer of shirt, I climbed the big dune, dragging my tired, wheezing, and hideously out-of-shape carcass up the most gradual incline I could see, feeling every cigarette and mouthful of food I'd had in the last six months. It took me a long time. I had to rest every fifty yards or so, gasping, trying to summon the strength for the next fifty. I picked my way slowly along the soft but dramatic edge of a sharply defined ridge, then fell onto my back at the highest point. Rising after a few moments onto my elbows, I looked, for the first – and probably last – time in my life, at something I'd never seriously imagined I'd cast eyes upon: a hundred miles of sand in every direction, a hundred miles of absolutely gorgeous, unspoiled nothingness. I wiggled my bare toes in the sand and lay there for a long time, watching the sun drop slowly into the dunes like a deflating beach ball, the color of the desert quickly transforming from red to gold to yellow ocher to white, the sky changing, too. I was wondering how a miserable, manic-depressive, overage, unde-serving hustler like myself – a utility chef from New York City with no particular distinction to be found in his long and egregiously checkered career – on the strength of one inexplicably large score, could find himself here, seeing this, living the dream.

I am the luckiest son of a bitch in the world, I thought, contentedly staring out at all that silence and stillness, feeling, for the first time in a while, able to relax, to draw a breath unencumbered by scheming and calculating and worrying. I was happy just sitting there enjoying all that harsh and beautiful space. I felt comfortable in my skin, reassured that the world was indeed a big and marvelous place.

I was eventually disturbed from my maharishi-style meditations by the familiar sound of bread being scraped. I took that to mean my snack was ready, so I loped down the dune and returned to camp, to find my Tuareg buddies brushing the last grains of sand off a fat cooked loaf of meat-filled bread. Not a grain of sand or grit remained when one cut me off a thick wedge, a waft of spicy aromatic vapor escaping from inside. We crowded around a small blanket, eating and drinking tea as the sun finally disappeared completely, leaving us in blackness.

The camels picked their way across the desert in the pitch-dark, moving slowly up and down the steep rises and dips. At one point, I could see the dark shape of poor Global Alan, asleep on his camel, nodding off, then nearly falling off his animal. He woke with a start and a cry, frightening the whole formation. We traveled for about two more hours in near-total absence of light, the only discernible sight the off-black surface of the sand sea. Then I began to glimpse a few winking lights in the distance. As the camels trudged on, the lights grew larger. I could make out a bonfire, sparks rising from the flames, the outlines of what looked to be tents, moving bodies. There was the sound of drums, and singing or chanting in a language I'd never heard. The spectral apparition disappeared as our camels descended into another hollow, where I could see nothing, the only sound – once again – the breathing and snorting of our camels. After a long, tedious climb over a last rise, suddenly we were there.

A vast floor of ornate carpets stretched out for fifty or sixty yards, surrounded by tents. A covered table, fabric-wrapped stools, and pillows waited under an open canopy. A mud-and-straw oven, like a giant cistern, or the muzzle end of a sixteenth-century cannon, glowed to the left, away from the tents. Musicians beat drums and sang by a huge pile of burning logs, everyone dressed in the same blue or black head-to-toe robes of our escorts. And wonder of wonders: A full bar, nearly ten yards long, stocked with iced bins of beer and a row of liquor bottles, shone under a string of electric bulbs next to a humming generator.

It was a good old time: the Blue Men whacking drums with hands stained blue from the vegetable dyes they use on their clothes, singing and dancing by the fire, a capable and friendly French-speaking bartender in full headdress. In no time, I was fully in the spirit of things, banging on the drums with my blue pals, rolling a fat blunt, watching as one of the tribe rubbed my whole lamb with onion, pepper, and salt, then wired it to a long pole. Assisted by two others, they hoisted my dinner onto their shoulders and walked to the smoldering, volcanolike mud oven.

'See?' said Abdul, nursing a Heineken in one hand while sticking the other hand into the glowing opening atop the oven. 'Something very special. Very hot.' The Tuaregs leaned down to the base of the oven, to another, smaller opening, and removed with a stick every ember of coal and stick of burning wood. Then they quickly sealed the opening with fresh, wet mud. My *meshwi* went in the top, straight down, securely held to the pole by wire, placed vertically into the wide, still-nuclear-hot oven, a round meat lid placed on top. The lid was sealed in place with more mud, the Tuaregs carefully examining the oven from every angle to see that it was completely sealed, pausing now and again to patch or reinforce any holes or weak spots, any flaw that might allow all that residual heat to escape. Abdul and I retired to the bar.

We were brought water and soap on a silver tray, as in Moulay Idriss, washed our hands, and were soon being fed with the usual array of tasty olives, salads, and bread. A thicker, lambier version of *harira* soup arrived in a tureen, very welcome on what was becoming an extremely cold night. Abdul had loosened up considerably after many beers, entertaining us with a high-spirited round of joke telling – most of which, sadly, led me to believe that jokes about Jews are very big in Morocco. I found that Polish and hillbilly jokes work just as well in the desert, if you substitute Libyans. Finally, after about an hour and a half of eating and drinking, the *meshwi* arrived, stretched out on a long, flat board, a Blue Man with a long and sharp-looking dagger right behind. Still sizzling-hot, the lamb had been roasted crispy and straight through – far more cooked than I would have done in the world of knives and forks. The skin was black in places, the rib bones poking through shrunken muscle. It did, however, smell amazing, and I found that well done, while almost never my preferred temperature, although, unfortunately, the chosen level of doneness for most of the unrefrigerated world, was in this case absolutely necessary to the kind of hacking, tearing, peeling, clawing, and sucking the meal required. There were no steak knives, after all, to be cutting tidy pink loin chops off the lamb.

The chef broke the lamb into primal sections, then broke those down into smaller pieces, small enough to wield with a fist. I invited the chef and my new Tuareg buddies to join me at the table, and after a few *bismillahs*, everyone was poised to dig in. The chef made a quick motion with his dagger and lifted free a dismayingly large testicle from the lamb's crotch. With some ceremony, and a few appreciative smiles from around the table, he deposited the crispy, veiny object in front of me, then sat down and helped himself to a thick slab off the other nut. Abdul contented himself with ripping steaming-hot chunks of shoulder and leg with his fingers while I, God help me, tore off a sizable piece of gonad and popped it in my mouth.

It was sensational. Tender, even fluffy, with a subtle lamb flavor less intense than shoulder or leg; the whole experience, the chewing and swallowing, was reminiscent of sweetbreads. It was certainly the best testicle I'd ever had in my mouth. Also the first, I should hasten to say. I enjoyed every bite. It was delicious. Delightful. I'd do it again in a hot second. If I served it to you at a restaurant, as long as you didn't know what it was, if I called it, say, 'Pavé d'agneau maroc,' you'd love it. You'd come back for more. I felt proud of myself. I'll try almost anything once, but I often feel let down when I fail to enjoy myself as much as I'd hoped. Telling people about the cobra bile you drank when you were in Vietnam makes a great story, but it's dismaying when the experience was just as unpleasant as it sounds. Sheep's balls, however, are great. I would recommend them unhesitatingly and without reservation.

Abdul, the crew, the Blue Men, and I made short work of the lamb, getting serious with our hands, until the thing was only well-picked-over fragments, looking like an autopsied burn victim. When the fire began to die down, as the musicians, servers, and camel drivers melted away to their tents, I was left with Global Alan and Matthew, and a big hunk of hash – and that classic emergency smoking device of sixties legend: the toilet paper roll and tin foil pipe.

As it was near freezing now, we wrapped ourselves in heavy camel blankets and staggered aimlessly into the desert, heading in the general direction of a waxing moon. With the blankets covering us from heads to shins, we looked like lepers, stumbling on uncertain feet into the dark. When we finally agreed on the right distance and the right dune – still reasonably certain we could find our way back to camp – we sat down on the cold sand and smoked ourselves into a state that once, many years ago, might have been mistaken for enlightenment, our coughs and giggles swallowed up by the dunes. I lifted the description 'a bewildering array of stars' once from a far better writer – I can't remember who now, only that I stole it – and that expression came to mind as I stared up at an awe-inspiring sky over the Sahara, the bright, penetrating lights, the quick drop of comets, a cold moon, which made the rippling patterns of sand look like a frozen sea. The universe was large all right, but no larger, it appeared, than the whole wide world ahead of me.

HIGHWAY OF DEATH

I JUST HAD THE closest near-death experience I've ever had.

And I'm about to have another one. Then another.

I'm hurtling full speed down Highway 1 on my way to Can Tho, sitting with Philippe in the back of a hired minivan, horn honking constantly, heading right up the center line into oncoming traffic. There's a water truck about a hundred yards ahead, coming fast in the opposite direction, showing no sign that he intends to pull back into traffic, also honking wildly. Linh and a driver are in the front seat, with two shooters behind us – and I'm convinced that any second we're all going to die.

During the war, Highway 1 was said to be dangerous: snipers, sappers, ambushes, command-detonated mines, the usual perils of guerilla insurgencies. I can't imagine it's any less dangerous now. Understand this about driving in the Mekong Delta: The thing to do is keep up a constant attack with the horn. A beep means 'Keep doing what you're doing, change nothing, make no sudden moves, and everything will probably be fine.' It does not mean 'Slow down' or 'Stop' or 'Move to the right' or 'Get out of the way.' If you try to do any of those things on Highway 1 after hearing a car horn behind you – if you hesitate, look back over your shoulder, slow down, or even falter for a second – you will immediately find yourself in a burning heap of crumpled metal somewhere in a rice paddy. The horn means simply 'I'm here!'.

And there are a lot of people here today, just like us, tearing down the two-lane road at full speed and hammering their horns like crazy. The water truck ahead is getting closer. And closer. I can make out the grille, the Russian manufacturer's logo on the hood. Our driver still has his foot on the gas, not slowing down in the slightest. We're right in the middle of the road, what would be a passing lane, if they had such a thing here. There's an uninterrupted line of fast-moving cars to our right, with no room at all between them in which to pull back in, a steady torrent of oncoming cars to our left, and the shoulders of both sides of the road are choked three-and four-deep with cyclists, motorbikes, water buffalo, and scooters – all of them loaded with crates of food, washing-machine motors, sacks of fertilizer, flapping roosters, firewood, and family members. So there is no room, none at all, should our driver suddenly decide at the very last minute to abort mission and pull out of the center. If he decides suddenly that the oncoming driver is definitely not going to yield in this maniacal high-speed game of chicken, that he's going to have to veer off the road to avoid collision, there is nowhere, nowhere, to go!

We're close enough now that I can make out the features of the truck's driver, the color of his shirt, the pack of 555 cigarettes on his dashboard. Just when our bumpers are about to meet, vaporizing all of us in an explosion of brake fluid, safety glass, blood, and bone, two cars to our right suddenly open up a space for us – and as if part of some hellish high-speed chorus line, we slip back into traffic. The water truck whips by with a terrific blast of wind, avoiding contact by less than a centimeter, and there's that peculiar vacuum pressure-drop effect you feel when on a train that is suddenly passed by another hurtling in the opposite direction. Philippe just looks at me, shaking his head, says, 'Are we still alive? . . . I . . . I was sure that truck went right through us.' He's not joking.

Every few moments, we do the same thing again, pulling out to pass – often pulling out to pass a vehicle that is already passing – taking up the whole highway, three-deep, screaming straight into cars and trucks doing the exact same thing in the other direction, horns blaring and honking, a sea of farmers and grandmas and children on rickety bicycles on both sides, the occasional added hazard of oxcart or water buffalo protruding dangerously into the road.

Again.

And again. This time, it looks like an army truck, olive drab, the back loaded with standing soldiers in fatigues. They're coming right at us, not slowing down at all. Our driver doesn't seem concerned. He's having a nice conversation with an equally oblivious Linh, hardly, it seems, paying attention to what must certainly this time be our imminent doom. He honks the horn. He keeps honking. He leans right on that thing like it's a magic wand that will somehow alter the laws of physics. His foot is still on the gas, the motor racing. I see Philippe's knuckles getting white, then whiter on the armrest of his seat, see Chris the shooter's eyes grow huge in the rearview mirror. There's a collective holding of breath among the Western contingent as we all brace for impact, think fleetingly of loved ones, prepare ourselves to be thrown through the windshield . . . Again, somehow, we're back in traffic, a momentary blast of air as the two vehicles nearly kiss paint. Then we're right back straddling that center line again, honking wildly at a slow-moving car in front of us, tailgating at 120 kliks per hour.

Whatever magic safety zone our driver thinks envelops our car, protecting us from harm, we're beginning to think he must be right. There's no other explanation for our continued survival. Again and again and again, we just miss colliding, so frequently and regularly that, after an hour on the road, we actually begin to believe it, even count on the idea that we are invincible – that some Vietnamese juju does indeed prevent us from slamming head-on into another vehicle. We run straight at the most unroadworthy twenty-year-old Soviet-made contraptions on four wheels, gas pedal flat on the floor each time, enduring that queer Doppler effect as they whip by, the horns going *WHOOoooANNnngggg* as the shock wave blows us sideways toward a family of four on a wobbly bicycle. On more than one occasion, we come so close to rolling right over a pedestrian or an overloaded bicycle that I'm sure we touched them. I think all of us, long ago, would have screamed at our driver to slow down, maybe even attempted to wrestle the wheel away from him (he's clearly a madman intent on destroying us all), but there isn't a single second when we're not paralyzed with fear, bracing for impact, or at least certain that if we were to speak, or distract him for even a split second, it would surely cause our instantaneous deaths.

Eventually, nerves shattered, blind faith takes over and we either try our best to ignore what's going on outside the thin layer of metal and glass around us or we simply pray, nearly hysterical with fear and nervous exhaustion.

The city of Can Tho is a low-rise river town with the colonial architecture of its French planners. We check into the Hotel Victoria Can Tho, one of the many luxurious foreign-run hotels one sees more and more of in Vietnam. It's stately, beautiful, with an airy whitewashed lobby, black-and-white marble floors, a pool and boathouse on the shores of the Mekong River, hardwood teak and mahogany rooms with comfortable beds, and satellite TV. There's a business center, a health and massage studio, a very decent restaurant and bar – and an anti-aircraft battery down the street. As we drive by the gun emplacement, Linh reminds the shooters, 'Not to photograph, please.'

I order a mango daquiri as soon as we check in. God, there's nothing like a fine hotel when you've survived multiple brushes with death. I splurge and send out my moldering clothes to be laundered, schedule an hour-and-a-half massage, and treat myself to a traditional Vietnamese lunch of chicken BLT club sandwich. Philippe, in a monogrammed hotel bathrobe, is already at the pool. Soon, I'm oiled up on a table, half-asleep, a tiny Vietnamese girl walking on my back, by now only vaguely aware how lucky I am to be alive.

I'm also beginning to think that there must be a lot of penile dysfunction in Asia. There's no other explanation for it. Just about every damn thing you can think of seems to have been thoroughly investigated for its potential wood-raising properties. If your waiter or a friend urges you to put something in your mouth that a few weeks ago you never would have thought of eating, chances are it is believed to 'make you strong.' Only desperation can account for what the Chinese, for instance, do in the name of 'medicine.' That's something you might remind your New Age friends who've gone gaga over 'holistic medicine' and 'alternative Chinese cures.' They say there are sun bears in China, hooked up to kidney drips like catsup dispensers, leeching bear bile into tiny bottles. Rhino horn. Bear claw. Bird's nest. Duck embryo. You've got to be pretty anxious about your penis to contemplate hurting a cute little sun bear.

And you've got to be really concerned about your penis to eat at the My Kanh Restaurant in Can Tho. Our waiter greets us and proudly takes us on the obligatory premeal tour of the grounds. It's a large wooded park with a narrow cement pathway that winds and twists around zoolike cages of menu selections. Everything here is available for dinner. I lose my appetite as soon as I see the sun bear. There are snakes, bats, lizards, crocodiles, cranes, an eighty-kilo python, monkeys, and dogs. The dogs, our waiter assures us – not too convincingly – are not for sale. We pass ponds where one can catch one's own elephant fish or catfish. And in the middle of this torture garden, where the cages seem to radiate fear, are cute little bungalows where Chinese and Taiwanese businessmen come for dirty weekends, their mistresses in tow. They come to eat animals that most Americans have seen only on the Discovery Channel, to absorb, I'm guessing, the animal auras at close hand – before killing and eating them. The plan, then, I can only assume, is to settle the check quickly, rush back to the bungalow, and endeavor mightily to produce a hard-on. The management of My Kanh, our waiter proudly shows us, is putting in a swimming pool. It's a horrifying theme park of cruelty. And I'm sickened by it all. Bad enough to want to eat some of these creatures. But to want to stay here, close to your victims, to lie in bed with your mistress, listening to animals die – what kind of romantic weekend getaway is that?

Philippe and I settle for catching our own elephant fish in a murky, stagnant pond covered with green film, a small boy helpfully pointing out exactly where to drop our hooks. It takes about thirty seconds to catch our entrées.

For appetizers, we go for the relatively benign curried frog legs, a little ground snake with shrimp cracker, peanuts, garlic, and mint, and some braised bat (imagine braised inner tube, sauced with engine coolant). We eat no animals with cute bunny eyes. I just can't take that today. Philippe and I pick at our food unenthusiastically, a strong cloud of fermenting fish from the nearby *nuoc mam* factory doing nothing to improve our appetites.

No one should come here.

Our waiter is a friendly-enough young fellow, soft-spoken and attentive, but I can't get it out of my head that if I should suddenly decide to order some monkey, he'll happily slit the little fella's throat with the same friendly expression on his face.

I'm in much better spirits the next morning when we board a riverboat to go to the nearby floating market at Cai Rang. It's beautiful out, the sun creating pink-and-orange coronas around the edges of the clouds, the light on the water hypnotic. Bamboo-frame houses with thatched roofs, tall palms, the crowded waterfront of Can Tho pass by. The river itself teems with activity. Net fishermen, their handwoven nets extended like the wings of giant moths over the water, dip and pull with ingeniously crafted levers of bamboo poles. Families in sampans pass by, sampans with lone women paddling from the stern and baby sitting aft, boats overloaded with cinder blocks and building materials. There are floating gas stations: a thousand-gallon floating gas tank piloted by a chain-smoking old man sitting on top. The river traffic gets more intense as we near Cai Rang. Sampans are so overloaded here, so low in the water, I can't imagine how they stay afloat. Boats are piled high with sacks of rice, fertilizer, produce, potted palms, cages of live poultry.

And there are floating food vendors.

A chugging sampan pulls alongside our craft and inquires if we'd care for coffee. He's got a whole Starbucks rig set up at the helm. Attaching his boat to ours with a frayed rope, he sets immediately to work filling our order, one hand keeping his boat aligned as we speed along the river, the other steaming, filtering, and pouring some of that fabulous Vietnamese coffee into tall glasses. Another boat, this one selling baguettes, comes along the other side, and we buy a few of those, too. They're still warm, crunchy, and delicious, as good as any you'd find in Paris. A boat selling *pho* joins us and soon Philippe and I are digging greedily into bowls of outstandingly fresh spicy beef and noodles, a slice of liver, those brightly colored and crunchy garnishes making the flavors pop. I could eat here all day. Just float along and everybody comes to you. Pâté sandwiches, roll-your-own beef, spring rolls, sweets – all this in the middle of busy river traffic. At the market, there are floating fishmongers, livestock pens, fruit and vegetable wholesalers, bakers, plant sellers, all of them in waterlogged, porous-looking, questionably seaworthy vessels of indeterminate age. Slurping down the last of my morning *pho*, I'm thinking that this is living. Everyone smiles. Children shout 'Hello!' and 'Bye-bye!' and 'Happy New Year!' – all wanting nothing more than to practice the few words of English they know. A dessert boat sells candied mango and banana, skewered melon, chunks of pineapple, whole jackfruit, durian, mangosteen, dragon fruit, and custard apple. Boats chug by with bundles of beautifully wrapped square and triangular *banh* dangling from the wheelhouse, an entire convenience store aboard, selling cigarettes, sodas, beer, and fruit juices in plastic bags. Women cook in woks of boiling oil on fast-moving boats, grill little packets of ground meat wrapped in mint leaves, fry little birds, boil noodles. Everything smells good. Everything looks good to eat.

Looking at the far shore, I can see doorless shacks built out over the water, nearly without furniture, except for an occasional hammock, the glow from a much-repaired television set. There are television aerials over medieval-style privies built out over the water. Watch the shore and you see every stage of domestic river life: mothers bathing their children, pounding laundry, scrubbing their woks in the brown water, laying out circles of rice paper to dry on rooftops, fastidiously sweeping their tiny primitive abodes, every inch clean and squared away.

It's something I'm seeing everywhere in Vietnam; what makes its food so good, its people so endearing and impressive: pride. It's everywhere. From top to bottom, everyone seems to be doing the absolute best they can with what they have, improvising, repairing, innovating. It's a spirit revealed in every noodle stall, every leaky sampan, every swept and combed dirt porch and green rice paddy. You see it in the mud-packed dikes and levees of their centuries-old irrigation system, every monkey bridge, restored shoe, tire turned sandal, litterless urban street, patched roof, and swaddled baby in brightly colored hand-knit cap. Think what you want about Vietnam and about communism and about whatever it was that really happened there all those years ago. Ignore, if you care to, the obvious – that the country is, and was always, primarily about family, village, province, and then country – that ideology is a luxury few can afford. You cannot help but be impressed and blown away by the hard work, the attention to detail, the care taken in every facet of daily life, no matter how mundane, no matter how difficult the circumstances. Spend some time in the Mekong Delta and you'll understand how a nation of farmers could beat the largest and most powerful military presence on the planet. Just watch the women in the rice paddies, bent at the waist for eight, ten hours a day, yanking bundles of rice from knee-deep water, then moving them, replanting them. Take awhile to examine the intricate interlocked system of Stone Age irrigation, unchanged for hundreds and hundreds of years, the level of cooperation necessary among neighbors simply to scratch out a living, and you'll get the idea.

These people survived bombing, strafing, patrols. They outwitted the CIA, the NSA, satellites, AWACS, blacked-out C-130 cargo planes that had been tricked out with sensors and Gatling guns, staffed by whole teams of airborne intelligence analysts searching the ground below on winking monitors, B-52 strikes, hired killers, special units of 'counterterror' teams, regime after regime of clannish leaders who cared nothing for them. They survived *The Beverly Hillbillies* and Bob Hope and the worst that America's lusts and America's culture had to offer. They beat the French. They beat the Chinese. They beat the Khmer Rouge. And they'll survive communism, too. A hundred years from now, the Commies will be gone – like us, another footnote in Vietnam's long and tragic history of struggle – and the rice paddies of the Mekong Delta, this market, and this river will look much as they look now, as they looked a hundred years ago.

I like it here. I like it a lot.

TOKYO REDUX

I'D ONLY BEEN TO Tokyo once before, but I knew that as soon as I hit the ground, I'd be tapping into that main vein again, a dead-bang, surefire, king-hell rush. For me, Tokyo is like one long film trailer – one of those quick-cut, fast-moving highlight teasers for a noisy action flick with only the best parts shown, in molar-shaking, heart-pounding surround sound, the pace getting quicker and quicker, the action more frenzied, leading up to sudden blackness and the promise of more excitement to come.

No place I've ever been, or even heard about, is as guaranteed to cause stimulation in the deepest pleasure centers of a cook's brain. No cuisine, broadly speaking, makes as much sense: the simplest, cleanest, freshest elements of gustatory pleasure, stripped down and refined to their most essential. Unlike Tokyo's streets – and much of its popular culture – the traditional sectors of food and relaxation are austere, uncompromising, devoid of all distraction and repetition, beautiful in the manner of a single long-stemmed calla lily: unknowable, serene. The Japanese, hardworking, hyperregimented, obsessively well scrubbed, and painfully repressed, live lives of powerful – even lurid – imagination and fantasy. Over the centuries, they have given a lot of serious thought as to what, exactly, is needed and desirable in the taking of pleasure. The unnecessary, the extraneous, the redundant, the less than perfect – these are discarded. What is left is often an empty room, a futon, a single perfect flower.

Their streets may be noisy, riotous Möbius strips of flashing

lights, screaming jumbotrons, rank after rank of tightly constrained, identically dressed humanity (this year, *all* young
women *will* dye their hair red!), their TV variety shows insanely
over the top, hysterical assaults by break-dancing reindeer,
hyperactive hosts, cloyingly cute, fluffy, pyschedelic-hued animal characters and doll-eyed cartoon heroines, their porn some
of the ugliest, most brutal, and most disturbing on earth, their
popular sexual obsessions may make even the Germans look
well adjusted, and they may indeed teach their school children
that all that nasty World War II nonsense never really happened,
but from a cook's perspective, who cares? I was there to eat.
When it comes time to sit at a table, or take a long weekend
relaxing in the countryside, no one on earth has figured things
out so well or so thoroughly as the Japanese.

It's all about fish, fish, fish, daddy-o. You like fish? You'll love
Japan. They've scoured the world's oceans looking for good
stuff to eat. And they'll pay anything – anything – for the good
stuff. (I watched my friend Taka at Sushi Samba in New York
unhesitatingly pay over eighty dollars a pound – wholesale – for
a hunk of *o-toro*.) I actually get high walking through their fish
markets; my pulse quickens even thinking about them. I missed a
lot last time I was in Japan. I wasted a lot of time working and
wandering blindly about. Early on, I'd been intimidated by the
strangeness, the crowds, the different language, I'd been reluc-
tant, at first, to throw myself into it, to plunge right into packed
noodle joints and businessmen's bars. This time, I was determined, at the very least, to miss less. My quest for 'the perfect
meal' would be put on hold. This was Japan. I knew I'd be
getting a lot of perfect meals here. That's what they do.

It was a packed flight out of JFK, and I was too excited to
sleep. After three movies, three meals, and fourteen hours to
Narita, with the plane's engines droning on and on, it reached
the point where I yearned crazily for that telltale change in the
engine's pitch, that moment when velocity slows, the plane
begins its final descent, every ticking second of monotonous
hum a fiendish form of torture. They ought to issue rubber chew
toys in coach class. I needed one by the time the flight attendants

started strapping down food carts and checking to see that our seats were in the upright position.

I was staying at the Hotel Tateshina in Shinjuku, a tacky businessmen's lodging on a side street. My dollhouse-sized room had a hard but comfortable bed, cheap bureau, a TV set, and a pillow that sounded and felt as if it were filled with sand. The walls were thin. Outside the room was a bank of vending machines selling my brand of cigarettes, coffee, Asahi beer, and plastic cards for the porno channels (Cherry Bomb). I showered in the hermetically sealed bath pod, dressed, and walked in the rain to Kabuki-cho, taking a hard right off a neon and billboard-lined street, ducking through a quiet Shinto shrine and into a bustling warren of pachinko parlors, hostess bars, pantyless coffee shops, yakitori joints, and whorehouses. Turning onto the Golden Gai, things were even narrower and the streets were bordered by tiny one- and two-table bars. Above, through a tangle of fire escapes, power lines, and hanging signage, skyscrapers winked red. Welcome to Tokyo. I squeezed into a phone booth-sized place, passed a bank of glowing hibachis, sat down, and ordered a draft beer.

A hot towel arrived with my beer. I ordered pickles and crudités with miso paste, a bowl of *onsen tamago* (a soft-boiled egg with mountain potato and seaweed), cooked collar of yellowtail with radish, some chicken wings, stuffed shiitake mushrooms, and some roasted gingko berries. Life was good again. The grueling hours in cattle class, knees pressed to my chin, staring at Mel 'Fucking' Gibson and Helen 'Two-Expression' Hunt – you know them from such films as *What Tony Does NOT Want*, costarring Gene 'He's Good in Everything' Hackman, playing (surprise) a gruff but kindhearted football coach, and Gene 'Me Again' Hackman playing a gruff but kindhearted former NSA agent – all of it faded into ugly memory.

That night, I woke up at 3:00 A.M. and made myself green tea in my room, on the thoughtfully provided *denji* server. I tried to write. I attempted to telephone my wife back in New York but got the answering machine (Elvis Costello singing 'sometimes I wish that I could stop you from talking'). I hung up, feeling, for the first time since I'd hit the road, truly and permanently cut off from my former life – a universe away from home, everything I'd ever been and done somehow an abstraction. I'd thought I was alone in the Tateshina annex, until a toilet roared through the thin walls. Soon I could hear the sounds of moaning. My neighbor was catching up on Cherry Bomb.

I slept for a while, and had a vivid dream that Nancy had renovated our apartment and thrown me a surprise party. All the guests were Asian. Everyone was doing a lot of hugging. For some reason, Leslie Gore was there, singing 'It's My Party.' When Nancy hugged me in my dream, I could feel it.

I woke up early and bought a hot can of coffee from the vending machine. Out front of the Tateshina, I met my fixer/translator, Michiko, a pretty, smartly dressed, extremely capable young woman the TV people had hooked me up with. Behind the wheel of a rented van was Shinji, my driver, a longhaired guy in a Yankees cap. Both spoke excellent English, and Shinji was completely up-to-date on his Yankees stats and recent trades, so I knew I was in capable hands. On the ride to the Ginza district, Michiko kept up a steady stream of patter on a slim silver cell phone, making arrangements, while Shinji and I worried over the implications of a possible Brosius trade.

This time around, I had a definite agenda. At the top of my list was Edomae sushi. Edo was the old name for Tokyo, and the term *Edomae* when used with the word *sushi* implies that it's old-school, Edo-style, the unvarnished grand-master version of sushi (in a culture where sushi is already revered). Michiko had introduced me to Mr Kiminari Togawa, the chef/owner of the Karaku restaurant in the expensive Ginza district and a master of Edomae sushi.

While I had visited the awe-inspiring, life-changing mother of all fish markets before, this time I would be going with an expert. The plan was to meet Togawa-san at his restaurant, run over to Tsukiji to do his day's shopping, then return to his restaurant and eat myself silly. I've written about Tsukiji in the past, and used up most of the superlatives I can think of. Just take my word for it: It's the Taj Mahal, the Colosseum, the Great Pyramid of seafood. All that unbelievable bounty, spread across acres and acres of concrete, wriggling and spitting from tanks, laid out in brightly colored rows, carefully arranged like dominoes in boxes, skittering and clawing from under piles of crushed ice, jockeyed around on fast-moving carts, the smell of limitless possibilities, countless sensual pleasures – I am inadequate to the task of saying more. There is nowhere else. Believe me.

This time, instead of simply gaping, slack-jawed, I was doing it right. Mr Togawa was with me, and when the fish sellers saw him coming, it got their attention. A friendly but serious fellow of about my age, Togawa-san was looking for a few select items today: fresh live eels, live octopus, sea bream, tiger prawn, and o-toro – the best of the best of the tuna – in season. We spent a lot of time yanking living creatures out of fish tanks and examining them. Mr Togawa showed me something I hadn't seen before. Lifting a flipping and flopping sea bream out of a tank, he took a knife and whacked it behind the head with the blade. The cut opened it up just enough to expose the spine. Mr Togawa quickly took a long, thin wire and inserted it into the fish's marrow, running it up and down its length like a deep root canal. He explained that he was basically paralyzing the sea bream. The fish would live – in a comalike state of suspended animation – until the very last second, back in Mr Togawa's kitchen, when he'd finish the job. Walking down one of the busy aisles, the chef caught sight of a large square of fatty *toro*, and he veered over to examine it more closely. After gazing at it reflectively for a while, and a little discussion with the fishmonger, the piece of tuna went in a bag. We bought a few kilos of very lively eels, an octopus – which very reluctantly released its grip on the glass walls of its tank – some brightly colored prawns, then headed back to Ginza.

The chef's cooks were waiting for us when we arrived, and they immediately fell on the morning's shopping. They salted and pounded the octopus for slow cooking in mirin (rice wine), then butchered the tuna and sorted various parts for different purposes. The small, stark cellar space was soon filled with the smell of steaming rice and freshly grated ginger and wasabi. There came the sound – beautiful really, almost musical – of a very sharp knife cutting through the tiny pinbones of a very fresh fish, the blade scraping quickly along the spine with an extended *ZiiiippppP!* The cooks' blades moved confidently through the eels, then finished off the sea bream with that distinctive sound: *Ziiip! Ziiip!* I sat at the sushi bar, watching them work, until, embarrassed by my growling stomach, I withdrew to a table.

Finally, as zero hour approached, Michiko, Shinji, and I took our places in a small, private tatami room. Hot towels and cold beer were served; then one of the doors slid open and we were off.

Octopus with fresh wasabi – the color and shape of a cherry blossom – came first; then grilled sardine with *ponzu* sauce and *yuzu*, the flavor electric, dazzling; followed by a platter of traditional sushi, each piece, as should be the case with Edomae sushi, containing a nearly identical number of grains of rice – and, as is also the style with Edomae, still warm and more loosely packed than the cold, gluey rice cakes you might be used to. I'd watched Mr Togawa make some of these earlier for another customer. His hands flew, twirled, an entire ballet with ten digits. It had taken him, he told me, three years, during his training and apprenticeship, just to be considered as having mastered rice alone. For three years in his first kitchen, it had been all he'd been allowed to touch.

Half-beak came next, a pointy-nosed transluscent little fish, silvery and alive-looking, then maguro (the lean section of a tuna), marinated twelve hours, tiger prawns, flounder, *o-toro*, all served over the sticky yet fluffy rice, which was still warm. Everything – every fish (except the toro) – was from the Tokyo area. All of it was of the absolute highest quality. No price is too high for the best fish. And with Edomae sushi, one always buys the best.

The meal continued in an uninterrupted flow of delights: a miso soup with tiny steamed cockles, a course of pickles and microgreen salad, a slice of *tamago* (omelette), big shell (whatever that is), abelone, sea eel. Was the meal over? No way! A tray of hand rolls came next: sea cucumber, ark shell, more eel, dried radish with powdered, dried king prawns, chopped *toro* with fresh chives. Bigger hand rolls arrived, each containing *tamago* (egg), shiitake, and cucumber, accompanied by a plate of dried, then pickled daikon. The sea bream appeared squeaky-fresh; it seemed alive on my plate. Then we were served a little bowl of butterfish roe poached in court bouillon, some luxuriously portioned *uni* (sea urchin roe).

The screen slid back and Mr Togawa joined us with a jumbo-sized bottle of frozen sake. He sat down and poured me a glass of frozen, delicious, slushy goodness. In keeping with local custom, I poured back, returning the favor. This usually initiates a lengthy back-and-forth, and that day was no exception. Just when the beer and the frozen sake had combined to give us all mild, blissful grins, a final dish arrived: a few pieces of that incredible *o-toro*, lightly seared, still raw in the middle, with a subtle sweet-and-sour sauce. Perfect.

Perfect. The best sushi ever. The best. Far and away. Let me repeat: the best, finest, freshest, best-prepared sushi meal I've ever had. It took every bit of discipline I had not to moan and giggle and gush throughout the meal. If you're reading this, Togawa-san, and you ever need a favor at four o'clock in the morning, anywhere in the world, I'm there for you. You showed me the light.

That night, my belly still distended from lunch, I strolled over to the old train station and Yurakucho alley, where the air was heavy with the smell of grilling chicken parts and caramelizing marinade. Every little chicken joint, every low-to-the-ground stool and upended beer-crate table, was packed with salarymen drinking and eating yakitori on skewers. I wandered for a while, amazed to find my appetite returning. Down one dark and narrow street, I found a single free stool next to a large and raucous group of business people, all from the same government office, letting loose after a hard day. One of them, in a gregarious mood, reached over and pulled my table near theirs, offering warm greetings and a big portion of hot sake. In a mix of broken English and slurred Japanese, we made introductions, and I found myself plunged unexpectedly into yet another orgy of drinking and eating. Trays of skewered yakitori – ground chicken balls, gizzards, marinated cartilage, and breast and leg meat – began arriving. As soon as my glass was half-empty, someone would fill it. Food kept coming, and soon everyone at the table was making jokes, telling stories, complaining about their spouses. One celebrant at the opposite end of the table slumped periodically onto his outstretched arm, unconscious, waking only for more sake. The others gave him little notice. My stated mission, to eat my way around the world, got a lot of interest. Suggestions rang out from every direction.

'Bourdain-san! You try *chanko*?'

'Bourdain-san! You go for *onsen*? *Kaiseki* food? Very good!'

A pile of stripped skewers accumulated at each end of the table. The sake kept coming. Soon, one of the salarymen was demonstrating what might have been the twist, others making incomprehensible (in any language) mother-in-law jokes. There was a spirited discussion on the subject of who was cooler: Iron Chef Morimoto (my choice) or Iron Chef Sakai (the popular favorite). I did my best to explain the American reaction to the Bobby Flay 'cutting board incident' during the first Flay/Morimoto face-off, an event seen by many Japanese, apparently, as the culinary equivalent of the Tyson/Holyfield ear-chewing debacle.

It turned into a very long night of backslapping, drink-spilling, and loud exchanges of '*Kanpai!*' (Cheers!). Just before the evening threatened to veer dangerously into karaoke, I made sincere gestures of gratitude and appreciation and staggered home, leaving at least two of the party sleeping deeply, face down in their seats.

We are barbarians. We are big, hairy, smelly, foreign devils, unsophisticated, loud, clumsy, overexpressive, and overfed, blundering thoughtlessly through life. At least that's how you might feel when preparing yourself for the *ryokan* experience. The Japanese – those that can afford it – like to unwind and relax. They like skiing. They adore golf. Fly-fishing is an obsession. But the traditional way to kick back is to spend a weekend at a *ryokan*, a country inn, usually in a rural area in the mountains, away from city life. There, one can spend a few days in quiet reflection, soaking in *onsen* (hot springs), enjoying the healthy benefits of a massage, perhaps taking in a little musical entertainment, and dining on *kaiseki*, the most refined, sophisticated style of eating in Japan. An outgrowth of the tea ceremony, *kaiseki* is the national version of haute cuisine, an experience designed to appeal to all the senses, and one's spirit, in equal proportion, as well as one's sense of history and location – a complete yin/yang workup. What better way for a stressed-out office drone to lose himself completely to pleasure than to step back for a few days into the sixteenth century?

Nervously waiting for the *shinkansen*, the bullet train, to the seaside town of Atami, I was becoming painfully aware of my otherness. *Kaiseki*, like no other Japanese cuisine, offers a mine-field of possible behavioral gaffes to the uninformed Westerner like myself. Now, I know how to use chopsticks. By New York standards, I'm impressive. But while reading up on proper dining etiquette at a *kaiseki* meal, the customary practices and procedures when staying at a *ryokan*, my heart filled with dread and terror.

- Don't point your chopsticks at anyone else.
- Do not allow the soles of your feet to be exposed to anyone else.
- Do not step on the wooden dividers between mats.
- Never leave your chopsticks sticking straight up out of your food.
- When drinking soup or tea, it's one hand under, palm up, the other cradling around from the side.
- If it's a soup with chunks, hold your chopsticks thus, and lift the bowl to your lips to sip from it.
- Do not drown your sushi in soy sauce; to leave granules of rice floating in your dipping sauce is the height of bad taste and brutishness.
- When your geisha pours you sake (hot sake with cold food; cold sake with hot), wash your cup after drinking and pour her some into the same receptacle.
- That was *not* a finger bowl.
- Wash for dinner. Really wash.

- Dress appropriately.
- Remember to remove your sandals before entering the room.

No experience is more guaranteed to make you feel like a nine-hundred-pound ape than a *kaseiki* dinner for which you are inadequately briefed. I was very jittery. Shinji had driven me to the station in his personal car, a tiny Renault two-seater convertible, top down. I'd sat in the miniature front seat, my head protruding out beyond the windshield, feeling freakish, huge, and bumbling. I knew I would soon be looking sillier and feeling more awkward than I had since sixth grade, when I'd briefly attended a ballroom-dancing class. The memory of that particular horror still makes my hands sweat and my face burn with shame.

The *shinkansen* are magnificent machines. They slide quietly into train stations, their great bug-spattered nose cones looking like space shuttles. A cleaning crew in pink outfits rushed on board as soon as mine arrived. A few minutes later, liftoff. I was on my way to Atami, gliding at high speed through the outskirts of Tokyo, a *bento* box of *unagi* (eel) and rice and a cold Asahi in front of me. The bullet trains can reach speeds of 270 klicks an hour. Mine moved like a high-speed serpent. From the rear of the train, I could watch the front of it as it whipped like a snake head past Mount Fuji's snow-capped peak, through mountains, fields, small towns, and tunnels, the sea appearing and disappearing to my left as the train hissed through space. About an hour later, I was in Atami, climbing the steep, twisting mountain roads in a taxi. It was sunny and relatively warm for wintertime. Up and up we went, one impossibly angled switchback after another, until we pulled into the hidden driveway of Ryokan Sekiyou, near a mountaintop high over the sea.

I removed my shoes, careful to kick one off, then place a stockinged foot on the raised interior platform before removing the other shoe. I selected the largest of the sandals provided, which still left my heel hanging out by three inches, did my best to bow gracefully to the two women and one man who had hurled themselves to their knees at my entrance and were bowing so deeply that their noses nearly touched the floor. While my luggage was taken to my room, I sat in a small reading room by the entrance, a few coals glowing in a round brazier, mandarin oranges in a bowl, a stargazer lily and a painting by a local artist the only decoration. In a moment, I was escorted to my room by a woman in traditional garb, her feet moving noiselessly over the floor mats in tiny, rapid steps.

My room was not so much a room as a collection of spaces: one large area to eat and sleep in (my futon would arrive later), another area with a low bureau and tall pivoting mirror and a few little drawers, and another area with a low writing table and a heating blanket called a *kotatsu* – basically a table you can bundle yourself up under and stay warm in while you write. There were a few flat pillows on the floor, a painting, and a single flower in an unadorned vase on a shelf. That was it. Sliding back one side of the room, I found myself looking out at a small garden, an orange tree, the mountains and valleys of Atami, and the ocean beyond. Every room at the inn had been ingeniously angled in such a way as to provide each visitor with a spectacular view – and yet maintain the illusion that one was completely alone, the only guest. I looked warily at the flat pillows on the floor. I knew what that meant. I'd be spending two days sitting exclusively on a hard mat floor, my long legs folded up beneath me. I was getting pretty good at contorting my six-foot-four-inch frame into correct Japanese dining position, my legs either tightly crossed or tucked under, knees in front. But getting up afterward was becoming tougher and noisier; the crunching and popping sounds of my forty-four-year-old legs reacquainting themselves with sensation after hours of numbness was not melodious to hear. Japan threatened to cripple me.

A server opened one of the screens from the long foyer to my room and motioned for me to sit.

Crunch! Pop! Snap!

At the low lacquer table in the main space, she gave me a hot towel, followed by green tea and a candied fig. She left for a while, reappearing later with a neatly folded stack of clothing. To my discomfort, she stayed to show me how, once I'd bathed, I should dress. A long gray-patterned *yukata* with billowing arms, a belt – which took many attempts for me to master tying and knotting correctly – an outer jacket, from which my arms protruded ludicrously, and little two-toed white socks, which on my size-twelve feet looked like particularly unflattering Mary Janes.

Left alone to bathe, I pondered my environment. I stared out the window, all thoughts of the outside world quickly banished. There was nothing in my room, just that single flower, the paper walls, the wide expanse of floor. In no time, I felt my metabolism shift, my whole system undergoing some kind of temporary metamorphosis from neurotic, hyperactive, short attention-spanned New Yorker to a character in a Kurosawa samurai flick. The surroundings were identical. I felt I could sit there forever in my *yukata* motionless, doing nothing more involved than contemplating an orange.

There were two parts to the bathroom. The toilet, a typically Japanese device overloaded with gadgets, was in one room. It looked like a regular toilet that had been tricked out by a bunch of speed-freak aerospace engineers. From the array of multicolored buttons, plastic tubes, non-English instructions and diagrams, I gathered that the thing could clean and sterilize itself after each use; spinning and washing the seat, it could direct various widths and pressures of warm-water jet at your rectum – a feature that might cause my old sous-chef, Steven, never to leave; it could wash, sanitize, powder, and emoliate every recess of your nether regions; and it could probably play a medley of popular show tunes while doing it. I was afraid to flush the damn thing.

The other part of the room was more in keeping with my idea of superior plumbing. A deep oblong cedar tub sat against one wall, next to an open window, from which one could gaze out at the mountaintops without being seen, along with an adjacent area in which to wash oneself prior to soaking in the tub. There were a small wooden stool, a scrub brush, a wooden bucket, and a high-powered-spray shower attachment. The idea was to squat on the wooden stool, soap up, scrub oneself down with the hard-bristle brush, pausing to rinse now and again with buckets of hot or cold water, as one liked, then shower. The whole floor, tiled in black granite, tilted conveniently into recessed troughs and drains. After one's outer layers of skin had been scrubbed off, one slid gratefully into the waiting tub, soaking for a long, long time, the window open just enough for a cooling breeze, a view of ripe oranges dropping from the trees in the outer garden.

After a bath, I nervously dressed myself in my *yukata*, socks, jacket, and belt, hoping to God that Steven – or worse, my cooks – would never see footage of this event. The *yukata* was long, ankle-length – and tight, constricting the legs like a long skirt, so I had to take short, quick steps. With the addition of the clunky, ill-fitting sandals one wore while moving from room to room, I felt like I was sashaying down a runway in an evening gown as I tottered off to the larger area of the room, which had been prepared for my dinner.

I would be dining alone at the long black table. By alone, I mean that I would be the only one eating. I would be attended to by two traditionally garbed geishas, who would assist me with my table tactics and food and drink service and provide musical entertainment. Mr Komatsu, the *ryokan*'s manager, in tie and tails, knelt in front of me at a respectful distance, observing and stage-managing the event. A server ran food from the kitchen, opening a screen and dropping to her knees with each course before sliding it across the floor to the geishas.

I managed to seat myself appropriately behind the low table, without exposing any crotch, and washed my hands with a steaming towel. A handwritten menu with a personalized water-color of a flower on rice paper (caligraphy and art by the chef) described in Japanese what I'd be eating. *Kaiseki* menus are a reflection of the region in which they are served and rely, to as great a degree as possible, on local products that are in season. The meal is in many ways a celebration of that season, the presentation, garnishes, plates, and serviceware designed to glorify that which is best about the particular place and time of year.

The meal began with an *amuse-gueule* of *hoshigaki abura-age goma-an*, dried persimmon and fried soy curd with sesame paste. The portions were small, intricately crafted, brightly colored, and, as it was wintertime, constructed around a theme of death and regeneration. Turned leaves appeared as garnishes, plates (square food on round plate, round food on square plate) appearing in groups reminiscent of an artfully strewn forest floor, with many strategic contrasts of color, flavor, shape, and texture.

Kisetsu no sakana goshu means an arrangement of five seasonal fish appetizers from nearby waters – either Ashi Lake or the Atami Bay area – five impeccable little plates and bowls exciting just to look at. I did my best with my chopsticks, looking to the nearest geisha for guidance as to what to eat first. She pointed out sea cucumber and its own liver – two little bowls, one containing what looked to be liver. The liver was gelatinous and golden-colored – like *uni* – and I dove right in with my chopsticks. Mr Komatsu was up in a flash, explaining – to much giggling – that the other item, the sea cucumber, was to be dipped in the liver, that I was basically eating the condiment straight. Blushing fiercely, I shamefacedly switched gears, feeling like I'd just walked into Les Halles, ordered pot-au-feu, and dug right in to the mustard with a knife and fork. I did better with a smoked trout dish with lotus root, the sake being poured by the geishas going a long way toward helping me relax. Oyster cooked in soy, I identified easily and ate with no problem (delicious). Dried mullet roe with radish – the roe salted for a month, then sun-dried – was also sensational. The geishas were helping me feel better about things, playfully teasing me and reaching over to help when I needed it, clearly amused by my ineptness but going to great lengths to make me feel okay about it.

Soup was in a beautiful ceramic bowl: *suppon-dofu*, a soft-shell turtle in egg pudding with green onion and turtle broth. I handled that course easily, doing the chopstick two-hand bowl tilt just fine, it appeared, as there were no giggles or looks at the floor.

The next course, however, presented real problems: *ise ebi*, grilled spiny lobster – in the shell. I stared hopelessly at the thing, all those tiny legs, even the tail meat resisting my first tenuous attempts to free it from the shell. A geisha was there to rescue me. Using her own set of chopsticks, she had every scrap of meat out and arranged in front of me in seconds. I began pouring the women sake after every one of mine, and the mood soon became more festive.

Another appetizer-sized offering appeared: *soba tsubu tororo mushi*, buckwheat in grated yam paste. This was a whole new taste terrain now, products I hadn't even imagined eating a few days earlier. *Amadai kabura surinagashi*, a fish course of sweet sea bream wrapped in *yuba* (a soy protein) with grated turnip came served in a clay pot, followed by a meat course – *gyu shiromiso nikomi*, a piece of tender beef wrapped in baby bok choy in white miso broth – and then another fish course – *komochi konbu*, seaweed marinated in rice vinegar and soy with herring roe. The herring lay their eggs directly into the seaweed, so I was enjoying the stuff nearly in situ. It was followed by *tokobushi daizu hijiki* – steamed rice with abelone, soy beans, and brown algae. Don't think algae sounds good? It is.

My head was swimming now, a pleasantly intoxicated dream state. I no longer knew or even cared what century it was. I was numb from the waist down, circulation long ago cut off to my legs. The heavily painted faces and costumes of my geisha companions, the spare black-and-white walls, the choo-choo train of tiny plates of jewel-like dishes – everything melted together into that rare full mind/body narcotized zone where everything/nothing matters. You know you're having one of the meals of your life but are no longer intimidated by it. Consciousness of time and expense go out the window. Cares about table manners disappear. What happens next, later, or even tomorrow fades into insignificance. You become a happy passenger, completely submitting to whatever happens next, confident that somehow the whole universe is in particularly benevolent alignment, that nothing could possibly distract or detract from the wonderfulness of the moment.

A small stone pot was slid across the floor on a tray and set up over a little stone brazier with two pieces of glowing charcoal. *Kuwai modoki*, grated and fried 'arrowheads,' served in red miso soup. I had no idea what an arrowhead was, but I was way past caring. I knew I was in expert hands. Whatever an arrowhead was, I knew it would be great. And it was. Many, many more sakes came my way – and were returned. I didn't know how the two geishas – tiny middle-aged women – were putting it all away so well. After a final course of dessert sorbets and local fruit, I was damn near goofy with pleasure. The two geishas retreated to the far end of the room and, standing in front of a shimmering gold lacquer screen, began to perform. One played a *syamisen*, a sort of long-necked string instrument she struck with a pick, while the other beat lightly on a drum, whose tone she modulated and manipulated by strings held against her shoulder. They played and sang. One danced. You've seen bits of this kind of traditional Japanese dance – on television or in movies – and you've heard that high-pitched warbling, and you've thought, Jesus! It sounds like someone's torturing a cat! You just hadn't had enough sake to appreciate it. You weren't sitting in that timeless dining room, after a long bath, reflecting on those mountains. You hadn't eaten the meal I'd just enjoyed. The music was lovely, the slow-motion dance mesmerizing to watch. I felt like a feudal lord. I no longer cared about the silly clothes I was wearing. In fact, I felt cool. It was good to be the king. I was ready to order out the cavalry, burn castles, strategize with my warlords in the rock garden, think deep thoughts while I watched the winter cherry blossoms bloom.

I walked carefully back to the sleeping area, where a futon had already been unrolled and turned down for me. I got under the covers, and one of the screen walls was pulled back. I was aware of an older woman entering the room in the dark. She gently drew back the covers and gave me what was easily the best massage of my life, an incredible hour-long treatment, her hands spinning, kneading powerfully through my *yukata* and over every muscle at undiminishing speed, like an agricultural thresher. A while later, half-asleep, half-awake, pleasantly drunk, freshly massaged, I slipped on my sandals and picked my way up a few stairs into a larger, communal version of my bathroom, where I squatted, scrubbed, and showered. It was midnight, and no one else was about. Leaving my clothes in a pile, I slid open another door, padded in the crisp night air across a few smooth flagstones, and lowered myself into the *onsen*, a hot spring-fed bath blasted into volcanic rock at the top of the mountain. I lay there in the water, breathing, listening to my heartbeat until even that seemed to disappear, happy as I'd ever been. When, an hour or so later, I finally climbed back under the covers of my futon and closed my eyes, I slept like the comfortably dead.

Dinner at the *ryokan* may have been the greatest thing ever. Breakfast was another thing entirely. At about 8:00 A.M., the screen slid back and an attendant removed the futon. A few moments later, I found myself, once again, sitting cross-legged at a low table, with a full spectrum of beautiful dishes coming my way. I was not ready, that early in the morning, for a large and challenging meal. I was not ready for Mr Komatsu again, dressed, as always, in his stiff black manager's outfit, kneeling a few yards away while I ate.

I was OK with the smoked fish, which was very good – the sushi, the rice. What I was not ready for, and never will be, was *natto*. The Japanese love *natto*, an unbelievably foul, rank, slimy, glutenous, and stringy goop of fermented soybeans. It's the Vegemite of Japan, dearly loved by everyone there, for reasons no outsider can understand. There were two kinds of *natto* for me that morning: the traditional soy variety, and an even scarier black bean *natto*. If the taste wasn't bad enough, there's the texture. There's just no way to eat the stuff. I dug in my chopsticks and dragged a small bit to my mouth. Viscous long strands of mucuslike material followed, leaving numerous ugly and unmanageable strands running from my lips to the bowl. I tried severing the strands with my chopsticks, but to no avail. I tried rolling them around my sticks like recalcitrant angel-hair pasta. I tried slurping them in. But there was no way. I sat there, these horrible-looking strings extending from mouth to table like a spider's web, doing my best to choke them down while still smiling for the attentive Mr Komatsu. All I wanted to do now was hurl myself through the paper walls and straight off the edge of the mountain. Hopefully, a big tub of boiling bleach or lye would be waiting at the bottom for me to gargle with.

Waiting in the wings, right behind the *natto*, was another concoction, described as 'mountain potato.' Of this, I could handle only a single taste. To this day, I have no idea what it really was. It didn't taste like a potato – and I can't imagine anything on a mountain tasting so evil. I didn't ask, frightened that my host might mistake my inquiry for enthusiasm and offer up another generous helping. The small, dark, chewy nugget can only be described as tasting like salt-cured, sun-dried goat rectum – unbelievably, woefully flavorful – garnished by small maggotlike wriggly things, so awful to my Western palate that I was forced, through the grim rictus of a smile, to ask politely that Mr Komatsu 'leave me alone for a while so I can fully appreciate this fine breakfast in solitude.' I had no choice. I thought I would die. Nothing, not bugs, not iguana, not live reptile parts, not tree grubs, *nothing* I'd ever eaten would approach the horror of these few not unusual Japanese breakfast items. I'm not sneering. I'm sure that natto *and* mountain rectum are, as they say, 'acquired tastes.' And I'm sure that over time I could learn to appreciate them. If I were incarcerated and *natto* was the only food provided. But for right now? Given a choice between eating *natto* and digging up my old dog Pucci (dead thirty-five years) and making rillettes out of him? Sorry, Pucci.

Fugu. The deadly puffer fish of legend. It's a delicacy. It's expensive. You must be licensed by the state – after a long and comprehensive course of training and examination – to prepare and serve it. It can kill you. And every year in Japan, it does kill a score or so of its devotees, who are poisoned by the potentially deadly nerve toxins in its liver. First comes a feeling of numbness around the lips, a numbness that rapidly spreads through the central nervous system, paralyzing the extremities. Quickly followed by death.

Sounds cool, right? If I'd had a top ten list of things I absolutely had to try while in Tokyo, fugu would have been right near the top. I had high hopes. I was ready. I wanted the exhilaration of a near-death experience. I'd scheduled my whole trip around fugu season. As I understood it – from careful study of barroom speculation and an episode of *The Simpsons* – a fugu meal was a game of chicken with all those delicious, if potentially fatal, toxins. There had to be a psychoactive, or at least a physical dimension, to the fugu experience, maybe just enough of the liver in each portion to give you a momentary peek into the void, maybe a sharp but pleasant sensation in the belly after eating, an artificial sense of well-being, a slight MDA-like high as traces of nerve toxin flirted with heart muscles and synapses.

I chose the Nibiki restaurant, run by chef/owner Kichiro Yoshida. Mr Yoshida's father was the first licensed fugu chef in Japan. Nibiki has been operated by the Yoshida family for eighty years without incident or fatality. You get one shot at running a fugu restaurant. One strike and you're out. Nibiki is a homey-looking little place with a large plastic puffer fish hanging over the door, an open kitchen with counter, and a raised dining area with tables and cushions.

Mr Yoshida welcomed me into his kitchen and gave me the short course in fugu. A large example of the fabled fish lay on a spotless white cutting board, looking similar to monkfish with its scaleless, slimy, and knife-resistant skin. The anatomy was similar to monkfish, as well: a center spine, no pinbones, skin that had to be peeled off, and two meaty tenderloin-shaped filets on each fish. Yoshida-san quickly zipped off the skin and began carving away some dark bits. A small metal waste container with a hinged lid and padlock stood next to the cutting board. The chef removed a key from a chain and gravely unlocked it. The toxic parts – every toxic part – of the fugu, he explained, must, by law, be disposed of like medical waste, segregated and secure at all times. He trimmed away any remaining skin, a few parts around the gills, some tiny, innocuous-looking dark spots on the flesh, then soaked the clean white meat repeatedly in cold water. The liver, I have to say, was lovely: creamy café au lait-colored, engorged-looking, with a foie-gras consistency. It looked appetizing, like monkfish liver. 'Do you eat any of the liver?' I asked hopefully. 'No,' said Mr Yoshida. Many are tempted, he explained. Most of the fatalities from fugu, he assured me, occurred among fishermen and fishmongers who were unable to resist the tasty-looking livers – and whatever holistic, restorative powers they might believe the deadly but attractive organ to have. According to Mr Yoshida, the problem is that there's no way to tell how much toxin occurs in any particular fish. A big fugu with a large, plump liver might have relatively little toxin in its liver. Take a nibble, or prepare a *nabe* (broth in a pot) with a tiny bit, and you might well be fine. Conversely, a small fish's liver might well be overloaded with toxin; take one lick and you keel over stone-dead. A daredevil fugu fan might become emboldened by the occasional nip of liver, only to take one toxin-heavy bite of another one and check out for good.

As the chef carefully cleaned and washed the fish again and again, I began to get the idea that I would not be risking my life at all. I sat down to a very nice, very fresh meal. There was a tray of fanned-out slices of fugu sashimi, arranged in a chrysanthemum pattern, with a garnish of scallion sticks and a dipping sauce. The flavor was subtle, bordering on bland. It needed the sauce and scallions. A *nabe* of fugu arrived next, served in a hot pot on a tableside burner – also excellent, but hardly the white-knuckle experience I'd hoped for. A batter-fried fugu dish was next, indistinguishable from a deep-fried fish filet at any of a thousand New England seaside seafood barns. Had I not been expecting a brain-bending, lip-numbing, look-the-devil-in-the-face dining adventure, I would have been thrilled with the meal. That it was only excellent was not enough. I had gotten it wrong. Maybe next time, I'll hook up with those fishermen. They sound like party animals.

Very early the next morning, I hit the Ota fish market. Michiko had arranged for a special treat. As I stood and watched the whirlwind of activity going on around me at 4:00 A.M., three workers wrestled a four-hundred-pound tuna up and onto a cutting board in front of me. With a man-sized serrated blade, the size of a forester's saw, they ran down the length of the still-in-rigor tuna, neatly removing the top half, exposing the pink and red meat inside, and the animal's massive spine. The main man behind the cutting board removed the heart, quickly whacked it into slices, and threw it into a hot wok with some ginger. Then, with a few deft motions, he cut away a selection of the tuna's flesh, each from a different part of the fish: head, loin, and two big hunks of that most treasured part of only the best of the best tunas in season – the *o-toro*. Relatively pale in color, heavily rippled with fat, and looking very much like well-marbled beef, this was sliced into manageable pieces and laid out in a maddeningly appetizing-looking buffet arrangement along the tuna's spine. Taking a soup spoon, he scraped along and between the spinal bones, removing buttery-textured peelings of transluscent, unbelievably tender meat. A small bowl of dipping sauce and some freshly grated wasabi was put down in front of me, along with a pair of chopsticks, and I was urged to dig in. The fish I was using as a service table would fetch somewhere in the neighborhood of twelve thousand dollars – the *otoro* constituting only about 12 per cent of total weight. I was right in the middle of *toro* season, when the fish are at their most relaxed and well fed, their flesh at its fattiest and most tasty. This particular tuna, I was assured, was an aristocrat among its peers. I stood there and ate about a pound and a half of the best of it, knowing I would never taste tuna this good or this fresh again. What is love? Love is eating twenty-four ounces of raw fish at four o'clock in the morning.

Down an alley, I slid open a door, took off my shoes, and padded across a small foyer to an inner door. Immediately, there was the sound of flesh slapping against flesh, grunts of exertion, the noise from hundreds of pounds of wet humanity colliding. I opened the inner door and sat on a cushion on a slightly elevated platform at the back of the room, next to a chain-smoking *oyakata*, the boss of the Tomotsuna sumo stable. I was center stage, painfully cross-legged, at the back of the hot, low-ceilinged room, witnessing something very few Westerners had ever seen. A few feet away, about twenty gigantic, nearly naked men swayed, stretched, and flexed; they pounded their great sweaty no-necked heads against columns, pawed their bare and bandaged feet against the hard dirt floor. In the center of the room was a ring of what looked like a slightly raised hump of woven straw or hemp. A novice wrestler swept the dirt with a straw whisk broom.

The noise! Two gargantuan wrestlers faced off at center ring, crouched down, knuckles resting on the dirt . . . then . . . *smack!* An incredible impact as two five-hundred-pound men crashed into each other at top speed, grappling, slapping with both hands, choking, striving for a hold, or leverage, momentum. Most matches were over in seconds, the winner remaining in the ring to meet one opponent after another until he was bested. The sense of bulk in the little room was overwhelming – a sea of flesh and muscle confined in the cramped space. Occasionally, when one of the mammoth athletes was thrown over another's leg, he'd come spinning or tumbling right toward me, threatening to crush my spine like a bag of taro chips. A huge wrestler frog-walked on bended legs in front of me, back and forth, while at the edge of the ring a young novice, still small in size, stood in a painfully bent crouch, holding a basket of salt in outstretched arms, beads of sweat sprouting on an exertion-reddened face. Punishment? Initiation? I didn't ask. Mr Tomotsuna, the boss, to my left – and an ex-sumo wrestler himself – did not emanate approachability and looked too focused on the activity in the room to disturb him with my witless questions. He hardly gave me a glance unless I was lighting his cigarette for him. Sumo wrestlers live as a family under one roof, all under the guidance and tutelage of the *oyakata*, who rigorously controls every aspect of their daily schedule and training: when they exercise, when they sleep, when they eat, what they eat. They rise early along hierarchical lines: novices first, higher ranks later. (You can distinguish rank by hairstyle.) The novices, much like kitchen interns, sweep, clean, and do household chores, including assisting with the cooking.

I was here to see *chanko*, the food of the sumo wrestler. Typically, I had all the wrong ideas about what they eat. When I'd heard about *chanko* food, I'd assumed, since we're talking about the stuff sumo wrestlers eat in order to blow up to refrigerator-sized grappling machines of fat and muscle, that daily fare would consist of vats of fatty pork and lasagna-density starches, big gulp-sized milkshakes, Cadbury bars between meals, brick-proportioned Snickers bars, whole pullets filled with lardons of bacon and cornmeal stuffing, Grand Slam breakfasts, and endless buffets. I was wrong about this, of course. As I was wrong about these wrestlers. They are not just really, really fat guys in diapers.

Sumo wrestlers are perhaps the most visible and obvious expression of all those dark, suppressed urges in the Japanese subconscious that I referred to earlier, that tiny voice inside every whipped salaryman that wants to make like Godzilla (Gojira) and stomp cities flat. They are a projection of Japanese power, and, make no mistake, they *are* powerful. Under all that carefully layered bulk, it's pure muscle, baby. It's like watching rhinos sparring as one fat bastard crashes into another, digs in low, and pushes the other guy – all six hundred pounds of him – straight back and out of the ring, or flips him onto his back. The momentum and the focus are so great that during practice sparring, when one wrestler fells another, or drives him out of the ring, the other wrestlers step in quickly, all yelling something that sounds like 'Hesss!' – indicating that the bout is over, settle down, cease fire – and restraining the aggressor from further assaults. You do not want to make a sumo wrestler mad at you.

In old-school *chanko* cuisine, four-legged creatures were rarely served, the idea being that sumo wrestlers who use all four limbs during a fight have lost the fight. Chicken – which stand on two feet, like a good wrestler – and fish were the preferred main ingredients. Mr Tomotsuna was making a soup of tuna and vegetables for lunch the day I visited – a fairly sensible choice for Calista Flockhart, I thought, but hardly the bulk-inducing pigfest I'd imagined. I'd have to wait until dinner to find out more.

The Edosawa restaurant in the sumo district is a four-story place where customers eat in private dining rooms. The walls are decorated with paintings of famous wrestlers, and the restaurant attracts a steady crowd of sumo wrestlers and former sumo wrestlers. Michiko, Shinji, and I sat down in a top-floor room, with a simmering hot pot in the center of the table. Mr Matsuoka, the owner, prepared our meal personally. Sumo wrestlers, I discovered, don't just eat that one bowl of soup, as I'd seen them do earlier at the stable. They eat often. They sleep in between meals, and the meal is a delicious multistage operation. Essentially, we had a *nabe* – a big pot of broth into which a procession of ingredients were fed and removed, replaced by other ingredients. Platter after platter of vegetables, meatballs, pork, fish, shellfish, and tofu arrived and were added slowly to the pot – according to cooking time – then transferred to our plates and consumed. The liquid was replenished from time to time as it cooked down or was ladled out, the added flavors growing more assertive over time. The less strongly flavored ingredients went in first; then, over time, things like anchovy paste were introduced.

It was a lot of fun. I'd never seen Michiko and Shinji enjoy themselves so much. It's a family-type thing, cooking *nabe* style, explained Michiko. At her family home, relatives might show up for a *nabe* meal with different ingredients – each relative bringing something – and the adding and removing and serving is casual and fun, like a fondue party. Fooled by the soup I'd seen at the stable, I ate with gusto early on, not prepared for the arrival of more and more plates of raw ingredients, scarfing up scallops and pork and tasty little meatballs with plenty of the hot spicy broth. Soon full, I was taken aback by the traditional ending to a *chanko* meal – the addition to the remaining broth of cooked rice and beaten egg, a mixture that quickly becomes a delicious but absolutely cementlike porridge. I groaned with apprehension as Mr Matsuoka ladled out generous portions of tasty gruel, but I soldiered on, my belly straining. When the meal was over, I needed help to get up. I was the first to exit the room, and as I painfully staggered down the hall, a door slid open across the way and a large party of about a dozen well-fed and slightly drunk businessmen came tumbling out. One of them looked at me with a surprised expression of recognition. He was one of the guys I'd gotten hammered with at the yakitori joint a week earlier. The last time I'd seen him, he'd been fast asleep in his chair, his face resting on the table.

'Bourdain-san!' he cried excitedly. 'You crazy man chef! Where you go? What you eat next?'

ROAD TO PAILIN

I WAS GOING TO the worst place on earth.

The heart of darkness.

'But what are you going to do in Cambodia?' asked the television executive, when I mentioned my destination. Not a bad question as we were, presumably, making a food show.

I had no idea.

'You should go to this place I heard about,' said the TV guy, excitedly. 'A war correspondent I know told me about it. It's this town in Cambodia, Pailin; it's in the middle of nowhere, all the way up by the Thai border. Almost no Westerners have been there. It's a Khmer Rouge stronghold. It's where they still live. It's the end of the world. You'll love it. It's rich in gems; the streets are supposed to be littered with uncut rubies and sapphires, which is why the Khmer Rouge like it. And get this: The Khmer Rouge is in the casino business now!'

Casinos? Run by the most vicious, hard-core Commie mass murderers in history? Well, why not check it out? I thought. Satan's Vegas: lounge acts, strippers, maybe a few new casinos surrounded by razor wire and militia. A town where anything would be possible. Lawless. A little dangerous. I liked the idea. The last outpost for international adventurers, spies, speculators, smugglers, mercenaries, and lovers of vast reasonably priced buffets. Sounded good to me. The cutting edge of extreme cuisine. What could the Khmer Rouge be serving to the legions of degenerate gamblers who were no doubt pouring into their former stronghold? What were their plans for the development of tourism? How were they reconciling their formerly stated hopes for a Stone Age agrarian Maoist Valhalla with the logistical necessities and showbiz glitter of running a profitable casino?

Uncharacteristically, I read the small section in the Lonely Planet guide on Pailin:

> Pailin occupies a curious position as a semi-autonomous zone in which leaders of the former Khmer Rouge can seek haven, avoiding the long arm of international law. There is little of interest to the tourist here, unless you know a bit about gemstones or like hanging out with geriatrics responsible for mass murder. It is indeed ironic that this one time Khmer Rouge model town is these days a center of vice and gambling.

'Vice'? 'Gambling'? This was going to be the kind of lusty adventure I'd read about in *Terry and the Pirates* as a kid! Roadblocks. Sinister guys with automatic weapons. A heart-shaped water bed in some Maoist version of Trump Castle. Even if it was a little rustic, how bad could it be? When Bugsy Siegel built the Flamingo in Vegas, things were still pretty rough out there. This could be fun!

I flew Air Vietnam into Phnom Penh. At Pochentong Airport, a long desk of uniformed military men examined my passport, documents, medical certificate, and visas. All of them were in full parade regalia: leather-billed hats, mortarboards with tassels on their shoulders, chests festooned with medals. It looked like the Joint Chiefs had gathered to personally inspect every incoming visitor. The first guy gravely scrutinized my papers, handed them to the officer on his right, who read closely, made a tiny written notation, then handed them to the man on his right, who stamped them and returned them to the first guy – where the whole process began again. My papers made it all the way down to the last guy. Then, after some tiny incongruity was noticed, they were returned, once again, to the beginning of the line.

Eventually, my documents made it through this ludicrously overdressed gauntlet and I was in. Welcome to Cambodia. This is the last law you'll see.

Once you've been to Cambodia, you'll never stop wanting to beat Henry Kissinger to death with your bare hands. You will never again be able to open a newspaper and read about that treacherous, prevaricating, murderous scumbag sitting down for a nice chat with Charlie Rose or attending some black-tie affair for a new glossy magazine without choking. Witness what Henry did in Cambodia – the fruits of his genius for statesmanship – and you will never understand why he's not sitting in the dock at The Hague next to Milošević. While Henry continues to nibble nori rolls and *remaki* at A-list parties, Cambodia, the neutral nation he secretly and illegally bombed, invaded, undermined, and then threw to the dogs, is still trying to raise itself up on its one remaining leg.

One in eight Cambodians – as many as 2 million people – were killed during the Khmer Rouge's campaign to eradicate their country's history. One out of every 250 Cambodians is missing a limb, crippled by one of the thousands and thousands of land mines still waiting to be stepped on in the country's roads, fields, forests, and irrigation ditches. Destabilized, bombed, invaded, forced into slave labor, murdered by the thousands, the Cambodians must have been relieved when the Vietnamese, Cambodia's historical archenemy, invaded.

One look at the abject squalor of the capital city's crumbling and unpaved streets and any thought that Cambodia might be fun flew out the window. If you're a previously unemployable ex-convenience store clerk from Leeds or Tulsa, however, a guy with no conscience and no chance of ever knowing the love of an unintoxicated woman, then Cambodia can be a paradise. You can get a job as an English teacher for about seven dollars an hour (which makes you one of the richest people in the country). Weed, smack, whores, guns, and prescription drugs are cheap and easy to find. You can behave as badly as you wish. Shy boys on motorbikes will ferry you from bar to bar, waiting outside while you drink yourself into a stupor. You can eat dinner, then penetrate indentured underaged prostitutes, buy a kilo of not very good weed, drink yourself stuttering drunk, and be driven safely home to your spacious apartment – all for under thirty dollars. Cambodia is a dream come true for international losers – a beautiful but badly beaten woman, staked out on an anthill for every predator in the world to do with what he wishes.

Phnom Penh's total population when the Khmer Rouge finished marching its citizens out into the countryside to dig irrigation ditches – and executing most of them – was a mind-boggling twelve people. That's down from about 850,000 only a couple of years earlier. Most of the survivors returned to the city, to find their former homes in shambles; looted, waterless, powerless hovels, often occupied by equally desperate squatters. Armless, legless, limping, and crawling locals struggle still to scratch out a living making handicrafts for tourists. Or begging. The average wage in Cambodia is under a dollar a day. Four-year old children wander the markets, begging, carrying their two-year-old brothers.

Where does one go in Phnom Penh? Just where you'd think the expats would go: The FCC (Foreign Correspondents Club), where you can have an American-style hamburger, and a cold beer, then retire to the rear balcony to watch the bats leaving the eaves of the National Museum at dusk – a nightly event where a stream of thousands and thousands of bats curls out and up into the purple-and-gold sky like fast-moving smoke. Then you can stumble into the street, where a crowd of skinny, underweight boys on scooters and motos wait, no doubt calling your name – as they know you and your predilections by now – brush by a few amputees, hop on the back of one of the boys' motos, and head off to 'the Heart', local shorthand for the Heart of Darkness Bar. After that, there are the nightclubs and brothels (a narrow distinction between the two), maybe some pizza seasoned with ganja, a bag of smack for a nightcap. With any luck, your Cambodian-made condom won't snap, you won't get rousted or shot at by the cops, and you won't run into any relatives of Hun Sen, the prime minister – any of which might

lead to tragedy. If you do get into trouble, don't look to the law
to help you out.

A story from the *Phnom Penh Post*:

Tha Sokha, 19, tried for the rape of a six-year-old girl, will
serve only six months in jail for indecent assault because the
rape of his victim 'was not deep enough' said Kandal Court
Judge Kong Kouy . . . After initially ignoring the girl's family's
complaints against Sokha, district police brokered a compensation deal between the families of the victim and the perpetrator. The girl's parents thumbprinted a contract in which
they would receive 1.5 million riel in compensation for the
rape of their daughter, but they never received the money.
Upon taking the case to the commune police station on Jan.
11, the victim and her sister reported receiving death threats
from a commune police officer named Lon if they continued to
'talk about rape.'

Another typical story from the *Phnom Penh Post* – same day
as the above:

ACID MUTILATION A MISDEMEANOR: The first case of a
viciously mutilated acid attack victim pressing charges against
her assailant has shocked legal observers by resulting in a two-
year suspended sentence against the suspect. Kampong Cham
Municipal Court Judge Tith Sothy dismissed a petition to
upgrade the charges . . . Sothy justified the ruling on the
grounds that [the perpetrator] had no intention of killing
the victim but only sought to 'damage her beauty because
of jealousy.'

Getting the picture? So who is in charge? Hard to say. The
easy answer is Hun Sen, the former Khmer Rouge officer who
defected to the Vietnamese and then was 'elected' prime minister, ousting his nominal competition by coup d'état. There's
King Sihanouk, back again, installed in the palace after playing
footsie with the United States, the Khmer Rouge, the Chinese –

and everybody else. He provides a thin veneer of legitimacy and tradition to what is essentially a military dictatorship. There are the remnants of the Khmer Rouge and its allies – a loosely knit coalition of convenience among various unlovely private armies, organized criminals, former Vietnamese stooges, and extremist groups. The Khmer Rouge 'defected' to the 'central government' (such as it is), awhile back, in return for amnesty, and was basically given control of its former stronghold and cash cow in northern Cambodia, free to pursue its traditional pastimes of gem smuggling and lumbering – and its new gambling ventures. Those in the Khmer Rouge were given central government uniforms when they put down their guns, which means that nearly every male Cambodian of draft age, it seems, wears the same fatigues in one form or another, making it difficult to tell exactly who is robbing and extorting you on any given day. There are the much-feared private armies (everybody's got one), which act mainly as security for various despotic scuzzballs and their relatives – with attendant hit men – making it a dangerous matter if some drunken lout steps on your toe in a nightclub and you voice your displeasure too expressively.

Driving out by the airport one afternoon, my cabdriver pulled his car over suddenly, as did everyone else on the road. A police escort whipped by, sirens screaming, followed in short order by a spanking new black Humvee with tinted windows.

'Hun Sen nephew,' said my driver with distaste. Hun Sen's family and friends are the subject of frequent stories of drunken beatings, stabbings, and pistol-whippings, when one of them gets cranky during an evening out in the discos. There's a famous tale of the time one business associate arrived at Pochentong Airport on a commercial airliner. Told that the airline had misplaced his luggage, he is said to have disembarked, procured a gun from a waiting flunky, then begun shooting out the airplane's tires until his belongings were recovered. Needless to say, this behavior did not result in arrest.

Shooting things, if you have enough money in your pocket, is perfectly all right in Cambodia. Drinks are free at the Gun Club. Ammunition, however, you pay for by the clip.

My waiter, a slim, friendly Khmer, stood over my shoulder as I perused the menu. A tray of Angkor and Tiger beers sat in the middle of the table. Under the thatched roof of the long, open shelter, a few well-muscled soldiers in paratrooper camos from the nearby base sat at another table, unsmiling behind their sunglasses, drinking sodas and beer.

'I think I'll start off with three clips for the .45 . . . three clips for the AK-47 . . . followed by an entrée of five clips for the M16 – can I have some grenades on the side?'

'You like James Bond?' asked my waiter, refilling my glass for me. 'You like James Bond gun?'

'Depends,' I said. 'Sean Connery or Roger Moore. If we're talking Roger Moore, forget about it.'

'Look!' said my waiter, dangling an automatic pistol in front of my face. 'Walther PPK! James Bond gun! . . . You like?'

'Sure,' I said, hefting the thing over a picnic snack of baguette and sausage I'd brought along. 'I'll try it.'

You've got to admire an establishment that invites its customers to get drunk and then fire automatic weapons indiscriminately. Next to the gun racks and the ammunition locker, at the Gun Club, there was a sign on the wall that said in big block letters PLEASE DON'T POINT YOUR WEAPON AT ANYTHING YOU DO NOT INTEND TO SHOOT. This being Cambodia, I thought the text left a lot of room open for interpretation. A Japanese businessman boozily pulling the pin from a grenade a few feet away gave a glassy-eyed look in my direction, smiled, and hurled the thing at a target about fifty feet away. *Boom!* Next time I looked over, he was playing with an M16, trying to jam a full clip into the rifle – backward.

I'd be lying if I told you I didn't have a great time. Firing bursts from heavy weapons at paper targets of charging Russians is fun. I did surprisingly well with the AK-47 and the .45, hitting center body mass almost every time. At one point, his hands over his ears to protect them from the racket of my discharging weapon, my waiter tugged my sleeve and asked, 'So . . . whey you from?'

'New York,' I said.

'What you do?' he inquired.

'I'm a chef.'

My waiter looked at my target, which I'd pretty much shredded from neck to crotch, smiled encouragingly, and said, 'You could be a killer!' That's what passes for a compliment in Phnom Penh, I guess.

They had an impressive selection of armaments at the Gun Club. Ammunition cost between eight and fifteen dollars a clip. I favored the AK-47, as the M16 seemed to jam anytime I put it on full auto – and my marksmanship was better with the heavier gun. I sprang for a few tries on an ancient M50 machine gun, an old partisan weapon from World War II, they told me. It had a big drum canister, like a larger version of the old tommy gun, and discharged in one extended noisy squirt, kicking up and away. The first time I tried it, it raked the target area from floor to ceiling, very difficult to keep steady, sandbags blowing apart in smoky bits as the bullets chewed through. They used to let you play with a mounted M60, but no longer, my waiter informed me. The high-powered shells were tearing right through the sand berm separating the pagoda next door from the Gun Club range, causing mayhem among the bonzes. If I wanted to shoot a cow or a water buffalo, however – maybe with a B-40 rocket? – one could be provided.

I learned a few things at the Gun Club. I learned that when you see Bruce Willis or Sylvester Stallone in a movie, firing for what seems like forever with an automatic weapon, he must be changing clips a lot. When you squeeze down on the trigger of an M16 with the selecter on full auto, it's all over fast, all the rounds gone in seconds. Sly and Bruce would have a problem with overheated barrels, too, I'm guessing, as even on an AK-47, firing on semiautomatic, the gun gets very hot. And any idea that someone can competently handle two machine guns – one in each arm – with any kind of control or accuracy is ridiculous. Try firing two M16s at the same time and you'll blow your own feet off – at best.

We crossed over the Japanese bridge to the other side of the river. A strip of gigantic, football field-sized restaurants had been built on sagging wooden platforms over wetland. At the place we were eating, there were seats for at least five hundred people, yet Philippe and I were the only customers. A Khmer band played a mix of traditional Khmer and pop standards on a large soundstage with disco lights. A menu the size of a telephone book contained laminated full-color photographs of at least 150 offerings – mostly not very good-looking takes on stir-fry. We ate *chrouk pray* (wild boar), *popear* (grilled goat) in hot sauce, and *chilosh* (venison) with a salad of cabbage, tomato, and eggplant. A bus pulled up outside and the 'beer girls' arrived. Buying beer in a restaurant or nightclub can be tricky. Every beer brewer or importer hires teams of attractive girls in distinctive, presumably sexy uniforms to work the places the brand is sold. They arrive together – the Angkor girls, the Tiger girls, the Carlsberg girls – and representatives of two or three other brands. They're paid by the can or bottle sold, so competition is fierce. Within minutes, Philippe and I were surrounded by a throng of aggressive young women, all trying forcefully to get us to order their brand. When we ordered Tiger, the other girls melted away, leaving just the Tiger girl to work our table. Every time I'd get halfway down my bottle, she'd snap open another one.

That night, we went out with some expats. Misha, a Bulgarian; Tim, a Brit; and Andy, an American, sat at a table with me, drinking warm beer over ice, comparing bullet wounds. ' '97,' said Misha, pointing at a puckered, shiny spot on his neck. ' '93,' said Andy, pulling back his shirt to expose an ugly recess in his chest.

Along the wall, twelve or thirteen girls sat silently on folding chairs, looking as enthusiastic as patients waiting for the dentist. One of them cuddled an infant.

'Look at that little scrubber,' said Andy, pointing out a sad moonfaced girl hunched over in her chair under a flickering fluorescent light. 'She's a chunky little beast, isn't she?' he said in English, then translated it into Khmer for the girl's benefit.

We stopped at three or four bars, FCC, the Heart, a nightclub filled with underage whores. At the end of the night, I asked Tim how much to tip my moto driver, a kid who'd been hustling me around town on the back of his bike all night, waiting for me outside until I was ready, then taking me to the next place.

'Give him three dollars,' he said.

I gave him five. What the hell? Two extra dollars, right? He needed it more than I did.

'What are you doing?' complained Tim. 'You'll ruin it for everybody!'

Psar Thmei is the central market, a fetid, sweltering mess with heaps of room-temperature food sweating in the crowded aisles beneath heavy canvas tarpaulins – none of it looking (or smelling) any too fresh.

The difference between this market and markets in Vietnam was like night and day. But then, the Vietnamese have the luxury of pride. I passed by reeking cloudy-eyed fish, limp vegetables, slimy, graying poultry. Philippe, however, was undeterred. He dug into a towering pile of lemongrass tripe and tongue with a blissed-out expression on his face. 'Mmmm! Yummy!' he said to the tripemonger, clasping his hands together and affecting a short bow. 'Tony! You should try some! It's delicious!' He came at me with a steaming, dog-smelling mouthful of tripe pinched between chopsticks. I opened my mouth, and bit down, reminding myself to call Nancy later and ask her to make an appointment with the gastroenterologist. Philippe was trying to kill me.

He tried to kill me again at the 'Jello-O' stand at the market, insisting I try the nasty-looking gelatinous kelp-colored stuff they were eating from iced bowls. But Philippe is an adventurer, a gourmand, in the best senses of those words. He is afraid of absolutely nothing. He'll put anything in his mouth. Maybe it's because he's French. We visited a Vietnamese floating village off Tonle Sap, or Great Lake. We drifted past floating homes, businesses, livestock pens, catfish farms. 'What is she eating?' asked Philippe, pointing out a woman cooking in a wok on the small porch of a dingy floating house, naked children squatting next to her. He made us take our boat over. He smiled broadly and asked the woman if she'd be willing to share a small portion of her meal with us. She very nicely obliged, spooning up a serving of ground fish and pork cooked in sugar syrup with dried shrimp. It tasted pretty decent. As we pulled away after a rudimentary but filling meal, I pointed something out to Philippe. The woman was rinsing the wok in the brown river water a few feet down from a floating livestock pen, and a child washing nearby. 'How do you say *E-coli* in French?' I asked.

I knew it was close. I could smell it. The fabled durian fruit. You can smell it a hundred yards away. Imagine a big green menacingly spiked football – only it exudes an unforgettable, gassy, pungent, decomposing smell. It's an odor that hangs over markets and produce stalls all over Asia. It is said to be delicious. I was intrigued. Expensive, ugly, difficult to transport – it's against the law to take durian on most planes, buses, and trains – it is said to be one of the most prized delicacies of the East. I had to try it. I bought a nice big one; it looked much like the relatively benign jackfruit, except spikier. I'd planned on taking it back to the hotel, but after ten minutes in the car with the reeking, foulsmelling object, the crew were crying for mercy. We had to pull over by Wat Phnom, a pagoda and park in the center of town, where, under the watchful eye of an elephant, I carved up my durian, sawing through the thick skin and cutting myself on the stegaosauruslike armor. God it stank! It smelled like you'd buried somebody holding a big wheel of Stilton in his arms, then dug him up a few weeks later. After sawing through the skin, I pulled apart the fibrous yellowy pulp, exposing, around the avocado-sized pits, lobes of cheesy, gooey, spreadable material that looked very much like whole foie gras. The smell inside was less intense. I took a thick smear of the stuff – it had the consistency of a ripe St. André – and was shocked. It was fantastic. Cheesy, fruity, rich, with a slightly smoky background. Imagine a mix of Camembert cheese, avocado, and smoked Gouda. OK, don't. That's not a very good description. But tasting the stuff, one struggles for words. It didn't taste anything like it smelled; the flavor was much less assertive, and curiously addictive. Durian was one of the first truly 'new' flavors I'd encountered – unlike anything else in its uniqueness, its difficulty. Remember the first time you tasted caviar? Or foie gras? Or a soft ripened cheese? There's that same sense of recognition that you're in new and exciting territory. You may not love it right away, but you know you've tasted something important and intriguing.

Licking the delightful gleet off my blade, I wondered what I could possibly do with this information. What could one make with durian back in New York? How would one store it? Even wrapped in six layers of shrink-wrap, buried in foil, and encased in cement, the odor would escape like an evil spirit. You'd have to treat it like fissionable material, keep it segregated in a special locker in some specially ventilated subcellar constructed just for that purpose. But it's a tantalizing product. Someone, some New York chef, someday, will harness durian's strange and terrible powers. And I'll be there to eat it. Probably alone.

I flew President Air to Siemreap. It was a forty-year-old Antonov cargo plane with passenger seats bolted clumsily into the cabin. The seat belts were broken, hanging uselessly on the sides. When I took my assigned seat, it fell back immediately into the reclining position. The cabin filled up with impenetrable steam as we taxied down the runway. When the flight attendant handed out the in-flight meal, a cardboard box containing plastic-wrapped mystery-meat sandwiches, the entire planeload of passengers burst into nervous laughter and discarded them untouched under their seats without a second thought. Chris and Lydia, the shooters, sat paralyzed, their eyes bugging out of their heads as the plane wobbled and shimmied over Tonle Sap, then slowly descended over the mud flats as we approached Siemreap. Misha, the likable but sinister Bulgarian from Phnom Penh, was on the same flight, on the way to some 'business.' From what I'd understood from previous meetings, he was selling exotic snakes to a Russian clientele. But Kry, my translator/fixer, was dubious. 'He going to see KR,' he said. 'You don't wanta know. Believe me. I don't wanta know.'

Misha exhaled as the plane touched down. 'When I was in

Bulgarian paratroopers – we like this plane very much,' he said. 'Of course, we were all wearing parachutes.'

I stopped taking photographs at Angkor Wat. No camera is adequate to the task. It's too big, too magnificent to be captured in any frame. There's no way to convey through simple images the sense of wonder when you encounter the cities of Angkor looming up out of the thick jungle. Mile after mile of mammoth, intricately detailed, multileveled temples, bas-reliefs, jumbo Dean Tavoularis-style heads, crumbling stone structures choked in the root systems of hundred-year-old trees. This was the center of the mighty Cham empire, which once extended as far as Nha Trang and the sea to the east, all of what is now South Vietnam to the south, to occasional sections of Thailand and the Indian subcontinent. The work, the time, the number of artists, craftsmen, and laborers it must have taken to construct even one of the hundreds of structures is unimaginable. Looking at the densely populated reliefs, you are utterly intimidated by the impossibility of ever taking it all in. The KR did its best to ruin Angkor for all time, laying mines all over the grounds, destroying statues and shrines. Looters and unscrupulous antiquities dealers knocked off as many heads as they could, stripped the temples of what they could carry, and sold them on the black market in Thailand and elsewhere. But the UNESCO people are there now, painstakingly restoring what they can. The mines have, for the most part, been removed, and you can wander the interior of the dark stone piles, a waiflike Khmer kid by your side, telling you what it all means, pointing out the two-tongued figures in dark corners, urging you to give the saffron-robed bonzes tending to small Buddhist shrines a few riel. The dark, clammy interiors smell of burning incense and go on and on forever. Standing at the foot of a great stone head, I could only imagine what the first Frenchmen who'd stumbled onto the place must have felt like.

The cheap bastards from the TV production company had booked me into yet another depressing sinkhole in Siemreap. I took one look at the lobby, and, fully aware that I would be staying in even rougher environs over the coming days, decided to splurge. I checked myself into the Raffles-operated Angkor Grand a mile down the road. I figured one night living like a colonialist oppressor would be good for me. I had never enjoyed a high-pressure shower with unlimited hot water the way I did that night – glorious after all the lime-encrusted dribblers I'd been standing under in recent weeks. There was an enormous pool, three restaurants, and a bar and sitting room, where uniformed help in pointy hats and green *kromahs* made girlie drinks decorated with umbrellas. When I returned to my room after a massage, a swim, and a croque monsieur, there was a garland of fresh jasmine flowers on my pillow.

I took full advantage of my luxurious surroundings, because tomorrow the ordeal would begin. The crew was nervous. I was nervous. The plan was to take a hired boat out onto Tonle Sap, cross over to the mouth of a river, and chug upstream to Battambang. The following day, we planned to rent a 4 × 4 and driver and travel seventy to eighty kliks over the worst, most heavily land-mined road in Cambodia to Pailin, near the Thai border. This was not an auspicious time to be visiting with the Khmer Rouge. Recent developments in the capital indicated that the government was planning to revoke its agreement with Ieng Sary, the leader of the KR's Pailin faction, and bring him before an international tribunal for war crimes. The mood in town, we assumed, would not be good.

The road to Pailin. It's not a Hope/Crosby movie – and Dorothy Lamour is definitely not waiting in a tight-fitting sarong at the journey's end. I'd wanted to go up a no-name river to the worst cesspit on earth and, for my sins, I got my wish.

I set out from Siemreap in the early morning, along with Chris, Lydia, and Kry. Kry, who is something of an expert on the Khmer Rouge, had been to Pailin before, during the last fighting. But the moment we set out for Battambang from a muddy creek off the lake, he was struck dumb, nearly speechless for the duration. From the very get-go, things did not go as planned. Our skipper and a mate, who concerned himself mostly with a noisy, clanging, and dubious-sounding engine, couldn't agree on exactly where to find the mouth of the river. After crossing open water, we floated around the lake, looking for landmarks, broiling in the late-morning sun. I ate a packed lunch from the Angkor Grand of *saucisson sandwich*, Camembert cheese, and a nice bottle of Côte du Rhône and waited.

The river, when we finally found it, was wide and clean and pretty to look at. But after about thirty miles, as we approached a floating village, our skipper, without warning or explanation, pulled over to a waterborne police station bobbing on fifty-five-gallon drums. A few uniformed officers in death squad-chic sunglasses and two very dodgy-looking characters in red *kromahs* and olive drab fatigues stood there waiting for us. Without asking, the two fellows in *kromahs* and military clothing boarded our vessel and sat down by the skipper at the helm. The cops waved us on.

Now, the red *kromah* is an almost universally worn accessory all over Cambodia. It's worn as headgear, as a scarf, as a bustier top for women, as a sarong. In a pinch, it can be used for pulling an oxcart out of a ditch, as a carryall, or as a diaper. But when worn by unsmiling, unfriendly strangers with bloodshot eyes, attired in military garb – who've just boarded your privately engaged boat without asking – the red *kromah* takes on a sinister aspect. One's mind naturally flashes back to footage of the newly victorious KR riding into Phnom Penh on the backs of tanks – just before the mass murdering began.

A few moments later, I noticed that our boat had slowed almost to a standstill and that our new additions were arguing with the skipper, pointing in a direction decidedly opposite from where the river was taking us. I looked to Kry to translate, but he wouldn't meet my gaze. Not a peep. He stared off at some fixed point in space, apparently oblivious. When, at our uninvited guest's instruction, the boat changed course, coughing and clanking up a narrow no-name creek perpendicular to the river, I barked to Kry, 'What's happening? What's going on?'

'We take shortcut,' said Kry, quickly slipping back into what seemed to be a coma.

'*Shortcut.*' The word filled me with dread. When has a short-cut ever worked out as planned? The word – in a horror film at least – usually precedes disembowelment and death. A 'shortcut' almost never leads to good times. And in Cambodia, with our skipper suddenly piloting the boat up a shallow, twisting, foliage-choked, water-filled ditch, deep into who the fuck knows where, with two who the fuck knows who giving the orders, I was not feeling too secure. I consulted my Lonely Planet guide and was dismayed to find that this particular body of water did not appear on the map.

Upriver we went. For hours and hours, with no end in sight. The trip was supposed to take six hours. It had been nearly nine. The terrain grew rougher, then narrowed with each three-point turn. We pulled and pushed in waist-deep muck, tearing free of clinging vines, just barely clearing sandbars and mud flats. This trip was beginning to make the river journey in *Apocalypse Now* look like the Love Boat as the scenery got more primitive, the few signs of life becoming more backward and desperate-looking as we pushed farther and farther into the bush. The few sampans or boats coming in the opposite direction squeezed by without any of their passengers even acknowledging us. They eyed our olive drab-garbed passengers, then turned away, their faces showing what surely looked like fear. There were no longer greetings of 'Hello' or 'Bye-Bye' from the riverbanks, just glowers, stunned looks, silent hostility, indifference.

I saw nothing for hours but the occasional hut protruding from the water, or high atop stilts on the bank, men and women in rags, near naked in *kromahs*, squatting by the water's edge, rubbing unguent into sick pigs, washing clothing in the brown water, sharpening machetes against stone. I was becoming concerned. I hadn't seen a single house, not a single building with what could be called walls, not a TV aerial, not a power or phone line in hours. We could have been traveling up the same body of water a thousand years ago, with no discernible difference. What if our engine breaks down? What if our propeller fouls? What if one wing nut shears off, leaving us dead in the water? Whom could we call? Even if we had a cell phone? (Which we didn't.) No one on this boat, I suspected, could even have described our location. Which of a thousand similar gullies, canals, streams, creeks, and ditches were we on? And how far up? My American Express representative was not waiting at the next stop. Where would we sleep if we had to spend the night out here? There was nothing but water, mud, flooded rice paddies, jungle, and the occasional construction of bare sticks and bamboo – like a child's collapsed and forgotten tree house. And my mysterious fellow passengers, what about them? Who were they? Where were they going? What were their intentions? The scarier-looking of the two, who'd been smoking Alain Delon cigarettes, gave me something that looked like a smile when I offered him a Marlboro, but that's all I had going for me.

Deeper and deeper into the weeds we went. Mile after mile of nothing but demolished huts, muddy riverbanks, waterlogged and useless sampans. Once in awhile, there would be a chicken, a rooster, a water buffalo, or a pig, and a few of the tall, bare sugar palms in the distance. We rounded another turn, and there, in a village now sagging and sinking into the water, two more passengers were waiting for us with their bags packed. One of them was wearing a Tweetie Bird T-shirt and camo pants. Great, I thought. My executioner. Killed by a guy in a Warner Bros. T-shirt.

It was getting darker, and still there was no sign of Battambang – or anything else even resembling civilization. I wasn't looking for minimalls or office buildings any more. Evidence of electric power would have sufficed. Bugs were feasting on me. As the light failed, wood smoke began to curl over the water, and the river began to widen a bit. A few families bathing together on the banks provided some encouragement. More smoke, coming from cooking fires. I saw a house on stilts with actual walls. Another good sign. The river became busier. Flat rafts pulled by rope towed motorbikes and their drivers across the river to the other side. More homes and shelters. The skipper was listening his way upriver now, all light almost gone. The smoke thickened, and then I saw my first electric light, hazy in the distance. Soon, torches, more lights, a surreal image in the heavy smoke and near-total darkness. Shrill Khmer music and drums echoed out over the river from distant loudspeakers.

After tying up at the bottom of a steep, muddy bluff, hands reached out from nowhere and helped us off the boat and up a slippery slope. Dark figures grabbed at our bags and hauled them up the hill. Soon we were loaded into a van and taken to the fabulous TEO Hotel, Battambang's 'best.'

White tile floors, white tile walls, white stucco ceilings. The hotel was a big four-story blockhouse, free of decorative features. A sign by the front desk depicted the black shape of an AK-47, circled and bisected in red. The usual Cambodian hotel industry's hospitality features were in evidence: A door off the lobby with a sign saying KARAOKE MASSAGE in red letters. Translation? 'Whores available.'

My room was more white tile, a central floor drain – as if the whole room had been designed to be flushed with the press of a lever. The bathroom worked on the same principle: Turn on the shower, hold the calcified showerhead over your body while sitting on the toilet, and everything goes. The single roll of toilet paper was waterlogged from a previous guest. A smooshy packet of something that could have been either soap or a condom sat on a shelf over the sink. In the bathroom drain, a wadded-up Band-Aid floated on a raft of hair and soap scum. I didn't mind. At least I wouldn't be sleeping out in the bush with the cobras and the banded kraits and the mosquitoes. I showered as best I could and bounded down to the TEO's empty restaurant, where an eager waiter helped me select dinner from another colorful menu of photographs. *Congee*, green curry, *pad Thai*, *amok*, the usual collection of stir-fry and hot pots, the menu about half Thai, the check payable in riels, dollars, or baht. My waiter, after hearing that I was en route to Pailin, volunteered that he had been there once, having hoped to strike it rich in the gem trade. He came back with only malaria to show for his efforts. He said sadly, 'Bad people in Pailin. Bad people.'

You saw the signs first.

Little orange ones, every hundred yards or so, all along the road. WARNING! LAND MINES! There was a helpful picture of a skull and crossbones.

Try to imagine the worst road in the world: sixty miles of unpaved trail, alternately bone-dry ruts, hillocks, potholes, and crevices so deep and so steep that one's vehicle nearly topples over onto its side. The cars only a few feet ahead actually disappeared from view into ruts and depressions in the road. Trucks so dangerously overloaded with wood and hay that they towered ludicrously nearly fifty feet in the air – with whole families sitting on top. Vast pools of puddinglike muck, stagnant water from adjacent flooding rice paddies. And, of course, the usual road hazards of broken oxcarts, diverted streams, check-points, roadblocks, crumbling bridges, and armed bandits.

Black SUVs bounced by us, KR gangsters and illegal timber merchants behind tinted windows, armed goons riding shotgun. The occasional white 4 × 4s were the good guys, the minesweeping outfits, still hard at work in northwest Cambodia. The occasional full-color billboard depicted on its left-hand side a happy farmer walking with his son through their fields. On the right-hand side, the same farmer and son were shown being surprised by an explosion, the stumps of their arms and legs sprinkling brightly colored blood. Our vehicle was a hired white 4 × 4 with a very worried-looking driver. He didn't like us. He didn't like where we were going. He seemed unhappy about what the road was doing to his car.

From time to time, we crossed a bridge over a deep gorge or rocky stream. Rotten, moldering planks bounced and crumbled under our wheels, the rocks and water below visible through gaping holes as we slowly edged forward. Some bridges were actually suspended from cables – so we had to worry not only about the planks disintegrating under our tires but also about the whole structure swinging unreliably from jury-rigged supports. Overloaded trucks came to a full stop at each bridge as driver and passengers assessed their chances, then sped across as quickly as possible, hoping that it would be the next vehicle that might plunge through the splintering planks onto the rocks below.

Bounce, jolt, lean, grind, crumble, drop, bounce, jolt. We often had to stop and wait for an old woman, a pantless child, or an armed teenager in fatigue top and *kromah* sarong to remove a big rock or a row of sticks from our path – makeshift roadblocks and tollgates – and wave us on.

I began to see more guns at the checkpoints. And skulls. Arranged on display atop small birdhouselike platforms and shrines by the roadside were small piles of human skulls and thighbones. A warning? A remembrance? I don't know. As we got closer to what used to be the front line of the last armed conflict, I saw a rusted-out, bullet-pocked APC (armored personnel carrier) by the side of the road. Then a burned-out Chinese-made tank.

The armed guys at the last checkpoint did not look happy to see us. What about the casinos? Didn't these people want our business? I began to get the idea that I would not soon be enjoying a mai tai in the main lounge, entertained by the comedy stylings of Don Rickles. The likelihood of a buffet or a station to make your own omelette seemed increasingly remote. My driver kept looking in the rearview mirror as he drove along at a breakneck clip of ten miles per hour, echoing my waiter from the TEO with occasional remarks that there were 'bad peoples . . . bad peoples' here.

We stopped in a small village to eat and to stretch our ruined backs and necks. At a roadhouse next to a market, a group of agitated Khmers were rather too enthusiastically watching a Thai kick-boxing match on a television in the dining area, shouting and pumping their fists in the air anytime anyone got hit. I had a bowl of some warm beer on ice and some *tom yam*, a sort of Thai noodle soup. It was the best thing I'd had to eat since arriving in Cambodia – Thai food. Everything was increasingly Thai here, the closer we got to the border. Thai food, Thai money, Thai television. After a meal and a rest, we set out again, with about two hours to go until Pailin.

'This was where the front was,' said Kry awhile later, speaking up for the first time in memory. He pointed out a craggy mountain peak and a pagoda. 'KR used to dump bodies in this mountain. Thousands of bones up there inside the mountain.'

Just outside Pailin, the road was actually graded – probably to accommodate the lumber trucks. (They're cutting down every tree in Cambodia to sell off to the Thais, a practice that is leaving the countryside even more devastated and that threatens, each rainy season, to flood Tonle Sap, Bassac, and Mekong, drowning the capital.) We sped along the road, no one speaking, and then we were there.

Pailin. Unpaved, littered streets, mangy dogs, sullen locals who glared at our arrival. A few signs indicating karaoke massage, a barber, a few gem retailers selling chip-sized rubies and sapphires, a run-down, hopeless market. No casinos. No neon. No jumbo parking lots, new entertainment centers, dog tracks, or air-conditioned necropolises filled with one-arm bandits and Keno. No Seigfried and Roy. No Debbie. No Steve and Edie. Nothing but naked hostility, squalor, and scary-looking guys with guns. The Hang Meas, Pailin's only hotel, was a smaller, drearier version of the TEO. Same cautionary sign in the lobby about AK-47s. Same karaoke massage booth. Same white tiles, creepy stains, drain in the floor.

I ate some soggy stir-fry in the hotel restaurant, then took a ride around town on the back of a motorbike with a young man who wanted to show me where I could score some good rubies. There wasn't much to see. Ramshackle buildings, two-story businesses, a pagoda. The homes with the satellite dishes and the SUVs and new 4 × 4s out front belonged to the KR. Apparently, only Communists get to make money in Cambodia. I bought some overpriced and undersized rubies. Yes, there are uncut rubies strewn everywhere – by the riverbanks, in front yards, in the soil – but they cut the gems in Thailand, and they rarely make it back from the other side of the border – like most of the country's resources.

We sent Kry off to talk to the official in charge of tourism and information, a former high-ranking figure in the KR. Unsurprisingly, considering recent developments in Phnom Penh, he didn't want to talk about Pailin's future as a destination resort. He was not interested in showing us the casinos. The casinos, it turned out, were about thirty kliks beyond Pailin, in the jungle and mountains near the Thai border.

'He say you want to go there to shoot film? Maybe you get shot,' said Kry when he returned. The KR official did not care to talk about economic development or Hard Rock hotels or anything else to do with tourism. He wanted to talk about what the KR would do if Ieng Sary was in fact indicted and dragged before the courts. He wanted to talk about returning to the jungle. Rearming. Going down fighting with their leader in a blaze of glory. Not what we wanted to hear.

That night, at 3:00 A.M., someone began pounding violently on Chris's and Lydia's door. Lydia, whom I had seen leaning out of fast-moving cars to get a shot, who has filmed on paratrooper bases, in jungles, and in minefields without fear, told me later that she jumped out of bed and huddled in a corner, shaking as Chris finally opened the door. Fortunately, it was a drunken Thai businessman back from an evening of karaoke massage, confused as to which floor his room might be on – not a KR security cadre with radiophones and alligator clips.

The next morning, I ate breakfast in the hotel. I was depressed. Things had not turned out as I'd hoped. Two days of travel up a no-name river and across the worst road in the universe – and for what? This was no gamblers' paradise. The 'vice capital' was the same collection of dreary whorehouses and bars as everywhere else, only less welcoming. The citizens seemed stunned, lethargic, frightened, angry – not what you want in a destination resort. My dreams of becoming some kind of Southeast Asian Bugsy Siegel were shattered. Everyone wanted to leave, Kry and our Khmer driver more than anyone. The food, particularly compared to the delights of Vietnam, was uninteresting – mostly watered-down Thai, served under conditions incompatible with freshness. While I sipped my instant coffee, two guys in fatigues pulled up on a motorbike and dumped a dead deerlike creature on the ground with a *plop*! They dismounted and went to talk to the chef. Two children in rags hurried to the carcass, probing the large exit wound by the creature's neck with their fingers, then sniffing them while flies gathered.

'That's an endangered species, actually,' said a voice in English.

Tim and Andy stood there in head-to-toe leather motocross outfits, covered in road dust, behind me in a dark corner of the hotel's dining room. Tim has penetrating pale blue eyes with tiny pupils, and the accent of an Englishman from the north – Newcastle, or Leeds maybe. Andy is an American with blond hair and the wholesome, well-fed good looks and accent of the Midwest. Behind them, two high-performance dirt bikes leaned on kickstands in the Hang Meas' parking lot.

Tim owns a bar/restaurant in Siemreap. Andy is his chef. Go to the end of the world and apparently there will be an American chef there waiting for you. Kry, looking exhausted, joined me for breakfast, saw the two men in dusty leather, and nodded hello.

'Kry! How's it going, you bastard?' said Tim.

'Not bad, Tim. How are you?' replied Kry.

'Still hanging at Happy Herbs?' asked Andy.

Everyone knows each other in Cambodia, it seems. We were on the other side of the country – in the middle of nowhere – and Kry and the two motorheads were acting as if they bumped into one another like this all the time.

'You see Misha?' asked Tim.

'We saw him just now, coming in, talking to some KR guys,' said Andy.

'He was on the plane with us to Siemreap,' I offered.

'How'd he get here from Battambang?' asked Tim. 'We didn't pass him on the road.'

'Maybe he take helicopter,' said Kry.

'Ahhh . . . yesss,' said Tim with an evil cackle.

The two men were on a road trip across Cambodia's back roads – a daunting obstacle course for most travelers, but rollicking good fun for dirt bikes. They'd intended to travel from Pailin down to Sihanoukville and the sea but ran into trouble after encountering an illegal logging camp in the jungle and had had to turn back.

'We're going to try another route,' said Tim, 'but if things don't work out, we'll see you in Battambang maybe.'

We couldn't get out of town fast enough, but our driver misunderstood Kry's instructions and headed toward the Thai border, grumbling under his breath. It was an hour before we figured out that we were headed in the wrong direction, inching along miles of jungle road, passing small farmhouses with satellite dishes on the roofs, the telltale black Toyota Land Cruisers, Land Rovers, and SUVs sitting outside of neat homes in the middle of nowhere. Everywhere were felled trees – as if an army of indiscriminate lumberjacks had simply waded through, chopping down everything in sight. The clouds hung low around the mountaintops, and the people, when they saw our car and our cameras, appeared shocked, as if we'd disturbed them while bathing. Our driver looked frantically unhappy. When Kry finally pointed out that we wanted to go in the opposite direction – back to Battambang – the driver nearly wept with relief.

The whole way to Pailin, our driver had kept his vehicle at a steady ten miles per hour. On the way back, he tore along at a reckless thirty miles per hour, oblivious to any damage he might be doing to his suspension or undercarriage. He's scared, I realized. Really scared. When we passed a company of black-clad militia in full parade formation a few yards from the road, their heads turning in unison to watch us, our driver sped up even more, glancing nervously in the rearview mirror for the next twenty miles. At a checkpoint we'd passed the day before, there had been one or two rifles – clapped-out M1s or Chinese knockoffs. Now, the same checkpoint bristled with AK-47s. The whole way back, our driver was spooked. Every innocuous-looking civilian we passed on the road seemed to fill the guy with terror, a potential lookout radioing ahead to the ambush party. I never thought I'd be happy to see the Hotel TEO again, but I was. When you've been to Pailin, Battambang seems like a megalopolis.

Midnight in Battambang.

Tim drove one motorcycle, with me on the back, hanging on for dear life. Andy drove the other, with Misha behind him. We raced through Battambang's quiet streets at high speed, making a god-awful noise, roaring over a narrow pedestrian bridge toward the far end of town to a strip of bars and brothels.

Generally, when you're a Westerner encountering a roadblock, you try to bull your way through. Fully aware of your privileged position as a white man with money in his pocket, you slow down, just enough to be polite, maybe smile a little, then try to breeze through – as if roadblocks and checkpoints and armed police or military can't possibly be intended for the likes of you. And this usually works, I was told. It was certainly what Tim and Andy expected when we came upon a floodlit square, a line of uniformed policemen stopping traffic. We slowed down a little but, in typical expat style, did not stop.

Suddenly, things got very dicey.

'*Stop! You stop now!*' screamed a uniformed cop with more confetti on his chest than the others in firing position around him. It's unusual in an Asian country to see someone visibly angry. It's just not done. When one loses one's cool and one's control, starts screaming and yelling and making faces, one is usually considered to have lost the argument. Hence the term *losing face*. The rule did not apply here. The cop doing the screaming was absolutely livid, his voice cracking as he shrieked in English and Khmer for us to stop and get off our bikes. His face was contorted with rage, muscles twitching beneath his skin like a nest of rattlesnakes in a thin cotton sack. There was the sound of *klick, klack, klick, kachunk* as six policemen flicked off their safeties and racked rounds into their weapons.

'Oh shit,' said Misha, who'd been shot already at one of these impromptu affairs.

'Fookin' 'ell,' said Tim, stopping and turning off his engine. Andy did the same.

'*You stop! You get off now!*' screamed the lead cop, the others yelling along now in Khmer, their weapons fully extended. I dismounted first and immediately got a gun barrel thrust in my face, five or six people screaming at once. Another rifle prodded me to turn around, the little cop indicating he wanted me to put my hands on my head. Misha got off the back of Andy's bike and, familiar with the drill, calmly placed his hands on his head, too. Andy and Tim were last, as it takes a minute to put down kickstands. All the while the screaming and the threatening continued, the gun barrels becoming more intrusive, no longer a prod, but a shove. When all of us were standing there in the middle of the street, our hands clasped on top of our heads, bikes silent, the little cop demanded to know if we had any guns. This seemed to please Misha, who translated.

'*Where you go?*' demanded the little cop, his face still red and twitching.

'We're going to the brothels,' said Tim in English, following that up with a few words in Khmer and that evil laugh again.

As if by magic, the cop's face relaxed, the picture of instant serenity and congeniality. Smiles all around. Like the maître d' of an expensive restaurant, the little cop, who only seconds before had looked like he would most certainly be shooting us dead any moment – or at the very least dragging us off to jail – stepped back and to the side, arm extended in welcome, and ushered us theatrically through.

FIRE OVER ENGLAND

ENGLAND'S BURNING.

Turn on the telly, open up a newspaper, and you'll see or hear about smoldering mounds of stiffened livestock, quarantines, checkpoints, disinfectant, and body counts. No one seems to know when the killing will stop – maybe, it sometimes seems, when every edible creature in the UK has been executed, burned, and bulldozed into a pit. Just when diners were learning to live with the remote possibility that the beef they're eating could riddle their brains with spongiform bacteria, turn their cerebral cortices into loofahs, the foot-and-mouth thing (which does not affect humans) comes along, causing fear and uncertainty among the populace and giving yet more comfort and succor to the forces of darkness and evil.

The battle lines are drawn. Good and evil have met – and the front line is England. Nowhere else can the threat be so clearly defined. Nowhere else are good guys and bad guys so visible and apparent, the choices so black and white, devoid of gray.

I love England. I'm there a lot. So I have a vested interest in the outcome. Few cultures are as resolutely grounded in the appreciation of a nice thick slab of fatty meat, a well-brewed beer or ale than the English.

No country was experiencing the kind of foodie gold rush, that boomtown mass psychosis that suddenly causes everyone to become obsessed with all things to do with food, restaurants, chefs, and cuisine, that England was (except maybe Australia). Things were going so well. Now? Everything hangs in the balance. It's war. A fight for the hearts, minds, and souls of future generations. If the dark forces win? They'll be looking across the Atlantic; don't doubt that for a second. They already have their operatives in place. They'll be looking at your plate, inspecting your refrigerator. They already are. They want to take your meat away.

They even want your cheese.

Japanese porn is ugly, violent, and disturbing. German porn is ugly, fetishistic, and disturbing. American porn is stupid, slick, and produced in multiple versions (how explicit depends on what major hotel chain you're staying at) – sex as a mass-produced corporate endeavor. Brit porn, however, is the absolute bottom of the barrel – stuff so witless, brainless, joyless, and strange as to remove from the imagination immediately any possibility that sex might ever actually be fun.

The actors are crude, fat, and saggy and have bad teeth and dirty feet. Even their tattoos are artless. The cast members, apparently, are compelled to have sex through their underwear, tonguing saliva-soaked Jockey shorts until the questions about why Brits have historically been so fucked up about sex are answered: Judging from the videos I saw, it's all about bum whacking and undies. There is no hope. Bear with me here; I'm leading up to an allegory.

Eventually.

One can be forgiven, I hope – on first look – for thinking that the only people getting laid in England are rock stars and chefs. (Which is entirely appropriate. The two professions have traditionally been at the vanguard of sexual adventurism.) In England, as in America and Australia, the population has gone chef-crazy, reading about them in the tabloids, watching them on TV, buying their recipe books, losing themselves in lurid fantasies of cutting-board penetration and sweaty tangles in the larder. If food is the new porn – a less dangerous alternative to the anonymous and unprotected shag of decades past – then the mission is even more urgent.

A sampler of England's hottest 'chefs' would include a mostly hairless young blond lad named Jamie Oliver, who is referred to as the Naked Chef. As best as I can comprehend, he's a really rich guy who pretends he scoots around on a Vespa, hangs out in some East End cold-water flat, and cooks green curry for his 'mates.' He's a TV chef, so few actually eat his food. I've never seen him naked. I believe the 'Naked' refers to his 'simple, straightforward, unadorned' food; though I gather that a great number of matronly housewives would like to believe otherwise. Every time I watch his show, I want to go back in time and bully him at school.

Another TV demigod is Nigella Lawson – the object of desire of nearly every male I met in England – and the apparent dream of perfection for most women I encountered. She's a wealthy and beautiful widow who cooks in a denim jacket. When she leans over the workbench, her breasts are the focus of intent contemplation and rhapsodic praise by the male television audience.

Last time I was in England, it was all anyone seemed to want to talk about: 'Nigella's breasts . . . have you seen them?' While she may not look like too many cooks I know, she does seem to cook a lot of exuberantly cheesy, fatty, greasy stuff – not shying away from the butter and cream – which puts her on the side of the angels in my book. How many upper-crust widows do you know who say, 'Fuck it! Let's eat what's good!' Not many. I like her.

There's the Martha Stewart-like Delia Smith. There's the gel-headed Gary Rhodes. And then there's Ainsley Harriott – a man who makes Emeril look like William Buckley. Harriott, who tried his act in New York for a while, specializes in eye rolling, cooing, squealing, flattering, and mugging. It makes me cringe to watch a grown black man doing shtick, capering and coddling an audience of bison-sized white women who, were Harriott not on TV, would probably call the cops if he wandered into their neighborhoods.

The big dogs in England, the good guys, the people actually cooking in restaurants (which is what chefs are supposed to do, isn't it?), the folks actually fighting the good fight are what's really interesting about the English food scene. Swaggering, eccentric, aggressive, competitive, often brilliant, they're a refreshing change from their US counterparts in the celebrity chef racket.

In our country, when a blue-collar goof scores any kind of commercial success, he immediately strives to stop dropping his g's, to begin enunciating consonants, to stop using the word *fuck* as a comma. He may, as in the case of one much-praised colleague, immediately hire the services of a personal hairstylist and voice coach. In the UK, it's different. There, once a measure of success has been attained, the chef feels free to become the badly behaved, borderline-violent hooligan he always wanted to be, freely displaying the inner rude boy. Which is one of the reasons I feel very much at home in London.

It's competitive over there. When I casually mentioned to an English pal that I had lent a case of mesclun to the chef at the restaurant across the street from me in New York, he was outraged.

'*What?* Bloody hell! We'd never do that here.'

What happens if he runs out of mesclun? Would he borrow?

'Wouldn't give the bastard the satisfaction.'

Camaraderie is somewhat rarer. To associate too freely with other chefs is to trade with the enemy. When a sous-chef leaves a position to start his own operation, it's like he defected. He becomes the Person Never to Be Mentioned Again. In New York, if the chef across the street steals your saucier, you don't harbor too much of a grudge. Everybody knows you'll be stealing his grillardin if you get the chance. And everybody involved is probably going to end up working together some day anyway – so get over it. Stealing of cooks and recipes is part of the game – even part of the fun for some of us. In England, feuding with food critics, commentators, and other chefs is encouraged – and may even be a good career move. In New York, the idea of throwing the *New York Times* food critic (if you are lucky enough to recognize him) rudely out into the street with his guests would seem suicidally foolish. In England it's good public relations.

I threw a late-night party awhile back at a place in London's meat district to launch my book. I invited a lot of chefs, a good number of the press, and booksellers. The hope was that the chefs would swing by after work and have some fun. They did.

A terrifying mob of blood- and sauce-spattered culinarians lurched in the doors, many still reeking of sweat and fish, made straight for the bar, and began baiting and bullying the vastly outnumbered civilians. On at least two occasions, I had to step in between some white-clad chef and about-to-be-ass-whupped journo or bookstore manager to avert senseless butchery. As the chefs' numbers swelled to a mob of alcohol-swilling madmen, their accents growing thicker and their tone more belligerent, the representatives of the press appeared to contract slowly into a defensive perimeter by the bathrooms. A good time was had by all.

On to the good guys.

'This was a happy pig,' says Fergus Henderson, looking down with pleasure at the head of a carefully roasted medium-sized pig. He emphasizes his pride and respect for what he knows is damned delicious (perfectly crispy skin, buttery sweet – nearly ethereal fat, tender, ropy cheeks) by moving his arms up and down robotically. Behind clear glass lenses, his face is a little flushed, the corner of his mouth a little stiff, and one leg is pretty much checking out for the day – he's dragging it the last hour. Fergus represents England's best hope for salvation, the man at the spear point, a warrior, pioneer, philosopher, and fearless proponent of what's good – and has always been good – about English cooking; he knows about the pure enjoyment of high-quality pork and pork products.

Hours ago, we returned from Smithfield Market, where we spent the early-morning hours looking at meat, poking at entrails, prodding carcasses, and waxing poetic about animal fat. The day began in a cellar pub at 6:00 A.M., the chef and I enjoying a hearty breakfast of Guinness and deviled kidneys, the room filled with meat cutters in white plastic helmets and long white lab coats. Now, standing over my table, Fergus is tired.

He's been up since God knows when, was at his restaurant for lunch service, and is now presiding over an elaborate procession of nearly everything on the menu for my dinner. There are surely better chefs in England, but Fergus is my favorite – he's a hero to me, one righteous, solitary soul-surfing, daredevil motherfucker. I hesitate to mention that he's struggling with Parkinson's disease, because he was already a titan in my eyes, long before I knew. If there's one real hero chef in this book, a man who deliberately put himself outside the pack, staked out a position, and then held it – against all comers – it's Fergus Henderson, chef of what is maybe my favorite restaurant in the world: St. John, in the Smithfield area of London. Never has his country needed him more.

Years ago, when the prevailing wisdom among foodies dictated quaint, tiny, sculpted portions of brightly colored odd bits – light on the protein and heavy on the veg, Fergus was reveling in pig – pig fat, pig parts, and pig guts – his plates rustic-colored palettes of browns, beiges, and earth tones – maybe the occasional flash of green – simple, unassuming, unpretentious – and absolutely and unapologetically English.

While most of his contemporaries, newly empowered by Michelin stars and a suddenly food-crazed public, rushed to the squeeze bottle and the metal ring, to Japanese and French classics for inspiration, Fergus was alone on the hill, running up the Union Jack. He went to a neighborhood where nobody wanted to go, set up shop in an all-white abattoir-looking space down a seemingly uninviting alley, and began serving what he refers to as 'nose to tail' eating, a menu so astonishingly reactionary for its time, he might well – in another country – have been imprisoned for it. Today, while lesser mortals cower around their veggie plates in hemp sandals, cringing at the thought of contamination by animal product, St. John's devotees – and there are a lot of them – flock to his plain, undecorated dining room to revel in roasted marrow, rolled spleen, grilled ox heart, braised belly, and fried pig's tails.

It was a very ballsy position to take back in the early nineties – and it's an even ballsier proposition today, when the Evil Axis

Powers of Health Nazis, Vegetarian Taliban, European Union bureacrats, antismoking crystal worshipers, PETA fundamentalists, fast-food theme-restaurant moguls, and their sympathizers are consolidating their fearful hold on popular dining habits and practices.

Fergus is an exception to my general observations of chef behavior – as he's an exception to nearly all the rules. Standing by my table, he lovingly, even serenely, describes the lovely little pig's tail I'm about to eat and how much he's sure I'll like it.

'This was a very noble pig,' he says, looking like a thoroughly charming mad scientist in his white jacket and apron, his movements stiff, formal. He speaks quietly; shy, wry, sounding way too educated to be a chef, he's the last guy in the world you'd picture as the proprietor of an establishment that celebrates nothing less than guts and glory.

These are dire times to be a chef who specializes in pork and offal. The EU has its eye on unpasteurized cheese, artisanal everything, shellfish, meat, anything that carries the slightest, most infinitesimal possibility of risk – or the slightest potential for pleasure. There is talk of banning unaged cheese, stock bones, soft-boiled or raw eggs. In the States, legislation has been suggested, mandating a written warning when a customer requests eggs over easy or a Caesar salad. ('Warning! Fork – if placed into eye – may cause injury!') A woman in the States won a lawsuit, claiming her coffee was too hot, scalding her as she stomped on the accelerator exiting the McDonald's parking lot. ('Warning! Deep-fried Mars bar – if stuffed down pants – may cause genital scarring!') The result of this unrestrained fear mongering, this mad rush to legislate new extremes of shrink-wrapped germ-free safety? Much like it was after Upton Sinclair's *The Jungle* scared the hell out of early-twentieth-century meat eaters – the absorption of small independents into giant factory farms and slaughter domes. Try and eat an American chicken and you will see what looms: bloodless, flavorless, colorless, and riddled with salmonella – a by-product of letting the little guys go under and the big conglomerates run things their way.

You have only to visit an English pub in, say, Bristol or Birmingham – once-proud strongholds of British culinary tradition at its simplest and most unvarnished – to see that the enemy has reached the gates and is pounding on the door. A vegetarian menu! Right there – next to the steak and kidney pie and the bangers and mash! Worse – far worse – is when you look over at the bar and see Brits, brewers of some of the finest alcoholic beverages in the world, gorgeous beers, ales, and bitters, once served in that most noble of drinking vessels – the pint glass – sucking Budweisers from long-necked bottles.

It's war. On one side, a growing army of hugely talented young British, Scottish, Irish, and Australian chefs, rediscovering their own enviable indigenous resources and marrying them with either new and brash concepts or old and neglected classics. On the other? A soul-destroying tsunami of bad, fake reproductions of what was already bad, fake New York 'Mexican' food. Gluey, horrible nachos, microwaved never-fried 'refried' beans, fabric softener margaritas. Limp, soggy, watery, and thoroughly dickless 'enchiladas' and catsupy salsas. Clueless 'Pan-Asian' watering holes where every callow youth with a can of coconut milk and some curry powder thinks he's Ho Chi Minh. (Forget it. Ho could cook.) Sushi is almost nowhere to be found – in spite of the fact that the seafood in the UK is magnificent. You get more heart, soul, and flavor at an East End pie shop than at any of the rotten, fake, dumbed-down 'Italian,' 'Japanese fusion,' or theme purgatories. Even the cod – the basic ingredient of fish and chips – is disappearing. (I raised that subject with a Portuguese cod importer. 'The damned seals eat them,' was his answer. 'Kill more seals,' he suggested.)

Fortunately, Fergus and other like-minded souls are on the front lines, and they're unlikely to abandon their positions. Sitting at St. John, I ordered what I think is the best thing I have ever put in my mouth: Fergus's roasted bone marrow with parsley and caper salad, croutons, and sea salt.

Oh God, is it good. How something so simple can be so . . . so . . . absolutely luxurious. A few Flintstone-sized lengths of veal shank, a lightly dressed salad . . . Lord . . . to tunnel into those bones, smear that soft gray-pink-and-white marrow onto a slab of toasted bread, sprinkle with some *sel gris* . . . take a bite . . . Angels sing, celestial trumpets . . . six generations of one's ancestors smile down from heaven. It's butter from God.

A few years ago, the neighborhood around St. John was about as fashionable as a fistula. Now, there are faces and bodies one usually associates with tofu snacks and soy milk smoothies, skinny, well-dressed women, mussing their lipstick as they enthusiastically gnaw bones, ooh and aah over the glories of pork belly, pig's trotter, tripe – all that lovingly cooked offal. It's where the people who truly love food, who know what's good about wiping grease off their chins, can congregate without fear, safe from the dark clouds of processed food gathering over Europe. A meal at St. John is only one of the great dining experiences one can have in England. I'm not going to bother to give you an overview – reciting the names of all the sharp, ambitious, well-trained chefs who have, in recent years, completely reversed the widely held perception that English food was crap. Suffice it to say that most of these guys could kick their French counterparts' asses around the block. An Englishman in the kitchen – be it in New York, Melbourne, or anywhere else – is a promise of good things to come. A meal at St. John is not just one of the great eating experiences on the planet – it's a call to the barricades.

Because it will not end with the marrow (which already has to be imported from Holland). The enemy wants your cheese. They want you never again to risk the possibility of pleasure with a reeking, unpasteurized Stilton, an artisanal wine, an oyster on the half shell. They have designs on stock. *Stock!* (Bones, you know – can't have that.) The backbone of *everything* good! They want your sausage. And your balls, too. In short, they want you to feel that same level of discomfort approaching a plate of food that so many used to feel about sex.

Do I overstate the case? Go to Wisconsin. Spend an hour in an airport or a food court in the Midwest; watch the pale, doughy masses of pasty-faced, Pringle-fattened, morbidly obese teenagers. Then tell me I'm worried about nothing. These are the end products of the Masterminds of Safety and Ethics, bulked up on cheese that contains no cheese, chips fried in oil that isn't really oil, overcooked gray disks of what might once upon a time have been meat, a steady diet of Ho-Hos and muffins, butterless popcorn, sugarless soda, flavorless light beer. A docile, uncomprehending herd, led slowly to a dumb, lingering, and joyless slaughter.

I've never eaten Marco Pierre White's food, though I've lingered longingly over his cookbooks. He, I believe, no longer cooks personally at his restaurants – and is no longer the haunted-looking bad boy of the British culinary scene. Nowadays, he looks more like a well-fed Venetian merchant prince. But back in the old days, he was a hugely important figure in the UK culinary firmament and a crucial trunk in the genealogy of next-generation chefs. He remains a hero to me for two reasons. First, his food was important – defiantly retro (with his pig trotters, for instance), unapologetically French (he took them on at their own game – and won). His food was (and is) creative, beautiful to look at, and, I am reliably informed, delicious in every way. Second, he threw customers he didn't like out of his dining rooms – a move that caused shudders of pleasure among chefs around the world. And third – and most important to me – his was the first cookbook where the chef looked like the chefs I knew – gaunt, driven, unkempt. That groundbreaking photograph of Marco smoking a cigarette in *White Heat* made so many of us everywhere say, 'I am not alone! There are others like me!' (I'm not saying, by the way, that I can cook anywhere near as well as Marco Pierre White. Just that I smoke in my kitchen, too.)

Finally, there's England's greatest chef, or England's biggest bully, depending on which paper you're reading at the time – the fearsome and prodigiously talented Gordon Ramsay. I'd been hearing about this guy for years. Ex-footballer. Formerly with Robuchon, Ducasse, Guy Savoy, Marco Pierre White. A legendary wordsmith in the kitchen – famed for excoriating his

crew, ejecting food critics, speaking his mind bluntly and un-
diplomatically. A while back, I was told about the cinéma vérité
Boiling Point series, in which the beleaguered Ramsay was said
to behave monstrously to his staff. Intrigued, I managed to track
down a copy of the videotape series. To my mind, Ramsay was
sympathetic from beginning to end. I rooted for him as he
sweated out the beginning of a service period for a massive
banquet at Versailles, ill-equipped, with only a rent-a-staff of
indolent bucket heads to help him. I cheered when he summarily
dismissed a waiter for guzzling water in full view of the dining
room. *Pour décourager les autres*, I'm guessing. I suffered as he
suffered the interminable wait for his much-hoped-for third
Michelin star and was heartbroken when he didn't get it. (He
since has.) Those who can't understand why a chef operating at
Ramsay's level gets a little cranky, or who appears to be
operating at a higher and more self-important pitch than their
boss, simply don't understand what it's like to work in a
professional kitchen. They certainly don't understand what it
takes to be the best in that world. It is not only how well you
can cook that makes a great chef, but your ability to cook
brilliantly, day in and day out – in an environment where a
thousand things can go wrong, with a crew that oftentimes
would just as happily be sticking up convenience stores, in a
fickle, cost-conscious, capricious world where everybody is
hoping that you fail.

Is he really such a complete bastard? Let's put it this way: On a
recent visit to his restaurant in Chelsea, I recognized large
numbers of staff – both front and back of the house – from
Boiling Point. Years later and they're still there. When Ramsay
walked out of Aubergine, the entire staff, service staff included –
an incredible forty-five people – chose to go with him. That's
really the most telling statistic. Does he still enjoy the loyalty of
his crew? He does. No cook shows up every day in Gordon
Ramsay's kitchen, works those kind of hours, offers themselves
up daily to the rigors of a three-star service period, toiling in a
small, hot space where at any moment they could get a painful
and humiliating ass reaming because Gordon Ramsay is the

biggest bastard or the biggest bully in England. They show up every day and work like Trojans because he's the best. Because when they finally walk out that door to seek their own fortunes, they won't even have to write up a résumé. Say you worked for three years with Gordon Ramsay, and that's all any chef or owner should need to know.

There's another factor overlooked in the rush to brand Ramsay as rude, crude, brutish, and cruel. In the professional kitchen, if you look someone in the eye and call them a 'fat, worthless, syphilitic puddle of badger crap' it doesn't mean you don't like them. It can be – and often is – a term of endearment.

Bottom line is, his food's good. After all, it is about the food, isn't it?

I had two meals at his restaurant in Chelsea, and both were absolutely world-class. A great chef at the top of his game. There's yet another overlooked dimension to Ramsay that doesn't fit with the depiction of an uppity, lower-class lout overlyjacked on testosterone. Ramsay was trained as a pâtissier. This is significant – like discovering that a right-wing politician was a Bolshevik in his youth. Few chefs can really and truly bake. Most chefs, like me, harbor deep suspicions of their precise, overly fussy, somehow feminine, presentation-obsessed counterparts in the pastry section. All that sweet, sticky, messy, goopy, delicate stuff. Pastry, where everything must be carefully measured in exact increments – and made the same way every single time – is diametrically opposed to what most chefs live and breathe, the freedom to improvise, to throw a little of this and a little of that any damn place they want. Ramsay's food resonates with his training in pastry. It is precise, colorful, artfully sculpted or teased into shape (though not too teased). It is the product of that end point in a chef's development – the perfect balance of masculine and feminine, the yin and the yang, if you will.

What do I mean? Look at Roberto, my grill man. He's got a metal rod rammed through his eyebrow, a tattoo of a burning skull on his chest, muscles on his muscles. Rob Zombie and Metallica are his idea of easy listening. He's done jail time for assault. Not a guy you'd invite to an evening at the opera. But watch Roberto cook. He leans over that plate and delicately, carefully drizzles sauce from a favorite spoon, gently applies an outer ring of sauce, then sensuously drags a toothpick through it. He tastes everything. Looks at his plates with a decorator's eye for color and texture. Treats a filet of fish as tenderly and as lovingly as a woman's erect nipple. Piles cute, girly-little garnishes into high, cloudlike piles of gossamer-thin crunchiness. He's doing what everyone told him growing up that only women should do. (Ramsay's own father told him cooking was basically for poofs and that chefs were all ponces.) We work in aprons, for fuck's sake! You better have balls the size of jackfruits if you want to cook at a high level, where an acute sense for flavor and design, as much as brutality and vigilance, is a virtue. And be fully prepared to bulldoze any miserable cocksucker who gets in your way.

Both times I visited his restaurant, Ramsay was in the kitchen, supervising every dish that came out, riding his crew like rented mules. He wasn't gliding through the dining room, sucking up to his public. He's a cook in twenty-first-century England; that means he's an obsessive, paranoid, conspiratorial control freak. A hustler, media-manipulator, artist, craftsman, bully, and glory hound – in short, a chef's chef. That I found him polite, charming, witty, and gracious and am saying so here will probably be an embarrassment to him. For that, I apologize. His detractors should be so lucky as to taste the absolutely stunning braised beef and foie gras I ate at his restaurant – a dish so sumptuous that I am forced to use that word. A ham hock terrine of really extraordinary subtlety and flavor, a lobster ravioli with fresh green pea puree that revealed – as all food reveals its creator's true nature – a level of perception and sensitivity that can be a liability in the mosh-pit subculture of professional kitchens. Here's a guy who risked everything in his career, many times over. He walked away from a career in football when it was made clear he'd never play in the bigs. He endured a procession of stages in some very tough French kitchens. He bolted from his first restaurant, entangling himself in potentially enormous liabilities just when he was in sight of the mountaintop. He loudly announced he was going for three Michelin stars and then stayed on course until he got them. Rather than kiss the asses of all those people who might – under ordinary circumstances – be expected to be helpful to him, he has consistently kicked them in the teeth or even viciously sucker punched them. It's very hard for me not to like a guy like that. And every day those stars are sitting on him like six-ton flagstones, defying any who might choose to try knocking them off.

England's worst boss? I don't think so. England's worst boss is the boss who doesn't give a fuck, someone who's wasting his employees' time, challenging them to do nothing more ambitious than show up. Understand that in no-name pit stops and casual dining establishments, it's just a mistake when a cook forgets a single unpeeled fava bean or a tiny smudge of grease, but in a three-star restaurant, it's treason. In the cruel mathematics of two- and three-star dining establishments, a customer who has a good meal will tell two or three people about it. A person who has an unsatisfactory meal will tell ten or twenty. It makes for a much more compelling anecdote. That one unpeeled fava bean is the end of the world. Or it could be.

As most really good cooks or commis working in similar circumstances will readily tell you: Mess with the chef at your peril. It's his name on the door.

WHERE COOKS COME FROM

THERE'S A LITTLE TOWN in Mexico where cooks come from.

If you're a chef and you've spent any serious time working in professional kitchens, you know what to do when Hector, your saucier, gets pinched for assault and you suddenly need a replacement. Faced with a situation where you need a French-trained, ready-to-go, reliable, hardworking guy who knows what to do when you need a solid flounder special and have time only to describe sole *grenobloise* as 'filet sauté . . . with capers, lemon, *vin blanc*, shallot, butter,' you know where to go. Where do you tap into the source for the best French and Italian cooks? Not France. Certainly not Italy. If you're looking for a line cook who's professional in his work habits, responsible with your food, dependable, a guy with a sense of humor, reasonably good character, and a repertoire of French and Italian standards, and who can drill out 250 meals without going mental or cutting corners too egregiously, chances are you go to Carlos, your grill man, and say, 'Carlos, *mi carnale* . . . I need a *cucinero*. You know somebody for sauté?' In every likelihood, Carlos will think for a moment and say, 'Yeah . . . sure . . . I have a cousin.' Or 'Yeah . . . sure . . . I got a friend.' And a few days later, someone will show up at your kitchen door with features similar to Carlos's – or the now-incarcerated Hector's – and he'll step right into old Hector's station like it's a comfortable shoe. Hector, of course, was from the Mexican state of Puebla. As is Carlos. And just about every other cook and dishwasher in America. If there was a mandatory day of rest – or a public holiday for all Poblanos – a lot of restaurants in America would have to close their doors. As it is, the day after the fifth of May (Cinco de Mayo), half the cooks in America are hungover. Keep that in mind.

Fifteen or twenty years ago, we'd have been talking about cheap labor. You know, the old 'wetback' story: exploited, unskilled immigrant labor, toiling away for inhuman hours in menial jobs, paid cash under the table at minimum wage or less. Things have changed somewhat for the better. While we have yet to see as many mestizo-looking chefs with Spanish-sounding last names running high-end French kitchens as we should, all those dishwashers and porters didn't simply settle for spending the rest of their lives cleaning up after the rest of us. They watched, they learned, they trained on *garde-manger* and grill and prep and sauté – usually on their own time – and when some flighty white kid decided he wanted the winter off to go skiing in Colorado, they were ready to step in. When the French sous-chef appeared to be unable to work without a long, lingering two-hour lunch with his socialist comrades in the front of the house and the chef had finally had enough of his clock-punching, lazy prima donna act, the Poblanos were ready. Now, many areas of Puebla are like a talent pool of free-agent or draft picks in professional sports – pursued, protected, sought after by chefs who'd rather snip off a pinkie finger than lose them to the other team. They've been trained by a procession of French, American, and Italian chefs – most of whom come and go, turning over quickly, but who each leave behind a little knowledge, a new technique, a few more nuggets of information, some new ideas. So now, ask Carlos to do something with the soft-shell crabs and with that old asparagus and you can have a reasonable expectation that he will whip right into a salad of soft-shell crabs with asparagus and citrus vinaigrette in classic French nouvelle style. Stuck for a monkfish special or a soup? Don't worry, Carlos is all over it, remembering some long-gone French chef's preparation. (Old Henri-Pierre may have been a lazy Communist ratbag, but he could cook like an angel.) A lot of times, I'll walk into an unfamiliar kitchen to say hello to the cooks – or to thank the chef for a freebie – and I'll see the familiar posse of white-clad Mexicans listening to the Spanish station down by the dish-washing area, and of course I'll say hello, then casually inquire where, exactly, they hail from.

'¿ Poblanos?' I'll ask, pretty sure of the answer.

'¡ Viva la rasa!' will come the reply.

My cooks are almost all from Puebla, and not just from Puebla but from the same small area around the towns of Izúcar de Matamoros, Atlixco, and Tlapanala, situated downwind from the famous volcanoes of *Under the Volcano* fame. If there's an epicenter of fine French cooking, it appears to be Tlapanala, a sleepy little village surrounded by sugarcane fields and mango trees, about three miles outside of Izúcar. That's where my sous-chef, Edilberto Perez, was born. It's where Isidoro, my veteran grill man, hails from, and Antonio, my roundsman, and other cooks, runners, prep cooks, and dishwashers, past, present, and future. Their families still live there and they visit whenever possible. Over the years, I've heard a lot about the town, about Eddie's house, his ranch, about his uncle, the *heladero*, who makes ice cream the old-fashioned way, about Antonio's family, who live next door, about my prep cook Bautista's former street gang, the terrifying Vatos Locos, whose distinctive tag I often find scrawled on locker room walls, and whose hand signs (a '*V*' and an '*L*', signified by turning the right hand and making a sort of open-thumbed peace sign) I recognize. I heard about my prep guy Miguel's family's *pulquería*, Isidoro's family's candy store. I heard a lot about the joys of *barbacoa* (Mexican-style barbecue), *mole*, *pulque*: I wanted to go. I wanted to go very badly. I told my cooks how I'd visit their parents and tell them all what *desgraciados* their sons have become, now that they're living that *vida loca* in New York. So, when I first started putting together my '*Borrachón* Abroad' pitch for my publisher, I knew one of the places I absolutely had to go. I huddled with my sous-chef and said, 'Eddie, I want to visit your town. I want you to go with me, to show me your town. I want to meet everybody's families. I want your mom to cook for me, if she's willing. I want to drink *pulque* and *mezcal* and eat *menudo* and *pozole* and real *mole poblano* – like from Puebla – and *barbacoa* like you been tellin' me about all these years. I want to wear a cool-looking cowboy hat, ride a horse, find out where that serial killer Bautista really comes from. I want to go down there with you and have a really good time. We'll get the TV people to pay for it.'

'Let me call to my wife,' said Eddie, inspired. 'I send her down first to making the preparations.'

Which is how it happened that I found myself sitting by the *mercado* in the small central square of Tlapanala on a languid late afternoon, the sun slowly setting, watching as the women and children of the village lined up at the telephone kiosk, waiting to receive prearranged calls from kitchens in New York and apartments in Queens.

The streets were quiet and dusty, kids kicking around old soccer balls, shooting hoops in the court by the *mercado*, where old women sold chilis, squashes, *chayote*, yucca, and vegetables. Occasionally, an old man passed by, driving a few head of cattle, a herd of goats, a few donkeys down Tlapanala's tidy streets. A stray dog wandered over to see if I had any food. Young mothers sat with their babies. Children, still in their school uniforms, played on the back steps of the kiosk, the afternoon's silence broken now and again by the singsong music from a propane truck, playing along to the unforgettable chant of '*Gaaazzz! GaaaaAAAaazz!*' and announcements over a loudspeaker describing the products on sale at the *mercado*. At four o' clock, the peal of the bread alarm informed residents that fresh bread, hot out of the oven, was now available at the bakery.

A few yards behind me were the railway tracks. The train to Tijuana and beyond. Nueva York. The road out, the starting point, where generations of Tlapanala's young men began their long, hard climb out of poverty to become cooks in faraway America.

There were few young men left in the village. I saw only women, children, and much older men. In Tlapanala, you can tell the homes of families with a son or a father standing behind a stove in New York: They're the houses with the satellite dishes

on the roofs and metal rebars still protruding from the top of
new additions and annexes (instead of capping or removing the
extra lengths, they keep them sticking up out of the concrete;
should money come, they can more easily add a second floor). I
sat on my bench, contentedly watching and listening, an object
of curiosity, a lone *gabacho* drinking *cerveza* Modelo, grinning
for no apparent reason. Looking down the street, I spied my
sous-chef taking an evening stroll with his wife, new baby
propped on his arm, young daughter trailing behind, holding
her daddy's other hand. Thirteen years ago, Eddie took that
train behind me to Tijuana, swam and waded across the border,
then hopped a train to New York. He slept on the subway for his
first few weeks, slept on the floors of friends' apartments when
he could, until he got a job as a night porter. Now he's a sous-
chef, a title inadequate to describe his importance. He's opened
and worked at every restaurant in the company – Washington,
D.C., Miami, Le Marais – and, of course, for me – at the
mothership in New York. Long before I arrived on the scene,
he'd been the go-to guy for every chef who walked in the door.
Now he's a fully documented permanent resident (and soon-to-
be citizen) of the United States of America, and a newly enrolled
student at the French Culinary Institute, where he hobnobs with
culinary luminaries like Jacques Pépin and André Soltner. (He's
learning where all that French food he's been making brilliantly
for years really comes from – and why. Eddie knows how to
make a *gastrite*, he just didn't know what to call it. I wish I could
watch him in class, when they show him glaçage or how to make
a liaison, or explain the principles of déglacer. He'll say, 'Oh,
that! No problem. Same like for the ravioli at Les Halles.') Eddie
rents an apartment in Park Slope, owns both a house and a small
ranch in his home town of Tlapanala – and considerable livestock. He's an employer in Mexico, a role model and leader in
New York. And he's my friend. I wish I could take even the
slightest credit for the Edilberto Perez story. But I can't. He did it
all. Watching him walk the streets of the place he was born,
though, I was filled with pride just for knowing him, and for
being lucky enough to have worked with him. Before visiting

Eddie, however, I'd had a grim duty to perform. Yet another forced march to television entertainment. 'Tony . . . Tony . . . listen. It's a food show. It's going on the Food Network. We need some variety! We can't just show you hanging around in Puebla, getting drunk with your sous-chef! Don't worry! We're on it. We've got some really special ideas.'

That's why I went first to the state of Oaxaca. So I could be force-fed iguana.

Reasons Why You Don't Want to Be on Television: Number Four in a Series

I was in Puerto Angel, a fishing village on the Pacific coast, staying at a remote, kooky, overgrown retreat built around a ravine on the slopes of a mountain overlooking the sea. The only other residents were Martin, my driver; two shooters; a burned-out geriatric hippie known as 'Quiet Dave,' who spoke in a spacey whisper; the proprietor and his wife and assistants; and a former CIA chief of base for Nha Trang during the Vietnam War and his Chinese girlfriend. As I'd just been to Nha Trang, we had a lot to talk about.

Here's what I hoped for in Puerto Angel: a neglected stretch of beach, a near-empty, far from luxurious hotel, a few straggling eccentrics. Down the road a ways was the resort town of Zipolite, a sort of Last Stop for well-toasted surfers, backpackers, beach bums, fugitive dope pilots from the seventies, the itinerant jewelry/handicraft set. It's the sort of place you wake up in – after dropping one hit of acid too many at your 112th Grateful Dead concert – not having any idea how you got there, and far from caring.

We shot a whole-roasted-snapper scene in Zipolite, watched the fishing boats come in at Puerto Angel, the whole town running to meet them as they skipped full throttle through the waves and onto the beach, hulls loaded with fresh tuna. We drove to Huatulco, about twenty miles away, with the idea of doing some snorkel fishing. It was one of those ludicrous, pointless exercises in television artifice so beloved by people who look at life largely through a lens: 'Get some cool underwater shots of Tony! We can have him fish with a local! Cut to medium shots of Tony, looking hunky in a Speedo, in chef mode, grillin' and chillin' on the beach, sun setting dramatically in the background!'

Video gold.

After two hours of useless and unproductive floundering in the sea, the underwater camera rig having filled up with water – after about six miles of footage of my concave chest wheezing on the beach while Leo, our hired fishing guide, continued, without success, to catch even a stunt fish for a faked shot – we gave up. Matthew settled for frozen fish at a nearby tourist strip, and the always popular 'Tony gets drunk on local beverage, then sits in sullen silence, hating himself and everybody to do with this production scene.'

I never wanted to eat iguana. 'Yes you do,' insisted the TV masterminds. I had no particular curiosity about iguana. I knew from talking to my cooks that people eat iguana when they can afford nothing else. It's cheap and plentiful. Even Leo, talking about how he went out a few times a week with his dog to sniff out iguana, admitted he did it only because he had no money for real food. I had no expectation that a big lizard would taste good – and I was not anxious to have one killed so I could find out for sure. But Matthew seemed to feel that the 'iguana scene' would be must-see TV, a guaranteed cable Ace for Best Reptile Scene in a Continuing Cable Series.

Now, maybe somewhere they're making delicious marinated, then barbecued iguana with crispy skin and well-grilled but tender meat. Maybe if you sear it and then braise it long enough and infuse it with enough other flavors, it might make a meal interesting to adventurous palates. Maybe. I didn't see it.

The owner of our hotel was dispatched to wrangle up a nice plump example of iguanadom at its very best. But after three or four hours of investigation, he came up as empty as Leo's fishing line. Instead, he decided to sacrifice the poor hotel mascot, a ten-year-old wrinkly, leathery, liver-spotted thing – he looked paralytic – with a bifurcated tail and a troublingly agreeable nature. I took one look at the creature and tried very hard to weasel out of the meal.

'Matthew! Jesus Christ, man! He's a pet, for fuck's sake! Let the thing live! How good can he be? Just look at him!'

The hotel proprietor was no help. Stroking the iguana's belly, he insisted, 'Look! He is ready. He wants to die.' I was appalled.

What arrived later were iguana tamales: the hotel pet, boiled, sectioned, then simply wrapped in corn husk with *masa* and sauce. Next to *natto*, it was maybe the worst thing I'd ever had between my teeth. The iguana was undercooked. When I unwrapped my tamale, I found that I had been honored with the head and a forearm – still on the bone. The texture was like chewing on GI Joe – if Joe had been resting at the bottom of a long-neglected turtle tank. There was almost no meat to speak of, just tough, rubbery skin, knobby, slimy little bones. When I managed now and again actually to winnow out a little meat from between bones and skin, I was sorry I had. It was dark, oily, and viscous, with the pungent aroma of steamed salamander.

In the thankfully brief scene you see in the edited version, I look like I'm eating at gunpoint.

I hit the city of Oaxaca next, a place justifiably famous for its food. It's a beautiful town: lovely hacienda-style hotels, exquisite Spanish churches and cathedrals, a picturesque *zócalo* where you can sit at a café table and watch the world go by, a fabulous *mercado*, nice people. It is also, unfortunately, a magnet for the world's ugliest tourists. Herds of squinting, sun-blotched fanny packers in black socks and sandals shuffled by, snapping pictures. Extravagantly pierced backpackers, filthy from the road, sat in the park, ineptly strumming old Dylan tunes on clapped-out guitars. Thick-ankled German women looking for love, and hordes of doddering tour groupers and serial shoppers, fanned out to buy the inevitable tonnage of papier-mâché figurines, hammered tin, cheap silver, ponchos, serapes, funny hats, T-shirts, and pottery. College kids, fresh from the donkey show in Tijuana, sulked noisily on benches, broke and frustrated, waiting for a Western Union money order from mom and dad. But as it got late and the tourists drifted off and the locals began showing up in clean white guayaberas and frilly dresses, filling the café tables around us, Martin, my driver, and I started to enjoy ourselves.

Mezcal was served like tequila, in shot glasses, accompanied by chasers of *sangrita*, a spicy tomato juice concoction. With the de rigueur wedge of lime came a mix of salt and dried, powdered, chili-roasted maguey worms – an unexpectedly delicious accompaniment. Martin and I sat in the café, nibbling on *tortas* (sandwiches) of fresh cheese and ham, drinking beer and *mezcal*, a mariachi band strolling from table to table. Behind us, a man in his fifties, with a face scarred by a youthful bout with smallpox and the fists and brows of a former pugilist, sat alone at his table, drinking Modelo Negro, his straight black hair plastered down over his forehead, staring into space with a look of infinite sadness. After a long while sitting in silence with the same brooding expression, he motioned the mariachis over to his table, handed them a few pesos, and made a mumbled request. They played beautifully, and when they were done with the song, the man, though outwardly unmoved, handed them more pesos and asked for another. Again, his demeanor remained impassive as he monopolized the six-piece band.

Then suddenly, mournfully, without raising his eyes from the table, he began to sing. Still seated, looking at no one else, he sang of love and loss and broken hearts, his voice rich, deep, and beautifully modulated. Every customer in the café listened with rapt attention. More pesos, another song. The sad-faced man in a guayabera shirt, eyes almost shut now, sang and sang, the crowd cheering wildly after each song ended. He seemed oblivious to their roars of approval, focused through slit eyes on some point far away – or deep inside his battered skull – his voice carrying over the now-empty *mercado* and into the night.

I ate well in Oaxaca. I had chocolate *atole*, a thick hot chocolate beverage with the texture of Cream of Wheat, made from local chocolate, cinnamon, and cornmeal. I tried an ice cream made with *leche quemada* (burned milk), which is surprisingly delicious. I sampled the mysteries of the seven *moles*, watched *queso fresco* being made – a fresh farmer cheese – saw how one batch can be taken along to make a drier, aged variety, and a soft-curd version. At the *mercado*, I bought *morcilla* and chorizo sausages from one of the butchers, had them grilled with the garnishes and tortillas available from the many 'make your own' taco stands. I had a marvelous *menudo*, a spicy tripe and offal soup/stew, returning later to try *pozole*, a similar dish with chick peas. Outside the *mercado*, I found a busy taco stand, packed with Oaxaqueños sitting on benches. A cook and an assistant were hard at work hacking up a freshly cooked pig's head, rolling up still-warm portions of tender pork in corn tortillas, then drizzling them with *salsa verde*.

I squeezed in between some locals and ordered a few. Best tacos ever. I could have sat there forever under a naked light-bulb, surrounded by enthusiastically eating Mexicans and their children. But there were people waiting for a spot. I returned the next night, and the next.

Off a dirt road in the farmland around Oaxaca de Juárez, the state's capital, Dominga made me tamales. She cooked in a small outdoor kitchen: a charcoal fire, clay saucepan, steamer, a *comal* for toasting, a mortar and pestle, and a stone rolling pin. Chickens and roosters wandered around the dusty back lot and small garden, near the pigpens.

We were going to the *molino*, the community mill, where for centuries Mexicans have gone, often every day, to grind their dried corn for *masa*, their dried chilis for *mole*, and their chocolate and their coffee beans on stone wheels. Dominga was a short, wide woman with mestizo features and strong arms and hands, which had seen a lot of work over the years. The corn soaking in a plastic bucket in one hand, a tub of chilis and garlic in another, she walked the few blocks in the hot sun to a small shed with a tin roof, where a line of women in similar frilled dresses and aprons waited for one of the two generator-powered machines to become available. Inside, the *molina*'s owner carefully fed handfuls of chilis into one machine and corn into the other, a rich, smooth paste issuing from both. *Mole, masa, atole, café* – made fresh every day by mom.

You may think you've tried Mexican food. Unless you've been to Mexico and eaten in a home, you haven't. Mexican food is not that sour two-day-old sludge foaming and fermenting in the center of your table next to a few stale corn chips, a little limp cilantro turning to slime among the long-gone onions. It is not graying or packaged guacamole, whipped in the food processor until it achieves the consistency of baby food. It is not heaped with cheddar and Monterey Jack cheese (you won't see any of that in Mexico) and served with allegedly refried beans. In Mexico, everything is fresh. Dominga owns no Cuisinart. She doesn't have a freezer. Her salsas do not arrive in jars, and her recipes are not faxed from Central, portion-controlled for multi-unit use. Mexican food is not particularly hot and spicy. It is not soggy, frozen chimichangas, already haemorrhaging ingredients into the deep-fat fryer. It is not the dull, monochromatic slop you see all over America and Australia and the UK.

Dominga made me Oaxacan-style chicken tamales – instead of wrapping the chicken and *masa* and sauce in a corn husk, as is usually done all over Mexico, she wrapped them in banana leaves. When she returned from the mill, Dominga removed a simmering freshly killed chicken from a pot and pulled the meat off in shreds. (*Pollo pelado.*) She mixed and kneaded her fresh *masa* with some rendered pork fat (packets of which are an essential ingredient around here), lightly toasted the banana leaves on the *comal*, and stirred her intoxicating-smelling *mole negro*, which had been simmering for hours and hours.

Proximity to livestock and animal feces, I have found in my travels, is not necessarily an indicator of a bad meal. More often than not, in recent experience, it's an early indicator of something good on the way. Why is that? It might have to do with the freshness question. Still living close to the source of your food, you often don't have a refrigerator or freezer. Equipment and conditions are primitive. You can't be lazy – because no option other than the old way exists. Where there are freezers and refrigerators, laziness follows, the compromises and slow encroachment of convenience. Why spend all day making *mole* when you can make a jumbo batch and freeze it? Why make salsa every day when it lasts OK in the fridge? Try a salsa or a sauce hand-ground with a stone mortar and pestle and you'll see what I mean.

Dominga's tamales were marvelous. I ate them hot out of the steamer under a small *palapa*, among the flies and the chickens and the pigs – and it was damn near a religious experience.

Martin, Eddie, and I stopped at a *pulquería* outside of town. It was a sky-blue hovel with a distorting jukebox and a lone addled drinker. The *pulque* – the fermented sap of the maguey cactus – sat in fifty-five-gallon vats behind the bar, smelling sweet-sour. The bartender ladled the thick, viscous, milky-looking sap into two plastic beach pails – the kind kids make sand castles with. We sat down at a weatherbeaten picnic table and poured ourselves drinks in tall, not particularly clean glasses. 'Ewww!' said one of the TV crew, watching Martin enthusiastically insert and withdraw a finger into the *pulque* to check consistency, a long mucuslike strand coming along for the ride. The finger test wasn't doing much for my stomach's sense of well-being, either. I'd dined earlier on generous portions of fried worms and sautéed ant eggs – a specialty of the area. The worms had been OK – buried in enough guacamole and *salsa roja*, and the ant eggs had been . . . well, OK, nutty-tasting, with a mealy feel and a lingering woody aftertaste. But the order of *chiles en nogada*, the national dish of Mexico – stuffed *poblano* peppers, loaded with ground beef, walnuts, dried fruit, and cinnamon, served with two sauces (the colors of the nation's flag) – had been terrible beyond words. I don't like beef with cinnamon, particularly accompanied by a sauce. Sitting in the *pulquería*, swilling bucket after bucket of the mildly hallucinogenic low-rent beverage of choice for Mexicans in need of an affordable buzz, I was all too aware that underneath the roiling hellbroth of *pulque* even now beginning to bubble in my belly was a less-than-solid foundation of ant eggs, worms, and that horrible *chiles en nogada*. The ride back to my room in Izúcar de Matamoros was agony.

Eddie's house in Tlapanala was a neat, clean one-story build-ing – two bedrooms, living room/dining area, large kitchen – with a nice backyard and an outer kitchen and shed. When I arrived, Eddie's wife, mother, children, and baby-sitter were sitting on a couch and in chairs, watching satellite television. In the kitchen, a table was covered with the makings of *mole poblano*: *poblano* peppers, plantains, chocolate, nuts, herbs. In the outside kitchen, the mother of my *tournant*, Antonio, was making tortillas, while next door, the mother of my former salad man, Gilberto, looked on. I knew I was in trouble when I stepped into Eddie's well-tended backyard and saw a twenty-four-pound turkey still strutting around energetically. Eddie smiled and informed me that, as guest of honor, it was up to me.

'*Matelo!*' he said, handing me a machete. I'd never whacked an animal before. I was decidedly squeamish at the prospect. But the pressure was on. I was, after all, Eddie's boss. If I looked like a punk, he'd look like a punk for working for me. I was well aware that any one of the women – and probably most of the kids – could easily step in and take out that turkey like they were brushing their teeth. I eyed him carefully. He was huge and lively. Brandishing the machete, I stepped forward and, with Eddie's help, managed to restrain him. Eddie tilted the turkey's head back and poured a shot of *mezcal* down his throat. His wife dragged the turkey over to a bench, gave his neck a turn so he was pinioned flat to the board, and let me take over.

Now, I knew that turkeys are stupid. I knew that when you chop the head off a chicken, for instance, it takes some time for it to die, that it flaps around the yard for a while, too dumb to know it's dead. The phrase 'running around like a headless chicken' comes to mind. And I knew that I should expect the turkey to be no smarter than a chicken. Turkeys drown, sometimes, looking straight up into the rain, forgetting to close their mouths (kind of like Bon Jovi fans). I knew all this. I intended – as the gentle and sensitive soul I am – to dispatch this particular bird to turkey heaven as cleanly, quickly, and painlessly as possible. I would not waver, hesitate, or falter. I raised the machete over the struggling bird's neck, absolutely resolved to whack clean through, to end his life with one firm stroke. I came down with a resounding chop, the blade going *Thunk!* into the wood.

The turkey's body went insane, flapping and flailing and bouncing around! Oh my God! I thought, I've missed! I've botched it! Convinced that I'd somehow missed a major artery, cruelly and ineptly only wounding the animal, I began swinging the blade again and again in a terrified frenzy, like a novice serial killer, hacking blindly at a tiny strip of connecting skin that still held head and body together. A gout of blood erupted onto Matthew's lens – a shot, by the way, that he missed. Spray decorated me from forehead to sandals. I looked down and saw that the contorting head was in my hand, but the body, still flapping wildly, had been taken by Eddie, who nonchalantly hung it from the shed ceiling to be plucked. I was now a killer. I sat next to my victim for a long time before pitching in and yanking feathers from the still-warm body, wondering what the hell had happened to me.

It was a long, sleepy afternoon while the food cooked. Relatives showed up for the meal; a table was set up in the backyard. We eventually sat down to a very fine *mole poblano de qua jobte*, accompanied by enchiladas, salsas, salads, and beer. I looked around at the faces at the table and saw the faces of my cooks back in New York.

'Welcome to my little rancho,' said Eddie.

He'd arranged for a Mexican Woodstock at his little ranch in the foothills outside Izúcar. It looked like it would be the biggest thing the town had seen since they'd risen up and slaughtered the French – the Triumphant Return of Eddie Perez. He'd hired mariachis, a pop band, a singing vaquero with dancing palomino, a lariat act. A soundstage was in the finishing stages of construction in the dusty, sun-washed lot behind a row of low structures. Chickens, roosters, cattle, pigs, donkeys, and goats roamed freely among the accordion cactus in the surrounding hills. He'd invited the whole town: the mayor, a representative of the local criminal fraternity, notables of every stripe. He'd hired the entire off-duty police force of the neighboring town to act as security, and an army of women had been pressed into service. Rancheros dug a pit for *barbacoa*. Little boys in button-down shirts and little girls in Communion dresses ran messages and shuttled cooking equipment to and fro. Cases and cases of beer, tequila, and *mezcal* had been laid on. Gallon upon gallon of fresh-fruit *ponche* was in the works. Long tables had been set and arranged under the thatched roof of a *palapa*. This was going to be some party.

Meanwhile, I was having my own Marlboro Man moment. It's one thing to wear denim and cowboy boots in New York; it's quite another to kick dust and dung off your Tony Lama boots, sit back in a shady corner against a plain adobe wall, tilt back your chair, and put your feet up on a post. A cowboy hat, in New York, is a fashion accessory never, ever to be worn – unless you're a Chippendale's dancer. In Puebla, in the midday sun, however, it's a necessity. I tipped the brim of my spanking new hat down over my eyes to provide shade for my already-roasted nose and felt pretty damn cool. Sauntering into a spare outbuilding where some rancheros were already free-pouring tequila into dirty shot glasses, I brushed the dust off my hat and rasped, '*Tequila . . . por favor.*'

Sitting with Eddie and Martin – all of us in full ranchero dress with our hats and boots – watching a woman with Antonio's face making tortillas on a *comal* a few yards away, recognizing the features of people I worked with and had worked with in the faces of the women cooking rice in a clay pot over an open fire, the girls cleaning cactus for *ensalada de nopalitos*, the old *heladero* handcranking fresh lime sorbet over ice in an old wooden churn, I had never felt so happy to be part of my strange dysfunctional family thousands of miles away, back in my kitchen in New York.

The big event began with the digging of a pit the size of a large grave.

A fire was built at the bottom and allowed to burn down to glowing coals. When it was ready, some rancheros lowered big pots of goats' head soup into the pit, the stripped skulls dropped into the liquid at the last second by their horns, a pile of avocado leaves arranged around them. Sheep's stomachs, stuffed with blood, spices, and mint – a sort of Mexican version of *boudin noir* – were carefully placed inside. Then five whole goats, cleaned and butterflied, were stacked one on top of the other and covered with more avocado leaves. (The goats had been slaughtered earlier in the day. Their skins were even now stretched and drying on Eddie's roof.) The pit was then covered with a woven straw mat, which had been soaked in water, and carefully shoveled over with dirt. The various components would cook like this for about three and a half hours.

All over the arid lot, the pace quickened. From a sleepy, sun-drenched space, the ranch was quickly becoming a hive of activity. Everywhere, things were coming together, guests beginning to arrive. The mariachis began to play; pop singers drank beer and tuned their instruments; a kid I recognized as a former busboy in New York arrived with floral arrangements. Couples began to dance. Kids played tag. Men sat down at the long tables, women and children to the rear on folding chairs. Eddie, who never touches a drop back in New York, was already drunk – doling out the already-lethal *ponche*, he insisted on floating another inch of raw tequila on top. The rancheros, too, seemed well on their way, and the party had only just begun.

'Don't worry about nutheeng,' said Eddie, gesturing to the armed figures standing guard up on the surrounding hills. 'Drink! Anything you want. Tequila, *mezcal, mota*. You having a good time? Don't worry. You go asleep? No problem. You sleep anywhere. On the ground. With the chickens. Anywhere. You safe. Policía right there. Nobody bother you.'

'Jesus, Eddie,' I said, 'you should be proud . . . I can't believe you did all this, put all this together.'

The goats' head soup was fabulous – one of the best things I'd had anywhere. Platters of roughly hacked roasted goat arrived, surprisingly tender and absolutely delicious. The stuffed stomach was revelatory – a wonderful spicy jumbo sausage of bloody, oniony goodness. I tried to eat everything, including the *ensalada de nopalitos*, salsas, grabbing for food with still-warm tortillas from the readily available stacks in napkin-covered baskets everywhere. I ate rice, more salads, enchiladas, tamales, an incredible quesadilla of fresh zucchini flowers and *queso fresco*. And is there any music on earth more sentimental, more romantic, more evocative of place than Mexican mariachi? (OK, maybe samba gets the edge.) But that evening, as the sun set over Eddie's hills, with the sounds of music and laughter and Mexican-inflected Spanish all around me, I had never heard anything so beautiful.

The vaquero performed lariat tricks. Another sang on horseback, his horse dancing under him, rearing, lying down, kneeling at his lightest touch. Under rented floodlights and a string of Christmas bulbs, the sun long gone, the mounted vaquero dismounted, held his microphone with an officious gravity, and, in the tone reserved for announcers at sporting events, bellowed, rolling his 'r's' at maximum volume and gesturing toward me, '¡ Señor as y señores . . . el hombre, el chefe norteamericano, el chefe de Nueva York muy famosooo! Anthony . . . BouRDAIN!'

Uh-oh.

The crowd cheered. The music stopped, the mariachis looking at me expectantly. I knew what was required as I sauntered over to the horse waiting for me in the center of a ring of light. There was some hooting and HeeYaaaing coming from Eddie, the camera crew, and a few other smart-asses in the audience. I put one boot in a stirrup and hoisted myself smoothly into the saddle. (A few weeks at summer camp and two riding lessons at the Claremont stables served me surprisingly well.) I was drunk, unsteady, but it was a magical horse under me. Trained to dance, he responded to my every touch, breaking into a slow canter at the slightest movement of boot, turning on command. I made a reasonably competent turn around the yard, doffing my hat to all assembled, stopped at the appropriate spot, and swung down from the saddle like a rodeo dude, feeling both utterly foolish and thoroughly delighted at the same time.

Eddie's pal, whom he'd introduced as the head of the local Mafia, forcefully insisted the camera crew and I join him in a few rounds of what he called 'cucarachas.' It would be a friendly match – USA versus Mexico. One at a time, the two cameramen and I, followed by the Mafia guy and his two associates, were presented with a fifty-fifty mix of Kahlúa and tequila – ignited and still flaming. The idea, it was explained, was to stick a straw into the flaming elixir and drain it in one go, before the flames subsided. This was to continue until one team cried uncle or collapsed unconscious.

The USA team did well. To our credit, we acquitted ourselves with honor, each of us downing five of the devastating concoctions without igniting our hair or choking. The Mexicans, though, were right in there. Finally, through some thankful manifestation of international goodwill, it was wordlessly agreed that at the appearance of a sixth round, all the contestants – from both teams – would together stick in their straws and suck down a final round, saving face for everyone, as all of us, I think, were on wobbly knees by now.

Matthew made it out the gate of Eddie's ranch on two feet with the rest of us, but by the time we were in the car at the end of the dirt drive, he had his head out the window, begging for us to pull over. Now, Matt had, over the last few months and continents, been less than sensitive to my own moments of gastric distress. He had never hesitated to get me to choke down some cinematic but nauseating gleet – even when I was ill – if he'd thought it would make riveting television. He'd never had a problem shooting me sick in bed, crying for relief, crawling toward yet another cold tile floor. So when we pulled over so poor Matt could flop senselessly about in front of the headlights, then crawl into a drainage ditch on his belly, I had his camera in my hands. This was my moment. Payback. Video gold. All I had to do was aim, press the button, and then everyone back in the offices in New York – editors, producers, all of us – could play and replay the comeuppance of my longtime tormentor. The lighting was perfect. It couldn't have been more dramatic: a deserted country road, total black beyond the narrow circumference of the headlights, a dark canefield in the background. I raised the camera, pointed . . .

I just couldn't do it. I didn't have the heart.

We ended up hoisting the poor bastard back into the car, and carrying him to his room later. We took off his shoes. I left his camera and his exposed tape by his side.

When he woke, those would be the first things he'd be looking for.

He's a professional, after all.

CAN CHARLIE SURF?

I WAKE UP IN my room at the Bao Dai Villas, the onetime summer home of the last emperor of Vietnam. I hear reveille out the window, followed by patriotic music at a nearby school, and the sound of children assembling. Rain patters on leaves; roosters crow. Someone is chopping wood on the grounds and there's the familiar shush of a straw whisk broom sweeping tile. Out on the water, just around the point, a freighter's engines throb idly in the early-morning mist.

All my clothes are soggy and beset by mosquitoes. I remain under the netting over my bed until I can remember where I put the repellent. There's a knock on the door. It's Lydia, wondering if I have any Lomotil. I went alone to Nha Trang beach yesterday, ate whole sea bream with my fingers under a palm tree. Chris ate crab soup at the hotel. He's deathly ill with food poisoning. Of course I have Lomotil. The traveling chef's best friend. I give Lydia a few and wish Chris well. I know how he feels. It looks like I'm on my own this morning.

After locating the repellent, I spray down my clothes, find the driest ones I can, and get dressed. There's a scooter and motorbike rental by the desk, and I pick out the one with the most juice, hop on, then head into town for breakfast. Technically, foreigners aren't allowed to drive anything over a low-cc putt-putt, but the rental guy didn't give me any trouble, so in a few minutes, I've joined the thick stream of morning cyclists heading in on Nha Trang's main beachfront drag. It feels great. I'm surrounded on all sides by men and women in their conical hats, whipping by palm trees, a long stretch of white sand and gentle surf to my right, the beach mostly deserted. The Vietnamese are not really beachgoers. Pale skin is seen here – as it is in Cambodia and elsewhere in the East – as an indicator of high status and good family. A lot of money is spent on skin lighteners, acid peels, and various fraudulent and often-harmful procedures intended to make one whiter. Women in Saigon often cover themselves from head to toe to protect themselves from the sun's rays. So Charlie, it appears, does not surf. Not in Nha Trang anyway.

As I turn off the main road, away from the sea, the traffic intensifies. Cars, trucks, more and more cyclists – on motorcycles, bicycles, cyclos, and scooters – join the fast-moving pack. Crossing an intersection is a heart-stopping maneuver, frightening and thrilling at the same time, filled with the roar of engines all accelerating simultaneously as we swarm across a square, only a foot or two from people on both sides. I squeeze past a line of trucks on the bridge across the channel. In the water, the gaudily painted red-white-and-blue fishing boats are coming in toward shore.

Local legend has it that when Nha Trang was the base for US military activity in the area, the CIA and Special Forces used to kick prisoners out of helicopters over this channel – wire a few tire rims to their necks and out the door. Now, there's little evidence of what was once an enormous American presence. As elsewhere in Vietnam, there's plenty of infrastructure, which the Vietnamese have all too happily adapted to civilian use, but the obvious signs are gone. No more shantytowns built out of cans hammered flat and scraps of military detritus, housing whores and cleaning ladies and laundresses. Quonset huts, officers' clubs, barracks, and parade grounds are gone – or converted to more practical purposes. The large hotels and villas once used to house high-ranking military personnel are now the property of government officials or rented out to tourists. The only people on Nha Trang beach are a few French, Germans, and Australians, most staying in the modern foreign-built resort-type buildings clustered together at one end of the bay. Yesterday on the beach, a kid approached me with a box of used books in English. It was the ubiquitous Vietnam collection: pirated editions of Tim Page, Michael Herr, David Halberstam, Philip Caputo, Neil Sheehan, and Graham Greene – pretty much like the collection on my bookshelf at home. But among the crudely Xeroxed covers and the dog-eared copies of left-behind drugstore paperbacks, the kid extracted a novel by a Vietnamese author: Bao Ninh's *The Sorrow of War*.

'Not legal this book,' said the kid, looking theatrically in both directions.

Needing a good beach read, I bought the book. The author, a war hero, served with the NVA's Glorious Twenty-seventh Youth Brigade. Of five hundred officers and enlisted men who went into battle with him, only ten survived. It's a remarkable document. Change the names and it's an Oliver Stone movie. The members of the hero's platoon have nicknames, just as in every American war movie you've ever seen. The conflicts described are bloody, pointless, and horrific. The soldiers are frightened and superstitious. They get high on weed, on any psychoactive substance they can, whenever they can. Innocents are cruelly and foolishly killed. The 'good guys' are responsible for brutal rapes and atrocities. The hero returns to Hanoi cynical, embittered, and hopelessly screwed up, only to find his girlfriend has become a prostitute. He spends most of his time with other similarly screwed-up veterans – all of whom spend most of their time drinking and getting into fights, having lost faith in everything they once believed in. It's a remarkable book, mostly for its eerie parallels to similar American works. It's a Vietnam book – like so many Vietnam books – only told from the other side.

By a Cham temple on a hilltop, I turn right down a narrow dirt road, splashing through muddy puddles until I find the fish market. People are eating everywhere. Among the pallets of fish and fast-moving deliveries and the crowds of marketers, large groups of people – old, young, babies, and children – sit on low plastic stools and squat, leaning against walls, slurping noodles from bowls, drinking tea, nibbling rice cakes, and eating pâté between baguettes. There's food cooking everywhere. Anywhere there's room for a fire and a cooking pot, someone has food going. Little storefront *coms* sell *pho* and noodles and 'roll your own beef.' Street vendors sell spring rolls, shrimp on a stick, scary-looking pâté sandwiches, baguettes, fried fish, fruit, sweets, and steamed crabs. Others seem to have just settled down at random, fired up some soup or noodles, and dug in – along with a large group of friends and family. I'm taller, by at least a foot, than anyone for two miles. Walking through the fish market to the water's edge, I get a lot of stares. A woman smiles and holds up her baby, a healthy-looking kid in a bright knit cap and new clothes. The woman herself is nearly in rags. 'Hello!' she says, holding the baby's hand and showing him how to wave. 'Bye-bye!' She asks me, by pointing and gesturing, if she can use my camera to take a picture of her son with me. Sure. Why not? She hastily confers with a group of women from a nearby fish stall. Someone locates a stool and the kid is posed standing on top. I show the woman how to operate the shutter and she frames the photo, a large group of women gathering behind and around her, all trying to look through the view-finder, all beaming with pride that their best and brightest is having his picture taken next to the freakishly tall and strange-looking American.

Only women work here. The fishmongers, scaling and gutting at long wooden tables by the water's edge, are all women. The people mending nets, unloading their catch from the colorfully decorated boats (they look like Amish barns), and cooking food at the stalls are all women. Women in *thung chais*, perfectly round dinghies made of woven bamboo and pitch, paddle their wobbly vessels toward the docks – a difficult balancing act (as I'd soon find out). Where are the men?

I sit down at a table with a large group of fishwives and their kids. The cook smiles and carefully places some cooked fish, some rice noodles, a few fish cakes, chilis, sprouts, peppers, and cilantro in a bowl, then hands me some chopsticks, a dish of black pepper, a wedge of lime, some additional chilis, and *nuoc mam* and chili sauce. There's a pot of coffee brewing over coals, and she pours me a cup. As with almost everything I've tried in Vietnam, it's fresh-tasting, vibrant, and delicious. Women keep coming over to the table and introducing their children. What they want, I have no idea. They ask for nothing except to allow their babies and small children to touch my arm, shake my hand, wave, the kids gaping wide-eyed and confused as the women scream with laughter and obvious delight. All these women have been up since way before dawn, many of them out on the water for hours, hauling in fish, loading them into their little round basket boats, unloading on shore. Yet no one looks tired. No one looks beaten down or defeated by their work. New arrivals stand upright in their dangerously pitching basket boats, smiling broadly as they heave pound after pound of dripping fish onto the market floor. The cook asks me if I'd like more coffee and pours me another cup, making sure my can of condensed milk is not empty. Fish blood runs across the wet concrete floor; a basket of squid is dropped a few feet away, then another basket of fish. The channel is filled with incoming fishing vessels, the awkwardly bobbing *thung chais*. Clouds cling to the mountains surrounding Nha Trang like tufts of white hair. I love it here.

Offshore are the islands of Hon Tre, Hon Tam, and Hon Mieu. Beyond those, farther out to sea, are a few tall rocks, surrounded by rough, dangerous surf, constantly patrolled by gunboats. This is where the salanganes (a variety of swallow) build their nests, high on the perilous snake-infested cliffs. The nests, formed out of the hardened salivary secretions of the swallow, fetch up to four thousand dollars a kilo from Chinese 'medical' practitioners and are much sought after throughout the East for bird's nest soup. Chris and Lydia have already asked if I'd be willing to climb up a cliff, past poisonous snakes, and crawl hundreds of feet over jagged rocks and pounding surf so they can shoot a bird's nest soup scene. I pointed out that bird's nest soup is medicine – not really food – and that I have about as much interest in bird's nest soup as I do in the next Steven Seagal ecothriller. The gunboat thing finally dissuaded them from having me attempt rappelling from any cliffs, but I feared the issue was not yet dead. I did, however, want to see some islands.

Linh and his friend Dongh, our driver in Nha Trang, said they knew a place on Hon Mieu, a little fishing village called Ba Mieu, where the seafood is supposed to be spectacular. I put a lot of faith in Dongh's opinions on food. He is a foodie, and as soon as he'd met me, he'd announced that I was a lucky man, for I was in the best town in the country for food. When we'd eaten dinner the first night, he'd kept pointing out highlights of the meal, asking if I'd noticed the amount of roe practically bursting from the green crabs, the freshness and flavor of the local lobsters, the clear eyes and noble conformation of the whole fish. He'd already fed me really well at a fish joint by the beach, and when Chris had asked about the food at our hotel, he'd rolled his eyes at the ceiling and given a decidedly lukewarm response.

Chris, it appeared, would have been well advised to pay closer attention. I'm surprised Linh is willing to take me here, that he is allowing us to see this – and film it.

As our hired boat approaches the surf off the island of Hon Lon, Dongh calls out to two thin, shabbily dressed men on the beach. A long, narrow launch sets out from shore, straight into the breakers, and eventually pulls alongside. There's room for only two passengers at a time in the leaky, water-filled launch. Lydia and I clamber in and are ferried to shore, riding the waves the last few yards. Chris is still back at the Bao Dai, probably getting up close and personal with the plumbing. This is a Vietnam I haven't seen yet.

It's a hard-packed, finely grained white sand beach around a small cove, strewn with trash, flotsam and jetsam, an absolutely godforsaken strip. A small village lies back among the trees on the muddy banks of what looks like a drainage ditch. Huts, hooches, shacks – as soggy and fragile-looking as you could possibly imagine – sag into unhealthy-looking brown water. There is no sign of electrical power, telephone communication, television, or any modern development dating after the mid-seventeenth century. There are a few bundles of sticks, and a *thung chai* resting upside down on the sand. I see no signs of life.

Lydia and I are alone on the beach, and I'm thinking about a swim. The surf is high, with a nice shape, the waves breaking far enough out to get a good ride if I want to bodysurf. Suddenly, we're under attack. Women come running from their huts, holding baskets of cheap seashell jewelry (the same Macao-made stuff you see on every beach in the world). The women are screaming, desperate-sounding, waving babies in front of them, shrieking, 'Look! Look! Baby! Baby!' They surround us on all sides, pressing in close, aggressively shaking fistfuls of necklaces and bracelets in front of us. It's impossible to deter them. I shake my head, saying, 'No, no . . . thank you . . . no . . .' again and again, but it's no use. They're pushing in, tugging our clothes. I move away, but they follow wherever I go. Lydia looks nervously at the boat, Linh and Dongh still waiting for the launch to return. I make the mistake of buying two pieces, hoping that'll satisfy the women, but it only makes them more desperate and inflamed. They begin arguing with one another, screaming, shouting, waving their fists. A woman presents me with her baby, a beautiful child with a single gold earring with a tiny gold bell – probably more valuable than the entire village – and begs me to buy a flimsy string of shells. I give in, which causes the others to redouble their frenzied efforts.

'I have a plan,' I say to Lydia. I run down to the water's edge, peel off my clothes, and dive in, then swim as far out as I can. Lydia chooses to remain ashore.

Nice curl on the waves. No reason at all for Charlie not to surf. I'm sure he must – somewhere. Some American soldier must have left an old longboard behind. There must be a Vietnamese surfer somewhere. Next time, I'll check Da Nang. I stay in the water for a long time, finally coming back ashore, to find Linh, stripped to his undershorts, energetically jogging down the beach, doing calisthenics, looking as happy as I've seen him. He smiles at me and charges into the surf. The women have given up on us. Now they just sit and watch, without much interest.

Progress has certainly passed this village by. I can't imagine what must happen during the rainy season, when it can pour for weeks and weeks without pause. That ditch must become a torrent. The houses – already tilting on broken stilts and crumbling into the water – must flood. The roofs and walls, such as they are, can in no way keep out the rain. I see no animals, no crops or gardens. Other than the lone *thung chai*, there are no boats. I ask Linh later, 'Who are these people? How do they live?'

'Very poor people,' he says. 'Fishermen families.'

When we've finished up, it's back to the leaky launch. The trip to the boat is pretty dicey: straight into the surf, water up to our shins, waves crashing over the bow. There are open spaces between the planks, and I can't see how we're staying afloat. Aft, one man furiously yanks a single oar back and forth, propelling us into the waves.

Hon Mieu, only a few miles away, is a completely different story. I can see another village of low ramshackle structures on the shore, but the bay is filled with tourist boats and water taxis, fishing vessels and *thung chais*, women shuttling visitors to shore. As we draw closer and tie up alongside another large water taxi, I can make out a strip of waterfront restaurants. Crowds of Vietnamese tourists fill long tables on their raised decks.

'This way,' says Dongh. Linh, Lydia and I follow, climbing from boat to boat across the bay until we come to a series of large floating docks, a maze of pitching, rocking walkways built around square openings that have been sealed underneath with fishing net. A whole enterprise floating a mile out to sea. Boats are tied up, fishmongers argue over prices, and customers cluster around large underwater pens containing the most astonishing array of live seafood. I stand there in bare feet, trying to keep my balance with the rise and fall of the planks beneath me, looking at enormous squid and cuttlefish, a pen filled with thrashing tuna, grouperlike fish, sea bream, and fish I've never seen before. Giant prawns, huge blue-and-yellow spiny lobsters, and crabs scuttle about just below the surface, awaiting my selection. I kneel down, reach underwater, and pull out a three- or four-pound lobster. Linh picks out some squid and some tuna while Dongh makes arrangements for our transport to shore. Lydia and I walk out to the end of a swaying collection of planks and climb very carefully into a *thung chai*; the two women in charge show us just where to sit, indicating that we should balance on the narrow lip, to best distribute our weight. Linh and Dongh take another boat in.

It seems like the most poorly designed vessel ever dreamed of. Absolutely spherical, like big Ping-Pong balls sawed in half and thrown into water, the boats bob and pitch with every move inside or out, threatening to toss one into the sea at any moment. One woman paddles, leaning ahead over the side, while another, directly opposite her on the other side of the boat's circumference, paddles in the opposite direction. Back and forth, back and forth, in a zigzag pattern to shore. I take an immediate liking to my skippers, two ruddy-looking ladies in the standard conical hats, which are tied tightly by sashes under their chins. They chatter cheerfully all the way in. As we disembark, carefully, very carefully, standing up and stepping onto a slippery dock, everyone remaining in the boat has to move around quickly to compensate for the changing distribution of weight.

In one of those magic moments that makes you want to hug the whole world, when Dongh (landlubber from town) and Linh (Hanoi city boy in nice white shirt) try to leave their little round basket boat, Dongh loses his footing and pitches face-forward onto the dock, nearly capsizing the boat – and just escaping a good knock on the head. All the women burst out laughing. From other boats nearby, people hoot and tease, really enjoying Dongh's embarrassment. It goes on for a long time, all of us laughing hysterically. Every time any of us catch another's eye, it starts again. One of those rare crosscultural moments where one realizes we're not that different after all.

Right next to the dock, up a few slimy wooden steps, a cook from the Hai Dao restaurant gravely examines the sea creatures we've brought and then weighs them on a scale. One pays for one's dinner by weight. Seated at a large uncovered table, Dongh, Linh, and I are soon joined by the pilot of our water taxi. At Linh's urging, we order a bottle of Nep Moi, Hanoi vodka. A waiter approaches with my lobster, still kicking, holds it over a glass, and thrusts a short knife into its sexual organs. A transluscent, slightly milky white liquid pours out – and is quickly mixed with the vodka.

'*Ruou tiet tom hum* . . . lobster blood,' Linh volunteers. 'Makes you strong.'

The Hai Dao is packed with customers, every table filled with enthusiastic Vietnamese families chowing down, some visiting from America, some vacationing from Hanoi and Saigon. Everywhere, there is the sound of those plastic packages of cold towels popping, the floor littered with discarded lobster shells, cracked crab claws, fish bones, cigarette butts, rolling beer bottles.

Food starts to arrive at our tables: *tom hum nuong*, my lobster, grilled over a wood fire; *muc huap*, steamed squid with ginger and scallions; *ca thu xot ca chau*, tuna braised in tomato and cilantro; *banh da vung*, rice cakes studded with sesame seeds, in a bundt mold-shaped hot pot over a little gas burner at the center of the table; *mi canh ca*, a sweet-and-sour soup of fish, noodles, tomato, onion, cilantro, pineapple, and scallion, and a few humongous green crabs, overstuffed with roe. It is the perfect setting for a damn near perfect meal. I am now totally indoctrinated to the casual Vietnamese dining experience. I love the way you garnish and season your own food: the ground black pepper and lime wedges you mix together into a paste and dip your food into, the dipping sauces and fish sauce with chili paste, the little plates of tiny green and red peppers, the bottles of soy, the plates of chopped cilantro and scallions.

Dongh has made it his personal mission to make sure I fully enjoy every scrap of Nha Trang's bounty. He refuses to let me touch the lobster or the crab until he's tunneled through every claw and spindly leg and removed every micron of meat. When he lifts off the carapace of a jumbo-sized green crab, he beams at me as he points out the beautiful, fantastically plump roe, the crab backs swimming with delicious fat.

We eat with chopsticks. We eat with our hands. We smoke between courses. We smoke during courses. We drink vodka and beer, scattering our refuse all over the table, like everyone else. The food is wonderful. Nothing but happy faces as far as I can see, children and grandfathers avidly sucking the last bits of meat out of crab legs and lobsters, picking out the good stuff from between fish bones.

I am ecstatically happy. I love it here. I love this country. I consider, for the fifth or sixth time at least, defecting.

What else do I need? Great food. The South China Sea's beautiful beaches. An exotic locale. An element of adventure. People so proud, so nice, and so generous that I have to keep a cover story on tap, should a cabdriver or shopkeeper invite me to his home for dinner (bankrupting himself in the process). It's a wonderland of food and cooking. Everybody has an opinion. Linh, naturally, says the best food in Vietnam is in Hanoi. Dongh sneers dismissively and argues for Nha Trang. They have definite opinions in Can Tho. And Saigon speaks for itself. To the Saigonese, North Vietnam is a joke – unfriendly, uninteresting, filled with stuck-up idealogues who underseason their food. Anyplace where everybody feels so strongly about their particular community, their cuisine, and their cooks, you know you're going to eat well. I could live here. And it smells good. I've already come to like the odor of durian and fermenting fish sauce, promising, as they do, untold delights, constant reminders that yes, yes, I'm in Vietnam! I'm really in Vietnam!

But TV makes its own rules. When I get back to the Bao Dai Villas, still reeling from the feast, they're preparing something for me in the kitchen. Chris is still out of the game for a while. (In coming weeks, he became thin and pale, unable to eat, constantly feeling ill.) But Lydia has arranged for a meal of the dreaded bird's nest soup.

'You've been dreaming of bird's nest soup,' she begins.

'No, I haven't,' I say, interrupting her. 'I don't give a fuck about bird's nest soup. I thought this was settled . . . I'm absolutely stuffed. I'm feeling a little seasick from the trip back. Please don't ask me to choke down bird's nest soup. I just had one of the great meals of my life. Don't ruin it. Please.'

But Lydia's like a dog with a bone between its teeth when she gets a concept in mind. She's shot a lot of odd bits of film, closeups, kaleidoscopic scenes on 'progressive scan,' which she's convinced, after some additional *Apocalypse Now*-type footage of me lying in bed, shot from behind a slowly revolving ceiling fan, will make hilarious viewing.

'You've been dreaming about bird's nest soup,' she begins again, undeterred. 'It's the dream sequence.'

Far be it from me to stand in the way of art. I like Lydia. At the end of the day, I always end up doing pretty much whatever she asks. Looks like I'm eating bird's nest soup. And not just any bird's nest soup. Bird's nest soup from the same kitchen that put Chris on his back for the last twenty-four hours.

What the hell is in bird's nest soup? Bird's nest, for one. After cooking, it has the flavor, consistency, and appearance of over-cooked angel-hair pasta or cellophane noodles, slightly trans-luscent and, overall, pretty inoffensive. The chunks are the problem. Bird's nest soup is made by hacking up a whole rock dove (pigeon), putting the meat, bones and all, into a drained coconut, and then cooking it with the soaked nest, an assortment of Chinese medicinal herbs, dates, scallions, ginger, and the swallow's eggs. The coconut milk is poured back in and the whole thing is steamed for four hours.

It's disgusting. The nest tastes fine. The broth has a sweet-and-sour taste that's not too bad. But I just am not ready for the chunks. Not after my enormous seafood lunch on the island. Not ever. I struggle with chopsticks to pick my way through all the hard-cooked eggs, slurp strands of nest dutifully, if unenthu-siastically, managing to gnaw the meat off a few stringy bits of thigh and breast. But when the pigeon's head, beak, eyes, and all, comes popping up between the eggs and dates and bones and the rubbery sheets of coconut meat peeling off the shell, I have had enough. Linh and Dongh are digging into theirs as if they, too, have not just wiped out a monster-sized seafood feast. I eat as much as I can and hurry back to my room to lie under the mosquito netting and groan and toss, feeling like I'm going to die.

Two hours ago, I was dancing on the moon. Now? The horror. The horror.

WEST COAST

SAN FRANCISCO, AS ITS residents like to remind you, is nothing like Los Angeles. Anytime a snide, wise-ass New Yorker like myself starts slagging California, someone points out that 'San Francisco is different.' It's pretty. There are hills. Unlike LA, you can, on occasion, actually hail a cab by sticking a hand out in the street. Other than New York, it's probably got more talented chefs, and a more vibrant culinary scene, than any other American city. A good argument could be made that the whole renaissance in American restaurant cooking emanated outward from San Francisco, starting with Alice Waters and Jeremiah Tower. It's got a shabby, bohemian appeal, a rich tradition of bad behavior, good local ingredients. 'You'll love it,' my friends always told me.

So how come I can't fucking smoke? Somewhere north of San Francisco, I was sitting at the bar of a ramshackle roadhouse that, from all appearances, was exactly the sort of place I like. The bartender, 'Lucky,' or something like that, is in her fifties. She has a hoarse, rasping voice, two missing teeth, and a tattoo of a winged phallus above her wrinkled left breast. Charlie Daniels plays on the jukebox for a small group of regulars drinking bourbon and rye with beer chasers at ten o'clock in the morning. A chopped Harley sits out front and probably belongs to the guy in the cut-down denim jacket to my left, who offered to sell me crack a few moments ago when we passed each other in the septic bathroom – and I get the general impression that if I were to slide over to the left or the right, buy a few rounds for my fellow citizens, I could probably acquire an illegal handgun or two. This was the sort of place where I could walk over to the jukebox and play a couple of Johnny Cash tunes and nobody would say boo. Hell, they might even like it. This was the sort of place that when Johnny, singing 'Folsom Prison Blues,' comes to the line, 'I shot a man in Reno . . . just to watch him die,' people will sing along, getting wistful over similar golden moments in their own pasts.

On my second pint, I was getting into the ambience: the familiar smell of decades of spilled beer, a hint of Lysol, chicken wings in the deep fryer. Somebody down at the other end was drunkenly insisting, 'I barely touched the bitch! It was a fuckin' accident! Why she's gotta go and get a goddamn restraining order!' – before bursting into tears. I took another sip of beer, reached automatically into my shirt pocket, and fired up a cigarette. Lucky the bartender looked at me as if I'd just taken my pants off and begun soaking myself down with gasoline.

'Dude!' she wheezed, nervous, her eyes darting in all directions at once. 'You can't do that here! You gotta take that outside!'

You can't smoke anywhere in California. Rob Reiner says so. Celebrity fuckheads who live in walled compounds and use words like *working class* – never having sat down at a bar for an early-afternoon shot and a beer with any such animal in their lives – say so. For them, the bar is a place where we stupid, lumpen, and oppressed blue-collar proles are victimized by evil tobacco companies that have tricked us with their clever advertising into killing ourselves and our neighbors. For me, the bar is the last line of defense. 'It's an employee safety and health issue,' explained Lucky. The state is protecting her fry cook (I could see him in the kitchen, picking at an abscessed track mark) from the pernicious effects of secondhand smoke. Now, I can understand why they don't want me smoking in restaurant dining rooms. If I'm enjoying a delicate pairing of seared foie gras and pear chutney, I probably don't want somebody puffing away on a jasmine cigarette at the next table. I'm considerate. I can find a way not to smoke in the dining rooms of decent restaurants. Though bitterly resentful that I can no longer enjoy a cigarette with my fucking coffee in most places, I've learned to live with it. But the bar? The *bar*! What these miserable screwheads are saying is that it's OK to kill yourself with bourbon or tequila at nine o'clock in the morning – just don't enjoy yourself when doing it. It's only a matter of time before some well-intentioned health Nazi busts into your bedroom and yanks that postintercourse cigarette right outta your hand.

San Francisco is said to be one of the most 'liberal' and 'tolerant' places to live in America. That's a good thing, right? I'm avidly supportive of 'alternative lifestyles.' I'm 'tolerant'. But something's gone wrong here. It's a wildly expensive city to live in – even where I'm staying in the Tenderloin – too expensive for most people to afford. Yet San Francisco's acceptance of hopelessness, prostitution, and drug addiction as 'alternative lifestyles' seems to have ensured that many of its neighborhoods are choked with hustlers, junkies, the desperate, and the insane. I haven't seen junkies in such great numbers since the bad old days of Alphabet City – and in such bad shape. They're everywhere – dirty, diabetic, their limbs swollen, chalky, covered with suppurating tracks and infections. West Coast skells make my old crew from the methadone clinic look like the Osmond family. San Francisco's main employment sectors, at a cursory glance, are the countless whorehouses, massage parlors, clip joints, live sex shows, and crummy-looking strip joints you see everywhere downtown. A great number of women in San Francisco seem to be sex workers, and while perfectly OK as a 'lifestyle choice' in my book, there are so many of them, and so disproportionately Asian, it feels more like Cambodia then any American city. As rents are so high, there's nowhere to live – and the dotcoms ain't hiring like they used to.

With all their kind hearts and good intentions, San Franciscans, living in postcard-pretty houses atop high hills, seem to be sending a message: 'It's OK to come here. If you are prepared to lap dance for us . . . and then sleep on our sidewalks.'

Just don't smoke. That would be wrong.

I don't want you to think I don't like San Francisco. I do. It's a relief from Los Angeles. And some of my favorite movies were filmed there: *The Asphalt Jungle*, *Bullitt*, *Dirty Harry*. When I was a kid, reading *Life* magazine on a beach in France, all I wanted to do with my life was run away to the Haight and live in a house with the Jefferson Airplane, drop acid and draw underground comix. I grew up on R. Crumb's incredible line drawings of San Francisco, dreamed feverishly of all that free love I'd be enjoying with hippie chicks – if I ever turned thirteen. When it became clear that living in a commune, or sharing a crash pad, meant arguing over whom the last yogurt belonged to, when I realized, finally, that I'd been right all along, that the Grateful Dead really did suck, regardless of what my brainy friends said, and that 'the revolution' would never, ever, ever happen – and that that was probably not a bad thing – that particular dream died. The putative leaders of that revolution probably wouldn't let me smoke now, either. And of course, by 1975, when I first saw the Ramones, all thoughts of ever living in a city other than New York evaporated.

My first few days in San Francisco were fine. I ate oysters and Dungeness crab at the Swan Oyster Depot – exactly the kind of eating establishment I dearly love. I had durian ice cream at Polly Anne's out by the beach. I had a superb meal at Gary Danko – a too-precious dining room but very, very fine food, and a very likable group of hooligans in the kitchen. I visited a few New York transplants now working in the area, most lured by the town's reputation for good food and innovative restaurants and its selection of readily available fresh ingredients. I had a gluey, cornstarchy, dinosaur Cantonese meal at Sam Wo's in Chinatown, a throwback to my childhood forays to upper Broadway or Mott Street in New York. A cranky waitress hauled each course up a hand-pulled dumbwaiter. I purposefully ordered chop suey, wonton soup, and chow mein, not even having heard those words since 1963 – and thoroughly enjoyed myself – a little nostalgia for the old folks. I hung out with cooks a lot, as there are plenty of cooks in San Francisco. And one thing about cooks: Whether you're talking about New York, Philadelphia,

Glasgow, Melbourne, London, or San Francisco, we're the same everywhere. (Though I don't fully understand the Fernet Branca shot and ginger ale chaser thing.)

I was staying in a rock and roll motel around the corner from the O'Farrell Theater. There was a bar/nightclub set off from the pool deck and music pounded all night long; bearded metalhead band members sat in deck chairs while their roadies brought them drinks. I whuffed down a few cigarettes and then wandered into the bar for a drink. 'Are you Anthony Bourdain?' asked a security guy by the door. Knowing of no outstanding warrants or unsettled grudges on this side of the country, I said yes.

'Listen, man, my friend's a chef, and he really loved your book. He'd love it if you dropped by his restaurant. It's right down the street.' I'd heard about the place. Let's call it Restaurant X, a fairly swanky new joint a few blocks away. I'm always more comfortable in the company of chefs and cooks, so I figured, What the hell, maybe a few free snackies.

When I swung by, much later, the chef joined me and two off-duty shooters at my table. He was eager to send out some *amuses-gueules* and some drinks. A fairly young guy, in only his second or third chef's job, he was amiable but clearly stressed out, getting crispy from the pressure of opening a new restaurant, dealing with an overwhelming initial rush of business, and the responsibilities of managing a large crew. Nothing new there. We all have that look, to one degree or another. When he invited me in to see his kitchen, I gladly agreed. I like taking the tour through restaurant kitchens. (I'd been away from mine a long time – and I missed it.) He showed me a hot line of new Jade ranges, gleaming counters, an ice-cream machine and pasta maker, then took me through the walk-in, where he'd conscientiously organized and segregated the meat, fish, dairy, and produce. He introduced me to his cooks, the usual posse of pierced and decorated scamps, most in the final stages of kitchen breakdown.

The chef opened the door to his office and beckoned me in, as if to show me around – the familiar cluttered desk piled with invoices, schedules, old copies of *Food Arts*, *Restaurant Hospi-*

tality, faxed résumés, equipment manuals, stashes of saffron and truffle oil – and asked if I'd sign a grease-stained, food-smeared copy of my book, which I was all too happy to do. The greasier the better. Somebody shoves a book to be signed in my direction, and it's covered with food? I know it's for the home team. But when I looked up after scrawling my signature, the chef had closed the office door. He was sitting behind his desk, head in his hands, teary-eyed. 'What do I do? . . . I don't know what to do . . .'

I sat there, stunned, while a total stranger (I didn't even know his last name) cried in front of me.

'What . . . what's the problem, man?' I asked.

'My sous-chef,' he said, blinking away tears. 'He's . . . my best friend. But . . . he's like . . . talking behind my back. He's leaning on the cooks real hard. Yesterday, I had two cooks walk out 'cause a this guy! That's why I'm working the line tonight. I was supposed to be off . . . But I'm working the fuckin' grill 'cause two of my staff walked out. No notice, nothing.'

I felt my blood starting to percolate, simmer, threaten to boil. 'You tell this prick to lighten up?' I asked.

'Yes! I told him,' said the chef, clearly pained by the situation. 'He's my friend. My best friend. We came up together. I told him . . . I told him . . . But he just ignores me. He knows better . . . He says that to the cooks! I say one thing? He says another. The cooks can't take it anymore. I'm gonna lose all of them if something doesn't change.'

'You should fire the cocksucker' was my suggestion. I didn't have to think too long about it, either.

'I know . . . I know. I should . . . But . . . I just can't,' he said, rubbing his face.

'Listen. Let me get this straight,' I said. 'Just so we both know what we're talkin' about here . . . You're the chef, right?'

'Yes.'

'And your sous-chef, your underboss, is talking treason behind your back . . . disobeying your orders, causing discontent, disgruntlement, desertion . . . possible mutiny among the troops?'

'Well . . . yeah . . . I guess so. I mean, maybe he doesn't mean to. He's just trying to – '

'This guy's a fuckin' lone wolf! He's a loose cannon! He's gotta go!' I snarled, surprising myself with how viscerally involved I suddenly was in the chef's problem. 'I don't care if he's your bestest, dearest, closest buddy since you were babies. This mutt has gotta go. The sous-chef's number-one job is what? To make the chef look good. At all times. He's not there so that every time you come back from a day off there's some kinda problem you gotta deal with. Is he making you look good with this shit he's pullin'?'

'No,' admitted the chef. 'It's not good. Things are all fucked up.'

'That alone is enough . . . And he's talking trash about you when you're not around? Forget it! You gotta cut this cancer out before it kills you.'

'I know.' He sniffled. 'I know.'

'Look,' I said, softening. 'I know what you're going through. I fired my own best friend and sous-chef at least . . . what . . . three times. We're still friends. He's still my best friend. He's just not my sous-chef anymore. And you know what? After you kick this guy out, this kid'll go on and get his own chef's job. He'll be calling you up and apologizing for all the stuff he pulled when he was here. He'll know. He'll find out what a chef needs and expects in a sous. It's business. That's all. But it's serious business. That's what you forgot to tell him. Kiss this guy on the mouth and say, "Fredo, you broke my heart." Then whack him. But don't wait.'

'You're right . . . you're right . . .'

'Next time you're hiring a sous, do like I do. Take him out to a nice bar. Buy him a drink before you close the deal. Then give him the Talk. Let him know right up front. I say, "I'm the nicest, sweetest guy in the world. You call me at four o'clock in the morning needing bail money? I'm there for you. I'm not going to be riding your ass like some other chefs will. I won't humiliate you in front of your crew or anybody else. You don't have to address me as 'Chef' all the time. I've got a sense of humor – and in my off hours I'm a depraved, degenerate animal – just like you. You will like working with me. We'll have fun . . . But if you ever fuck me, talk shit about me behind my back, drop the ball, show up late, or show disloyalty in any way, I don't care if you're my dearest friend, I don't care if you saved my fucking *life*, I *will* fire your sorry ass like I'm blowing my fucking nose. Do we understand each other? Is that clear? And do you want me to write it down?" That's what's called "fair warning". You've drawn the lines. He crosses them and it's bye-bye. You let him know up front what a vicious, cold-blooded motherfucker you can be. That way, there're no surprises.'

The chef seemed considerably cheered by my inspiring little lecture. 'Thanks, man,' he said. 'I'm sorry for dropping all this on you. I knew what I had to do and all . . . It's just . . . I guess I needed to hear somebody else say it.' Then he reached into the pocket of his chef coat and offered me a bump from a big bag of white powder.

Maybe his sous-chef wasn't his only problem.

Reasons Why You Don't Want to Be on Television: Number Five in a Series

'C'mon, Tony! You've been to Cambodia, for Chrissakes! How bad can it be?' said the television producer. 'We can't do a whole show on one restaurant! This will be funny! They're looking forward to cooking for you!' What he'd arranged, what he had in mind, was for me to venture into the real heart of darkness, deep, deep into enemy territory, to Berkeley, and a vegan potluck dinner.

I've said some pretty hateful things about vegetarians, I know. In spite of this, many of them have been very nice to me over the past year. Though I think I have at various times referred to them as 'Hezbollah-like' and as 'the enemy of everything good and decent in the human spirit,' they come to my readings, write me nice letters. My publicist in England, whom I adore, is a veg (though I've forced her at gunpoint to eat fish a few times), as are a couple of the shooters I've worked with. They've shown remarkable good humor, considering how I feel about their predilections. There have been lots of vegheads who've been very kind and generous these last few months, in spite of the fact that they know that at the first opportunity, when they're drunk or vulnerable, I'm getting a bacon cheeseburger down their throats. That doesn't mean I wanted to sit in some hilltop A-frame eating lentils out of a pot with a bunch of Nader supporters and hairy-legged earth mothers in caftans. I certainly didn't want to visit 'them' on their home turf. If nothing else, I was reasonably certain that smoking would be a problem.

I'm going to try – really try – to be nice here.

I went along with the producer's scheme. Fair is fair. The opposition should be given every chance to prove the right-eousness of their cause – or at least the merits of their case. The people coming to the dinner, the folks who'd be cooking for me, were all serious vegans. Cookbook authors. Vegan cookery teachers. People who spent lots of time going to seminars, classes, corresponding with others of their ilk – on-line, in chat rooms, and at conventions and informal gatherings. Maybe, just maybe, they had something to show me. Maybe it was possible to make something good without meat, or stock, or butter, or cheese, or dairy products of any kind. Who was I to sneer? The world, I had recently found out, was a big, strange, and won-derful place. I'd eaten tree grubs and worms and sheep's testicles. How bad could it be?

Bad.

The vegans I visited did not live in a converted ashram on a hilltop, tending to their crops in bare feet or Birkenstocks. No one was named Rainbow or Sunflower. Only one person wore a sari. My hosts lived in a kempt modern luxury home in an exclusive area of the suburbs, surrounded by green lawns and shiny new BMWs and SUVs. They were, all of them, affluent-looking professionals and executives. Ranging in age from late thirties to early fifties, they were well dressed, unfailingly nice, eager to show me the other side of the argument.

And not one of them could cook a fucking vegetable.

Fergus Henderson, the grand master of blood and guts cookery, shows more respect for the simple side of sautéed baby spinach on some of his plates than any of these deluded vegans showed me in ten elaborate courses. Green salads were dressed hours before being served, ensuring that they had wilted into nutrition-free sludge. The knife work – even from the cooking teachers present – was clumsy and inept, resembling the lesser efforts of younger members of the Barney Rubble clan. The vegetables – every time – were uniformly overcooked, under-seasoned, nearly colorless, and abused, any flavor, texture, and lingering vitamin content leeched out. Painstaking re-creations of 'cheese', 'yogurt' and 'cream' made from various unearthly soy products tasted, invariably, like caulking compound, and my hosts, though good-humored and friendly to the hostile stranger in their midst, seemed terrified, even angry, about something nebulous in their pasts. Every time I asked one of them how and when exactly they had decided to forgo all animal products, the answer always seemed to involve a personal tragedy or disappointment unrelated to food.

'I got a divorce,' began one. 'I lost my job,' said another. 'Heart attack,' offered another. 'I broke up with my . . .' 'When I decided to move out of LA, I started thinking about things . . .'

In every case, it appeared to me (in my jaundiced way of thinking anyway) that something had soured them on the world they'd once embraced – and that they now sought new rules to live by, another orthodoxy, something else to believe in. 'Did you read about the PCBs in striped bass?' one whispered urgently, as if comforted by the news. 'I saw on-line where they're pumping steroids into cattle,' said another breathlessly, every snippet of bad news from the health front a victory for their cause. They seemed to spend an awful lot of time confirming their fears and suspicions of the world outside their own, combing the Internet for stories of radioactive dairy products, genetically altered beets, polluted fish, carcinogenic sausages, spongiform-riddled meat, the hideous Grand Guignol chamber of horror abattoirs and slaughterhouses.

They also seemed curiously oblivious to the fact that much of the world goes to bed hungry every night, that our basic design features as humans, from the beginning of our evolution, developed around the very real need to hunt down slower, stupider animals, kill them, and eat them. 'Don't you ever wake up in the middle of the night craving bacon?' I asked.

'No. Never,' replied every single one of them. 'I've never felt so healthy in my life.'

It was difficult for me to be polite (though I was outnumbered). I'd recently returned from Cambodia, where a chicken can be the difference between life and death. These people in their comfortable suburban digs were carping about cruelty to animals but suggesting that everyone in the world, from suburban Yuppie to starving Cambodian cyclo driver, start buying organic vegetables and expensive soy substitutes. To look down on entire cultures that've based everything on the gathering of fish and rice seemed arrogant in the extreme. (I've heard of vegans feeding their dogs vegetarian meals. Now that's cruelty to animals.) And the hypocrisy of it all pissed me off. Just being able to talk about this issue in reasonably grammatical language is a privilege, subsidized in a yin/yang sort of a way, somewhere, by somebody taking it in the neck. Being able to read these words, no matter how stupid, offensive, or wrongheaded, is a privilege, your reading skills the end product of a level of education most of the world will never enjoy. Our whole lives – our homes, the shoes we wear, the cars we drive, the food we eat – are all built on a mountain of skulls. Meat, say the PETA folks, is 'murder.' And yes, the wide world of meat eating can seem like a panorama of cruelty at times. But is meat 'murder'? Fuck no.

Murder, as one of my Khmer pals might tell you, is what his next-door neighbor did to his whole family back in the seventies. Murder is what happens in Cambodia, in parts of Africa, Central and South America, and in former Soviet republics when the police chief's idiot son decides he wants to turn your daughter into a whore and you don't like the idea. Murder is what Hutus do to Tutsis, Serbs to Croats, Russians to Uzbeks, Crips to Bloods. And vice versa. It's black Chevy Suburbans (which, more than likely, US taxpayers paid for) pulling up outside your house at three in the morning and dragging away your suspiciously unpatriotic and overopinionated son. Murder is what that man sitting across from you in Phnom Penh does for a living – so he can afford a satellite dish for his roof, so he can watch our *Airwolf* reruns, MTV Asia, and Pam Anderson running in slow motion down a Southern California beach.

Hide in your fine homes and eat vegetables, I was thinking. Put a Greenpeace or NAACP bumper sticker on your Beemer if it makes you feel better (so you can drive your kids to their all-white schools). Save the rainforest – by all means – so maybe you can visit it someday, on an ecotour, wearing comfortable shoes made by twelve-year-olds in forced labor. Save a whale while millions are still sold into slavery, starved, fucked to death, shot, tortured, forgotten. When you see cute little kids crying in rubble next to Sally Struthers somewhere, be sure to send a few dollars.

Damn! I was going to try and be nice.

But then, I wasn't in San Francisco to be nice. I wasn't there to investigate, experience, or explain the full sweep of NoCal culture and cuisine, to bring enlightenment or illumination or a new perspective to a complex and interesting subject. I was in the region for one reason and one reason alone: to eat at the French Laundry.

I was worried about this part of the jaunt. Even getting a reservation at the Laundry can be a lengthy and difficult process, and the prospect of chef/owner Thomas Keller allowing me, Mr Obnoxious Don't Eat Fish on Monday, to eat in his dining room at short notice – while a camera crew shot the kitchen and dining room during service – seemed doubtful. Keller, very likely America's greatest homegrown chef, had, as I pointed out in an E-mail to him, absolutely nothing to gain by allowing my spiteful presence through his doors. A journeyman knucklehead like me was hardly going to dazzle or impress. Instead, I threw myself cravenly at his mercy, pleaded for any consideration I could get: Professional courtesy? Curiosity? Pity? I'd take it, I told him, anyway I could get it.

Being the shrewd, conspiratorial, paranoid second-guesser that I am, I made damn sure, while Keller considered my request, to pad my guest list for the proposed meal with the heaviest-hitting, friend-in-common, high-octane bunch I could find. Even if Keller thought me an utter swine and an opportunistic hustler, my dinner companions would be sure to get his attention.

I put my end of dinner at the French Laundry together like a bank job. Enticed through threats, promises, and guarantees of an all-expenses-paid trip to what was sure to be a memorable meal, they came one by one. They knew who Thomas Keller was, just as he surely knew them.

From Palm Beach, dragged away from Easter dinner with his family, came Michael Ruhlman, the coauthor (with Keller) of *The French Laundry Cookbook*. We'd met only recently, at an evening of senseless debauchery and overindulgence at the Siberia Bar in New York. He'd written two other books, *The Making of a Chef* and *The Soul of a Chef*, which I'd really enjoyed; I'd found from his prose that Michael, like no other nonchef writers I know, understands the glories of veal stock, the grim realities of kitchen grease, the hard kernel of truth about what really makes people want to cook professionally – and why. He generously agreed to join me in my bold but weird venture.

Scott Bryan flew in from New York. He's an old crony by now. I'd met him through his food. I'm a regular customer at his three-star restaurant, Veritas, and we've become friends over the years. If you ever read in the papers about some ugly incident at a midtown bar involving me, a blunt object, and a vegetarian, chances are Scott will have been in the room when they clapped on the manacles. I'd written gushingly (and sincerely) about him in my earlier book, and I assured him that even though there would be TV cameras floating around like airborne pests, there was no script, no plan, and that all he had to do was show up in San Francisco, pile into a car, and eat what would very likely be a fantastic meal.

Eric Ripert, the chef of the four-star Manhattan restaurant Le Bernardin, flew in from Los Angeles. Here's a guy who is everything I am not: He has four stars, a résumé of nothing but world-class kitchens, incredible natural talent, top-drawer skills, and movie-star good looks. He's not even American; he hails from Andorra, a minicountry in the Pyrenees. That he entered my life after reading my book, I always secretly attributed to his all-too-well-remembered apprenticeship days, when he must have experienced something in common with the desperate, debauched hustlers, strivers, and journeymen discussed in its pages. (Though I have a very hard time ever picturing Eric knocking out eggs Benedict like I did for so many years.) He has, by the way, what is perhaps the best independent intelligence network running in New York – and maybe the whole country. The NSA has nothing on this guy. If it happens in a kitchen anywhere, Eric knows about it ten minutes later. He's also the most bullshit-free 'French' chef I've ever met.

They arrived, one by one, at my motel – all of us, it turned out, dressed for dinner in nearly identical black suits, dark ties, and dark sunglasses. Whatever collective coolness I may have thought we had evaporated immediately when I got a look at the car the TV folks had rented to take us out to dinner. It was a half-mile-long gleaming white stretch limo, a hideous rubemobile that practically begged for us to change into powder-blue ruffled shirts and pastel orange tuxes. I was mortified. Already extremely nervous about our reception and this much-anticipated meal, here we were, planning to arrive in the rural Napa Valley community of Yountville in a car more suitable to some lottery-winning yokel on his way to the county fair to sell off his prize hogs.

When you talk to most really talented 'star' chefs, the words *I* and *me* and *my* tend to come up a lot. Nothing wrong with that – it takes a big ego to do what chefs do, to keep them going in the face of absurd odds, uncertain outcomes, long hours in hot spaces.

'My cuisine . . .' 'My cooking . . .' 'My kitchen . . .' 'My cooks . . .' 'My approach to food . . .'

You've heard that before. I do it all the time. So it's striking to talk with Thomas Keller, to listen to this quiet, surprisingly modest man describe his restaurant as an institution – not as a personal enterprise or as the spawn of his own personal genius. Here's the guy whose cookbook is widely seen as the ultimate in food porn. Upon the mention of the chef's name, other chefs – no matter how great – become strangely silent, uncomfortable-looking, even frightened. In a subculture where most of us are all too happy to slag anybody at any time, you never hear anyone – even the French – talk trash about Keller. (One Frenchman, I believe, even called him the 'greatest French chef in the world.')

What's missing from all the wild praise of Keller, his cooks, his restaurant, and his cookbook is how different he is. You can't honestly use terms like *the best* or *better* or even *perfect* when you're talking about Thomas Keller, because he's not really competing with anybody. He's playing a game whose rules are known only to him. He's doing things most chefs would never attempt – in ways unthinkable to most. Everything about him and the French Laundry experience is different from most fine dining experiences; and Keller himself is a thing apart, a man hunting much bigger game, with very different ambitions than most of his peers.

Talking with the man as he walked through a small farm that grows him vegetables, watching his chef de cuisine pull baby leeks and garlic right out of the ground for that night's dinner – and later, as he showed us around the grounds of the French Laundry after dinner, when he sat with us in the dark garden, sipping an after-work glass of wine – it was evident how unusual his priorities are and to what lengths he is willing to go to attain them. The building itself looks like an unassuming country home, rustic-looking wood and stone, surrounded by green fields, farmlands, and vineyards in the small community of Yountville in the Napa Valley. There are two stories, an upstairs deck with a plain wooden balustrade, and a pretty garden. The decor, like the service, is unassuming, comfortably casual, with everything – the room, the wait staff, the view of the hills outside the windows and through the French doors – conspiring to put the diner at ease. The service, though relentlessly sharp and efficient, is not stiff or intimidating. The waiters are neither too friendly nor too distant.

'It looks like France,' said Eric, gazing out the window. For

Keller, the French Laundry is a cause. It is the culmination of a philosophy shared by the people who work with him. Every detail is inseparable from the whole, whether it's new steps to the porch or a new dish on the menu. He brought up the famous Taillevent in Paris as an example of the kind of place he aspires to leave behind someday. 'You don't know the chef's name at Taillevent, do you? No. It's the restaurant you remember – the institution. The tradition.' Though he's a legendary perfectionist, lives next door to his kitchen, and takes a hands-on approach to every tiny detail, what he has created in Yountville is a place inseparable from its community and suppliers, where the absolute best ingredients are treated with the highest degree of respect.

Think I'm exaggerating? Maybe I've gone over to the dark side – flacking for a chef I hope will someday throw me a freebie, maybe blurb my next book? No, you haven't seen how he handles fish, gently laying it down on the board and caressing it, approaching it warily, respectfully, as if communicating with an old friend.

Maybe you've heard some of the stories. That he used to make his cooks climb up into the range hoods each day to scrub out the grease personally. How he stores his fish belly-down, in the swimming position. That every fava bean in his kitchen is peeled raw (never soaked). How his *mise-en-place*, his station prep, is always at an absolute minimum – everything made fresh. Maybe you've heard about his unbelievably beautiful, elaborate *fifteen*-course tasting menus, seen pictures of food so perilously balanced, so perfectly posed, that you don't know how it ever gets to the table. They feed about eighty-five people a night at the French Laundry. They employ, all told, about eighty-five people. An army of similarly dedicated purveyors comb lonely stretches of the Pacific Northwest at night, some armed only with flashlights, looking for the telltale phosphorescence of a particular wild mushroom. People grow things to his specifications. The simplest-looking garlic chip garnish at the French Laundry can require the skills of a microsurgeon. Maybe you've heard all that.

There was a break between courses – a sort of seventh-inning stretch – and there we were: four grown men – three chefs and an author – standing outside Keller's kitchen in the dark, our noses pressed up against the window screen, spying on the man, whispering.

'SSssshh! . . . He'll hear us!' somebody said.

'Look,' said Michael. 'See how happy he looks!'

'My God! He's got no *mise* at all!' said someone else. Standing there in the shadows in the French Laundry's garden, it felt like we were kids on Halloween night.

'That's a happy man,' agreed Eric.

'How many chefs get to do this?' Keller had said earlier. 'We're just really lucky. And I don't forget that.'

A twenty-course tasting menu, under the most favorable circumstances, is a challenge to any chef. A twenty-course (including *amuse-gueules*) tasting menu for a party of fellow chefs is, for most of us, reasonable rationale for a nervous breakdown. But imagine – try to imagine – turning out four distinct and different twenty-course tasting menus for that one table of chefs, only two or three courses in common, over sixty different plates of food hitting one party of four – and doing it at the same time as serving a full dining room of regulars, many of whom are also having elaborate multicoursed tasting menus – and you get the idea when I say that Thomas Keller is different.

The meal took six and a half hours, with very little, if any, waiting between courses. Four different little oyster dishes would arrive, and we would all first look at our own plate, then glance longingly at the others'. For a while, we'd taste a little, sawing off a tiny bite of oyster, for instance, then pass our plates counterclockwise so the others could try. After many bottles of wine, and many courses, some of us just stopped passing. How do you cut a single oyster into four portions? It's hard. Some get more than others. In the highly charged atmosphere where everybody wants to try everything, this can lead to disputes – maybe violence. By the time the meat and fowl began hitting the table, I just hunched over my plate and said, 'Don't even think about it. You can try this one next time.'

There was a lot of head shaking and sighing going on. Who

among us in the whole wide world of chefs would attempt this? It was, far and away, the most impressive restaurant meal I'd ever had. Let me give you a closer look. Listed below is the menu for that evening, what I was served. Keep in mind that Scott, Eric and Michael were simultaneously enjoying equally elaborate and yet different dishes.

The meal began with the French Laundry's signature *amuse* – tiny little coronets of salmon tartare, served in a cone rack like at Baskin-Robbins (the inspiration for the dish). We all knew they were coming. We'd seen them in the cookbook – in my guests' case, they'd had them before. In addition to being delicious, it's psychological manipulation at its most skillful. You can't help but be charmed. The cute little cones, wrapped in tiny paper napkins, press long disused buttons in the sense-memory section of the brain. You feel like a kid again, your appetite jump-starts, and a breathless sense of anticipation comes over you. You want – you need – to know: What's next? Here's what I had next: puree of Robinson Ranch shallot soup with glazed shallots, English cucumber sorbet with pickled cucumber and a dill-weed *tuile*, Yukon Gold potato *blini* with shiitake mushrooms and chive butter, cauliflower *panna cotta* with Malpeque oyster glaze and osetra caviar, *côte de saumon*, an Atlantic salmon chop with russet potato *gnocchi* and Périgord truffles. Salmon chop? you're thinking. Salmon ain't got no chops! Yes, they do. Up by the head, there's an oft-neglected triangle of delicious flesh. It's a tricky little piece, usually discarded when chefs cut salmon for uniform portions of filet, because it's an awkward shape and riddled with annoying little bones. At the Laundry, a liability has been turned into an asset. There it was on my plate, a perfect little *côte de saumon*, looking just like a baby lamb chop, one bone extending from a tiny medallion of fish. Sounds cute? It is. A lot of Keller's dishes reveal an abiding sense of whimsy.

Whimsy and its unlovely cousin, irony, make appearances on a lot of menus these days, more often than not, unsuccessfully. You'll see a menu item with a 'cute' transposition of terms – for instance, 'tournedos of monkfish,' which means nothing more than that the chef is bored with the word *medallions* or feels insecure about titling his creation 'little pieces of monkfish.' Rarely does the finished product bear any resemblance to the term in its original usage. Now, if you were to serve that little disk of monkfish, larded with bacon, topped with a slab of foie gras, and drizzled with truffled *demiglace*, you might be able to get away with calling it 'tournedos of monkfish Rossini' – a direct reference to the old beef classic. But why? It's a dangerous game playing with your food like that. The line between cute and cloying (or worse – pretentious) is a very fine one.

But Keller, typically, is playing at something else here. He's not looking to elevate a less than worthy dish by associating it with a beloved classic. More often than not, he's taking something refined and giving it an ordinary – even clichéd – name (the best examples being his famous 'coffee and doughnuts' dessert, his 'Caesar salad,' and his 'grilled cheese sandwich.' 'The one compliment,' explains Keller, 'that I enjoy the most is someone saying, "This reminds me of" – and they'll tell you of this wonderful experience they had somewhere else. And I hope that when they go someplace else, they'll say, "This reminds me of the French Laundry." ' Memory – that's a powerful tool in any chef's kit. Used skillfully, it can be devastatingly effective. I don't know of any other chef who can pull it off so successfully. When you're eating a four-star meal in one of the world's best restaurants, and tiny, almost subliminal suggestions keep drawing you back to the grilled cheese sandwiches mom used to make you on rainy days, your first trip to Baskin-Robbins, or the first brasserie meal you had in France, you can't help – even the most cynical among us – but be charmed and lulled into a state of blissful submission. It's good enough when a dish somehow reminds you of a cherished moment, a fondly remembered taste from years past. When those expectations and preconceptions are then routinely exceeded, you find yourself happily surprised. Keller had a surprise for me.

He'd done his homework, I guess, gleaning from my book that I'm an absolutely degenerate smoker. There is no smoking at the French Laundry – maybe the only place on earth I don't mind refraining. But, to be honest, by course number five I was feeling a slight need. To my embarrassment and delight, they had anticipated this in the kitchen. When the next courses arrived, mine was called 'coffee and a cigarette': Marlboro-infused coffee custard (with foie gras). My dinner companions hooted. I blushed down to my socks, thinking this a cruel but very funny joke at my expense. I certainly didn't expect the thing to taste good. Goddamn the man, it was good. (He'd actually used the tobacco from a very decent cigar, he told me later.) Best of all, after I'd polished off my plate, I felt a very welcome, much-needed nicotine buzz.

Next?

Une salade fraîche au truffe noire with celery branch and celery root vinaigrette. Hand-cut tagliatelle with Périgord truffles and grated Parmigiano-Reggiano cheese. (The truffles were shaved tableside from a magnificent fist-sized monster.) Herb-roasted Chatham Bay cod 'shank' with a 'fricassee' of new-crop potatoes and applewood-smoked bacon emulsion. (Again, a liability turned into an asset, as the small, usually unservable tail section of fish had been cut across the bone and served like a lamb shank.) 'Lobster Navarin,' sweet butter-poached Maine lobster with glazed pearl onions, spring vegetables, and sauce 'Navarin' (another crosscultural reference – 'Navarin' is usually associated with a heavy, old-school French country classic of braised lamb shoulder). Brioche-crusted 'confit' of North American moulard duck 'foie gras' with braised fennel, fennel salad, and Tellicherry pepper. *'Gastrique'* milk-poached four-story Hills Farm *'poularde au lait'* with 'crème fraîche' dumplings and *'bouquetière'* of spring vegetables. Roasted Bellwether Farms spring lamb with a 'cassoulet' of spring pole beans and thyme-infused extra virgin olive oil. (These were the most fetching, tender little lamb chops I'd ever encountered.) 'Roquefort' ricotta cheese 'gnocchi' with a Darjeeling tea-walnut oil emulsion, shaved walnuts, and grated Roquefort cheese. Hayden mango soup *'et son brunoise'* (I love the *'et son brunoise'* thing – very funny). Haas avocado salad with Persian lime sorbet (of all the plates that made their way round our table that night, this was the only one that landed with a thud. Scott's comment was,

'This is waaay over my head. But then, I'm not that smart.')
'Coffee and doughnuts' – cinnamon-sugared doughnuts with
cappuccino semi-*freddo* (looking exactly like a coffee shop
doughnut sitting next to a Chock Full O'Nuts cup filled with
cappuccino, but marvelous). '*Mille-feuille à la crème de vanille et
son confit d'ananas mignardise.*'

It was an absolutely awe-inspiring meal, accompanied, I
should point out, by a procession of sensational wines. Unfortunately, I'm the wrong guy to be talking about wine. All I can tell
you is that Scott, who knows about these things, used the word
wow a lot. I remember a big brawny red in a cistern-sized glass,
which nearly made me weep with pleasure. Cooking had crossed
the line into magic.

Keller himself is quiet, with a bone-dry, gently sardonic sense
of humor and the wary, observant gaze of a totally centered chef
who knows what he wants to do – and is doing it – every day.

He seemed annoyed when asked about the roots of his drive
for perfection. 'Perfect is something you never actually attain,' he
said. 'It's something you search for. Once you reach it, it's not
perfect. You've lost it. It's gone.'

Gush too much about 'creativity' and you'll get: 'There's very
little creativity – in anything.'

But instead of *I*, *me*, and *my*, he uses words like *respect*, *hope*,
institution, *future*. Big words and big concepts in a trade where
most of us look no further down the road than the next star, the
next book deal, the next investor, the next busy Saturday night.

I was going to go on. I was going to blather on about the
seamless integration of restaurant and locale. I planned to
ruminate on the marvelousness of a chef finding, after years
of wandering and false starts, a home. I was in love with the idea
that a chef of Keller's unique abilities and ambition could
actually be content in a small town in wine country, marrying
place, purveyors, personnel, and personal vision into an idyllic
rural retreat, far from the carnivorous environs of the big city.
The whole concept had great appeal to me. An ideal accomplished, if not by me, then at least by someone I liked and
admired.

Then I opened up the *New York Times* and saw that Keller is planning a French Laundry in New York, that he's moving in across the street from Jean-Georges, down a ways from Ducasse, and realized I'd learned nothing at all.

'Unfinished business in New York,' said my chef buddies as we sat around a table at a Lower East Side joint.

'Rakel didn't make it,' said one friend, regarding Keller's failed venture in Manhattan many years ago. 'It was great – but the people weren't ready for it.'

'Jesus,' I sputtered, 'Keller coming to New York . . . That's an act of aggression! That's like Wyatt Earp coming to town. Everybody's gonna be gunning for him. Who wants that kind of pressure? He's already got it all. New Yorkers go to him! Why come here and have to put up with all the nonsense?'

Needless to say, when the new place opens its doors, every chef, critic, food writer, serious eater, and casual foodie in the city will have been hyperventilating for weeks. To say the restaurant will be 'eagerly anticipated' would be an egregious understatement. I cannot even imagine what will happen. I'm afraid. I'm afraid he'll fail (if that should happen, it would be for reasons having nothing to do with food, of course). But more, I'm afraid he'll succeed. I like the idea of having to travel to experience a French Laundry meal. The journey is part of the experience – or was for me – an expression of the seriousness of one's intent, and the otherness of everything Keller. I liked looking out the window and seeing hills and countryside. I don't know if I want to be able just to pick up the phone, make a reservation, and, sooner or later, simply hop in a cab and zip down to Columbus Circle. One doesn't take the A train to Mecca. That experience, like the French Laundry, should be a pilgrimage. Not that that will slow me down in the slightest when the new place opens its doors. See you there.

HAGGIS RULES

'WE'RE NUMBER TWO—BEHIND TONGA,' said Simon, talking about Scotland's position on the scoreboard recording the incidence of heart disease worldwide. 'We've got to get that sorted out. Where is Tonga anyway? I've got to go there!'

The Scottish, Simon tells me, will deep-fry anything. To prove his point, he was taking me to a chip shop for some 'suppers.' We were decidedly not in Edinburgh. 'Too European . . . too . . . English,' sneered Simon. They put brown sauce on their fish and chips there, Simon revealed, an outraged look on his face just from remembering the brown home-brewed Kitchen Bouquet or GravyMaster concoction.

'Brown sauce on fish and chips? No, no, no, no, no,' said Simon. It's malt vinegar all the way, and plenty of salt for Simon, a proud Glaswegian with a typically sardonic sense of humor. He'd been feeding me Guinness all day and showing me around Glasgow, and now it was time, he said, to visit a proper 'chippie.' We ate the traditional fish and chips first, a batter-dipped and deep-fried filet of cod – or more and more frequently, now that the cod population is in decline, haddock – usually served in either a paper cone or a plastic to-go container. 'You got to get a good bit of salt on it,' said Simon, following a very healthy sprinkling with a long squirt of malt vinegar. 'I could eat bloody Elvis – if you put enough vinegar on him . . . S' magic.' The fish was great, the chips, as everywhere in the UK, were needlessly substandard, limp and soggy. Few chip shop owners bother to blanch their fries in low-temperature oil before frying, so they are never, ever crisp.

The appropriate beverage for this kind of on-the-run Glaswegian repast, said Simon gravely, is Irn-Bru, the popular caffeine-jacked orange-tinted soft drink.

We were not really here to do the fish and chip thing. The real wonders, the full potential of the Scottish chip shop, lay some-where deeper: deep-fried haggis with curry sauce. The crispy cigar-shaped tube of sheep guts and oatmeal (more on that later) was wonderful – the perfect late-night munchie food after a long session drinking Red Bull and vodka, pints of heavy, or Buckfast (a cheap screw-top wine: the Ripple of Scotland). The 'king rib' – whatever that might be – was delicious, though its actual relation-ship to ribs seemed in doubt. Prefried orders of haggis, meat pies, sausages, and fish filets were crowded next to one another under bulb-lighted glass, ready to be snapped up by hungry drinkers.

Everything, everything at the chip shop, went into the same hot oil. Carlo, the counterman, unwrapped a Mars bar, dunked it in the universal batter, and dropped it into the oil. When it floated, golden brown, on the surface, he removed it, sprinkled a little powdered sugar on it, and handed it over.

'Careful,' said Simon. 'Inside, it's bloody napalm.'

Mmmm. I like grease. I like chocolate. And I like sugar. After addressing any concerns about potential mandibular or max-illary facial damage by allowing the thing to cool down a bit, Simon sawed off a half and presented it to me. It was still tongue-searingly hot – and not bad at all. Simon flashed me an evil smile and enjoyed telling me what was next. 'Deep-fried pizza?' I said, 'Oh . . . I don't know . . . That's maybe . . . I don't know, it seems somehow . . . unnatural.' I had a hard time believing that anyone would even consider such an atrocity. Sure enough, Carlo took a cold slice of premade frozen pizza, dipped it cheese side down into the batter, and dropped it into the all-purpose trough of grease.

'Not bad,' I said.

'Wait a minute,' said Simon as I made to leave. 'There's this one thingy we have to try.' He told a skeptical-looking Carlo to drop a pickled egg into the batter. We were breaking new culinary ground.

'I don't know,' I said. 'I don't . . . know about this.'

'This is where my granny would go "Holy Mary, mother of God,"' said Simon, taking a bite and handing me the rest. It was edible. I think one's enjoyment of the chip shop's more esoteric delights has a direct relationship to the amount of alcohol consumed prior to eating. Hot, salty, crunchy, and portable, the previously awful-sounding collection of greasy delights can become a Garden of Eden of heart-clogging goodness when you're in a drunken stupor, hungering for fried snacks. At that precise moment, nothing could taste better.

Glasgow has a working-class vibe and the familiar feel of parts of Brooklyn or the Bronx. In many ways, it's the antidote to everywhere else in the world, a city filled with gruff, no-bullshit, often very funny citizens with impenetrable but beautiful accents. On my way into town on the train, I fell asleep near a large group of Glaswegian football fans. When I woke, for a few disconcerting minutes, I thought, listening to the people talking and shouting around me, that I'd somehow stayed on the train too long, maybe slipped across the sea to Lithuania or Latvia or Finland. Only the repeated exclamations of 'Fook!' and 'Shite' brought me back to the correct time and place. (Note to travelers: Your choice of football team is an important one in Glasgow. Generally speaking, it's a Catholic versus Protestant thing, I think. Aligning yourself with one team over the other is a 'once in, never out' lifelong commitment. They take their footie seriously around these parts. It's a good idea to sound out one's friends carefully before saying what might well be the wrong thing.)

Edinburgh is, in my opinion, one of the most strikingly beautiful cities in the world. There's a castle sitting on top of a big rock promontory right in the middle of town. The place drips with history, a crowded tangle of cobblestone streets, ancient buildings, beautiful monuments, none of which weigh the town down. It's got good pubs, and bright, shrewd, very sophisticated, and often lavishly educated folks. I love it there (though I feel more at home in Glasgow).

This is mean of me, because I'm not going to give you its name

– and I'm certainly not gonna tell you where it is – or next time I go, there'll be a bunch of 'bloody Yanks' at the bar – but a friend of mine took me to his local awhile back, on a narrow cobblestone street in Edinburgh. My friend writes very fine novels set in the city, and his fictional hero, a mildly alcoholic civil servant, hangs out at this very real pub – in between murders. If there is a perfect place in the world to drink beer, this is it. It's a modest, unassuming corner pub with a small sign and smoked windows. One can't see the interior from the street. Just inside the door are an ancient small bar, weathered wood floors, hand-pumped beers and ales, a few middle-aged geezers drinking pints and chatting with the bartender. In a back room, there are a few tables and an electric fire in the hearth, some fading football posters on the walls. It is a place of perfect stillness and calm, the first sip of ale inspiring feelings of near-transcendental serenity. This was it, the perfect refuge from the modern world, and all its worries. Within moments of hanging my coat on a well-worn hook and sitting down, I turned to my friend and said, 'I'm never leaving.' I know it's terribly unfair of me to be so coy about the place. But don't worry, Scotland is loaded with great pubs – and I'm sure I'm overromanticizing. I do that a lot.

For Simon, it's love/hate with Edinburgh. He was not happy that I'd be having my first real haggis experience there. But he'd found us a very decent place on Edinburgh's High Street, just down from the castle, and he assured me that even though we were in (to his mind) the second-best city, the chef here knew what he was doing.

What is haggis, anyway? For one thing, it's the punch line to a thousand jokes in America. The Thing Never to Be Eaten Under Any Circumstances . . . What Groundskeeper Willie eats . . . It does sound terrifying to the uninitiated: a hot gooey mix of sheep's 'pluck' (the whole esophagus, lungs, liver, and heart, yanked out in one go, then finely ground), oatmeal, onions, and black pepper. This filling is cooked inside a sheep's stomach (which you don't eat) and then steamed slowly, covered in the oven, then served with 'neeps and tatties' – mashed turnip and potato. As with so many dishes, it originated with the leftovers of the rich landowners – turned into a proud classic by an enterprising and desperate peasantry.

A kilted bagpiper's performance preceded the arrival of dinner. (With his graying handlebar mustache, he looked suspiciously like the original 'Leather Guy' in the Village People.) Another few seconds of screeching pipes and I'd be reaching into my pocket for a hundred-pound note – just to make him go away. I may love Scotland, but the sound of bagpipes is as alluring as a dentist's drill hitting nerve. Fortunately, our haggis soon arrived, a big plump flesh-colored steaming balloon, tied at both ends and rupturing slightly in the middle, ground meat and oat mixture spilling out like a slowly erupting volcano. As I quietly struggled for words to describe its somehow violent-looking appearance, the fully costumed piper did me one better, yanking a sharp, menacing-looking dirk out of his scabbard, approaching the near-to-bursting membrane, and swinging right in to Robert Burns's 'Address to the Haggis.' I couldn't follow too many of the words, though I did catch the phrases 'gushing entrails' and 'a wondrous, glorious sack,' and then the piper slit the stomach fully open with his blade and retreated, leaving us to enjoy our guts.

After one mouthful, I couldn't disagree with Scotland's greatest poet. It was glorious. Haggis rules! Peppery, hot, meaty – it didn't taste of anything you might expect in a dish cooked in stomach. Not really tasting organlike at all, no bitter livery taste, no chewy mysterious bits, no wet-dog taste of tripe. It was in no way offensive to even the most pedestrian American tastes, but subtle and rich in a *boudin noir* sort of a way. If you can handle *boudin noir* or black pudding, or even sautéed calf's liver, you will love haggis. The mashed tatties and neeps provided a perfect counter to the hearty, peppery, oniony, oat flavor. The shepherd's pie in your old high school cafeteria was far more challenging to the palate. If haggis, right out of the oven, didn't look the way it did, we might all be eating it in America. They'd be serving it from street stands in New York, fried and battered with curry sauce. High-end restaurants would be making 'haggis sauce' and '*feuilleté* of baby bok choy, Yukon Gold potato, and haggis with a whiskey sauce,' and stuffing it into metal rings, decorating it with squeeze-bottle designs.

Scotland has far more to offer hungry pilgrims than grease and guts, however delightful they might be. The Scottish are going through the same foodie gold rush as elsewhere in the UK and Ireland (and Australia) – and, as elsewhere, they are rediscovering what was good all along about their country. The seafood is unbelievable. In Leith, the old waterfront on the firth outside Edinburgh, there are a number of modest-looking seafood joints serving absolutely smashingly good scallops, salmon, mussels, trout, oysters, and other fish from the North Sea, the Atlantic, and Scotland's many rivers, lochs, and streams. At the most ramshackle, touristy-looking seafood barn, where you'd expect, at best, to get a decent piece of deep-fried or plain broiled fish, they're piling tasty little stacks of fresh fish on piles of tasty indigenous vegetables – the technique as good as almost anywhere in New York or London, and the raw ingredients frequently better.

Scottish beef is justifiably famous. And Scottish game – venison, grouse, pheasant, wild hare, and rabbit – is perhaps the best in the world. I capped off my Scottish wanderings outside of Inverness, in the Highlands, on the 25,000-acre estate of the Cawdor family. For a guy like me, it's hard to fathom how the rich and the upper classes really live – especially when you're talking about the UK. For Americans, the aristocracy means any talented hustler who's got more than four cars and a beachfront pile in the Hamptons. In Scotland, I found out, it means something very, very different. The rich talk differently. They all seem to know one another. And in the case of the Cawdors, and Colin, the seventh earl of Cawdor, they tend to go back a ways. His family have been living on this particular Rhode Island-sized expanse of grouse moors, salmon streams, farmland, and forest since the late thirteenth century. There's a castle in the middle, a structure referred to significantly, if inaccurately, as the residence of 'Macbeth, the soon-to-be thane of Cawdor.' The Cawdors were kind enough to let me stay at their Drynachan Lodge, a hunting, shooting, and fishing retreat on their property, where I'd come to eat wild salmon and to try, halfheartedly at first, to kill a helpless little bunny rabbit or two.

Things really were different here. I don't know any rich people in America who count among their employees not just cooks and servers and housekeepers but also gamekeepers and foresters. I don't know any wealthy American families that can point to a magnificent forest of tall trees and deep gorges and rushing freshwater streams and say, 'My great-great-great-great grandfather planted that forest.' It was breathtakingly beautiful. From my big brass bed, I could see mile after mile of checkerboard-patterned grouse moor, the scrub and heather burned down in carefully controlled alternating square sections to provide optimum living conditions for the much-sought-after grouse. Pheasants wandered carefree just outside my door. Roe deer kept the underbrush to a minimum in the thick forest. Wild salmon literally leapt from crystal-clear streams. For mile after mile, an entire interlocking ecosystem was maintained – and had been maintained for hundreds of years – on the sprawling, seemingly never-ending grounds running all the way to the sea. Roddy, the gamekeeper, took me salmon fishing, and he showed me, as best he could, how to cast a line. I reeled it in across fewer than two feet of quick-moving water, hoping that a salmon would become enticed by the fly. The salmon were jumping out of the water, looking me right in the eye only a few feet away, but proved immune to temptation. Nothing like being proven – again and again – to be more stupid than a fish. But I didn't care. To stand at the edge of a Highland stream, casting across the water, reeling in, then moving slowly downstream on a brisk, clean, late-spring morning, had a hypnotic effect. I didn't mind if I caught anything or not. Fortunately, Ruth, the chef at the lodge, had a good supply of wild salmon on hand, so I wouldn't miss eating some.

I'd agreed – once again for purposes of television entertainment – to go rabbit shooting with Roddy. The plan was to bag a few rabbits, take them back to Ruth at the lodge, and have her make us a traditional poacher's stew of rabbit, venison, and cabbage, cooked in red wine and stock. Though by now I was reasonably comfortable firing automatic and semiautomatic rifles, handguns, and grenade launchers, given my Cambodian adventures, I had never in my life fired a shotgun. Nor had I ever fired a weapon at a living, breathing, fast-moving target. I am in no way supportive of hunting for trophies or sport – would never do it and don't like it that others do. But if you kill it, then eat it, it's fine. Still, I only agreed to take part in the senseless hunt because I was certain that I'd be hopelessly inept at shooting any rabbits, that I was sure to come up empty. I counted on Roddy, the seasoned professional, to provide enough bunny rabbits for the following day's lunch.

I don't know what happened. With my shotgun broken over my arm – so as not to shoot any of the TV crew or gamekeepers should I stumble into a pothole on the rough terrain – and the safety on, I spied a rabbit racing for cover about sixty to eighty feet in front of me. I quickly had to snap the gun closed, raise it, click off the safety, aim, and then fire – all this at a speedy, barely visible little critter that was running and leaping across his own turf. *Bam!* Very little kick. To my shock and no small amount of dismay, I'd blown the spine out of something that had once looked very much like Bugs.

'Well shot, sir,' said an assistant gamekeeper, retrieving the limp, still-warm corpse. Holding my prey, I couldn't resist the need to pet it, so cuddly and adorable; my voice actually cracked a little when I talked to the camera.

After each shot, I'd break my smoking weapon and an assistant would remove the shell and replace it. I saw a movement to my left, swung the barrel around, rapping Chris's camera in the process, and bagged another one tearing along a wall a long ways off. Jesus! I was a murder machine! Now I had two sweet-faced little bunny wabbits on my conscience . . . This was not right. But, God help me, I was having fun. Another few hours and I'd be signing up for grouse season.

Back at the lodge, Ruth prepared an amazing packed lunch of rabbit and venison stew, nettle soup, slices of air-dried beef, Scottish cheeses, and homemade breads. Then all of us, Chef Ruth, Gloria, the mad and wonderful Glaswegian housekeeper, an assistant gamekeeper, and the crew headed out over the moors to a fishing shack by the edge of a stream. Ruth set up a buffet on a picnic table inside and we helped ourselves, then sat down on the porch and devoured the fruits of the not-so-great white hunter's toil.

It was sensational. Sitting there watching cattle graze on a hillside across the water, listening to Gloria tell Glaswegian jokes, drinking red wine and watching the tall grass and heather move in the wind, I could hardly imagine a better setting for an afternoon meal. I did, however, begin to fear for my own safety. When this stuff hit the airwaves, when the PETA folks got a load of this, I could be looking at serious trouble. I don't want any vegan terrorists throwing blood on me – particularly not if I'm wearing an expensive jacket. Hopefully, my potential adversaries don't get enough animal protein to pose any real threat to my health or wardrobe. But I can't be sure, can I? Maybe I should buy a Taser.

VERY, VERY STRONG

IT'S BACK TO MY Saigon routine: Mornings at the market, 555 cigarettes and 333 beer. I'm holed up at the Continental (where I should have stayed all along), just across the street from Givral's pastry shop and the old Théâtre Municipal. Faded photographs of the hotel hang in frames on the walls surrounding the Orchid Garden bar in the courtyard. They date back to the 1880s, depicting straw-hatted French generals, white-suited colonists, satraps, and rickshaws. A much larger, later photograph, dated 1975, shows NVA soldiers resting out in front of the hotel. Across the square is the Caravelle, where journalists, spooks, and MACV brass once watched from the top-floor bar as B-52 strikes and airborne Gatling guns carved up the countryside beyond the city. Graham Greene stayed here. His character Fowler used to drink at the café downstairs, the Continental Shelf, where *le tout* Saigon used to gather each evening to drink and gossip.

I think I've gone bamboo, as they used to say about British military advisers who'd stayed too long in this part of the world. I've gone goofy on Vietnam, fallen hopelessly, helplessly in love with the place. I'm now accustomed to bowls of spicy *pho* for breakfast, strong cups of iced expresso over crushed ice with condensed milk at Trung Nguyen (sort of a Vietnamese version of Starbucks – only better), lunch at the *coms*, cheap eateries where I'd have bowls of rice with fish, chicken, or meat. I've come to rely on the smells of jasmine, frangipani, the durian and fish-sauce aromas at the markets, the constant buzzing and rumbling from the motos. I have a hard time letting any of the *don gah* pass me by – women carrying portable kitchens on yokes across their shoulders, serving bowls of soup or noodles that are always fresh. Everything is beautiful. Everyone is nice. Everything tastes good.

Linh has changed since introducing me to Madame Ngoc. A few weeks ago, he was all nerves and suspicion. When I told him, before leaving for Nha Trang, that Philippe might be swinging through town, maybe joining us in Can Tho, he'd stiffened at the prospect of an unannounced and unanticipated new arrival. He'd have to talk to the People's Committee, he said. People were watching us, he insisted, independently reporting on our activity. This addition to our party was an unexpected and potentially difficult development. Who was this Philippe? What were his intentions? Was he also a journalist? Was he a French or American citizen? During drinks at the roof bar of the garish Rex, when I left to go to the bathroom, Linh followed me, making an elaborate show of washing his hands while watching in the mirror to make sure I wasn't emptying a dead drop or whispering into a satellite communicator.

But since Nha Trang, he's been relaxed, and since he introduced me to Madame Ngoc, he's become an absolute pussycat.

Madame Ngoc is a force of nature. The relationship between the matronly middle-aged restaurant owner, dripping in jade and jewelry, smelling of French perfume, always smartly dressed in well-tailored businesslike Western attire, and Linh, the young translator and Communist functionary, is a mysterious one. When he first took me to her restaurant, Com Nieu Saigon, I couldn't figure out why he was so solicitous of her. At first blush, they couldn't seem more different: the cold, efficient Hanoi boy and the warm but mercurial Saigonese woman. Yet Linh never lights a cigarette without first lighting one for her. He pulls out her chair for her. He hangs on her every word, anticipates her needs. When she narrows her eyes, looks around the room, clearly desirous of something, Linh goes on full alert. But then so does everybody else. She may be a tiny Vietnamese version of a yenta, but underneath her soft features and almost overbearingly generous nature it's pure steel. She teases him relentlessly. She scolds, pokes, dotes on him, calls him 'Little Brother'. It is, I finally figured out after a few visits, love.

'Next time! You bring cookies. Chocolate!' says Madame Ngoc, pleased by my gift of flowers but preferring other things. 'Chris! Lydia! You happy? I love you . . .' she says, giving them both a big hug and a kiss. 'You too thin!' she says to Chris, who has never fully recovered from his crab in Nha Trang. 'Too thin! I think you sick.' She snaps her fingers, and across the room an assistant manager and a waiter rush over to serve her. She barks at them in Vietnamese, and a few moments later, the manager returns with packages of vitamins, Maalox, and herb tea. 'Tony, Chris, Lydia,' she says, looking worried. 'You must be very careful.' We each receive an identical package and a stern admonition to eat more carefully when outside of Saigon. A few days ago, it was bags of Vietnamese coffee (she'd heard me raving about how good it was here). When Lydia commented earlier on the toy dogs with bobbing heads on the dashboard of Madame Ngoc's chauffeured car, she'd presented each of us with a set later in the evening. We all love Madame Ngoc, and we think she loves us, too.

'I give my heart. Make people happy,' she says warmly, before snapping her head to the right and fixing a waiter with a brief look of withering scorn. Beers arrive at our table. Ashtrays are emptied. At Madame Ngoc's restaurant, people are happy. The clean white room is packed with Vietnamese families. Tables of eight, ten, twelve, fifteen people tear into food all around us, with new guests arriving every minute. They drive right through the dining room, three and four to a motorbike, then into the backyard parking area. Napkins are popping everywhere from their packets. Every few minutes, a clay pot shatters loudly on the floor and a sizzling-hot rice cake goes flying through the air. The colors on the plates at every table are electric, psychedelic, positively radiating bright reds, greens, yellows, and browns; and it smells good: lemongrass, lobster, fish sauce, fresh basil and mint.

Com Nieu Saigon is the slickest, smartest, sharpest restaurant operation I've seen in a long, long time. Madame Ngoc, a tiny little middle-aged woman, divorced, living – as she is all too willing to tell you – all alone, runs it like a well-drilled battleship. Every table, every corner, every crevice of latticework in the open-air dining room is clean, tight, and squared away. Underneath the broken crockery, even the floor is spotless. The cooks, the waiters, and the managers move like a highly motivated – even terrorized – dance troupe. It does not do, I have long since gathered, to disappoint Madame Ngoc.

She's figured out how to run a successful restaurant in a Communist country. Com Nieu is a loud, casual, comfortable family place with a distinctive gimmick. Madame Ngoc, reading up on Vietnamese culinary history, found a traditional preparation for rice baked in clay pots. The drill at Com Nieu is that when you order a rice side, a waiter retrieves it from the kitchen, smashes the crockery with a mallet, the pieces falling to the floor, then hurls the sizzling-hot rice cake across the dining room, over the heads of the customers, to another waiter, who catches the cake on a plate, flips it, sends it up in the air a few more times like a juggler, then cuts it into portions tableside, dressing it with fish sauce, peppers, sesame, and chives. The room resounds with the noise of breaking and broken crockery. Every few minutes, searingly hot disks of rice go sailing by my ear. It's a tightly controlled riot of food, folks, and fun, kids standing on their chairs, their moms feeding them, granddad and sons tearing apart lobsters, crabs, and giant prawns, grandmas and dads smoking between courses, everyone chattering, eating, loudly and visibly enjoying themselves.

Who is Madame Ngoc? As she tells you, she's just a lone hardworking woman, unlucky in love, who loves cookies, chocolate, stuffed animals (which she collects) and continental buffets in large Western hotels. (She took us as her guest to one of the bigger, newer ones – absolutely giddy around all those chafing dishes of French and Italian food, the cake stands of Austrian pastries and French petits fours.) She is driven everywhere in a new luxury sedan. When it rains, someone is waiting curbside with an umbrella. When she decides – at 10:30 at night

– that she wants us all to have our picture taken together, she
snaps her fingers, barks a few orders, and a frightened-looking
photographer arrives in a full sweat only a few minutes later, an
old Nikon and flash rig around his neck. Com Nieu is jammed
full every night – as is her other restaurant, a Chinese-themed
place down the street. And Madame Ngoc is at one or both,
reigning over her devoted staff and adoring public for most of
her waking hours.

'I so tired. Very hard work. Very tired. Sometime I don't want
to come. I want to stay in bed. Sleep. But no can. Always
watching . . .' She feigns a deeply suspicious inspection of her
rushing staff. 'I go to fish market to surprise. Maybe somebody
steal from me. I must find out. I say, "How much for crab today?
How much yesterday? How many pounds you sell me yesterday?" I must look. Careful.' She points to her eye, signifying
eternal vigilance. At the arrival of a large party by the front
entrance, she jumps up out of her seat and approaches them, all
smiles.

'I love everybody,' she says. 'You must give love. Give yourself
to be success. You love people. They love you back.' Food
arrives at our clean, newly varnished and polished table. *Canh
ngheu*, a tofu and dill soup. Platters of *bong bi don thit*, crunchy,
delicious golden zucchini blossoms that have been stuffed with
ground pork and seasonings, then batter-dipped and fried. *Cha
goi*, spring rolls, and *rau muong sao toi*, flash-sautéed spinach
with garlic sauce – an otherworldly bright, bright green. *Thit
kho tau*, a stew of pork and egg in coconut broth, the halved
boiled eggs tinged pink around the outer rim of white. *Tom kho
tau*, lobster stewed in coconut and chili, redder than red, the
plump tail meat a phosphorescent saffron yellow. *Ca bong trung
kho to*, a whole fish fried and dressed with chili sauce. *Dua gia
muoi chau*, stir-fried baby bok choy. And, of course, lots of *com
nieu*, the wedges of crispy rice cake from which the restaurant
takes its name. Everything is as fresh as I've seen it anywhere in
the world, fresher even. The flavors practically explode on my
tongue; the colors shimmer. At the end of the meal, platters of
ripe custard apple on ice arrive, accompanied by sliced mangoes,

papayas, dragon fruit, and pineapple. I have been Madame Ngoc's guest three or four times by now, and there is no question in my mind that hers has been the best food I've had in the country (this in a country where everything is already fabulous).

Like any really good restaurant lifer, Madame Ngoc's nervous system is hard-wired to every movement in both kitchen and dining room. She has the ability to sense a full ashtray on the other side of the restaurant, even when far out of view. One moment she's cooing over Lydia, or teasing Linh for being late to the airport the last time she was in Hanoi, or insisting I try the crab, or worrying over Chris's stomach – the very next second, she's giving orders to a shaking but very competent waiter who has somehow managed to displease her, rebuking him in terrifying imperious tones.

Then it's back to 'I love you, Chris, Lydia . . . Tony, you happy?' She places her hand over mine and gives it a pat. When she smiles, it's a broad, full-body grin. And I want to hug her like a beloved aunt. She's a cross between a Jewish mother and the head of the Genovese crime family, driven, relentless, smotheringly affectionate, dangerous, warm, complicated and attentive. Though very concentrated on money – and things – she has rarely, if ever, allowed us to pay for anything.

She's strong. She can be hard. She can be cold. But on our way out the door after dinner, as we say goodbye for the last time to our new best friend in Saigon, her face collapses and she bursts into tears. As our car pulls away, she is sobbing, her hand brushing the glass in a combination wave and caress.

New Year's Eve in Saigon is a jumbo-sized version of the *song tu do*, the weekend ritual of cruising downtown Saigon, circling the fountain at the intersection of Le Loi and Nguyen Hue boulevards. It's the Vietnamese equivalent of low-riding or cruising down Sunset Strip; thousands – tonight, hundreds of thousands – of young Vietnamese, dressed in their best button-down shirts, freshly laundered slacks, dresses, and *ao dais*, drive in perpetual slow-moving circles through the downtown city streets. They are going nowhere in particular. They don't stop. There is no place to stop anyway. Every inch of Saigon seems filled, tire-to-tire, with motos and scooters. It takes twenty minutes to cross the street.

My plan was to celebrate the New Year at Apocalypse Now, a promisingly titled expat bar a few blocks from the Continental. What better place to be when the ball dropped, I thought, than some sinister expat bar in Saigon? I expected opium-addicted ex-mercenaries, aggressive whores in silver minis, long-AWOL 'white VC,' black market hustlers, Aussie backpackers, shriveled French rubber barons, their faces teeming with corruption and the effects of malaria; I expected international rabble, arms dealers, defectors, and hit men. I'd had such high hopes. But from the moment I step inside, I am instantly disappointed. Apocalypse Now is a fern bar! There's food! A crowd of well-dressed tourists from America, Canada, and Taiwan sit in a rear dining room among potted palms and Christmas lights, near a buffet of hot entrées, salads, and what looks like Black Forest cake. They sell T-shirts with the movie's logo. Soccer is shown on an overhead projection screen near a small stage. Sunburned blondes with Midwestern accents and Tammy Faye hairdos drink colorful cocktails at a clean Formica bar.

I hate the place on sight and retreat back into the streets, finding somewhere to stand by a large stage set up behind the Théâtre Municipal. I recognize my moto driver from a few days earlier – from his Yankees cap – and we wave hello to each other. Onstage, a group of children are taking part in some kind of dance and theater presentation: patriotic songs, storytelling. No one in the crowd is watching; everyone has their attention fixed somewhere else. The constant growl of the motos and scooters drowns out nearly everything. Once in a while, loud techno-music plays over loudspeakers as the traditionally garbed per-formers leave the stage for a break. Everyone seems to be waiting for something, going somewhere, but nothing happens. As the hour approaches, I see a few people check their watches. One minute to midnight, and traffic has not slowed. No ball appears poised to drop. There are no fireworks. Midnight passes – indistinguishable from five minutes before or after. No one cheers. No one kisses. Not a single raised fist, shout of 'Happy New Year,' or any acknowledgment that another year has passed in the Western world. It's true the Vietnamese celebrate the Chinese New Year (Tet), but for weeks there have been signs everywhere reading HAPPY NEW YEAR, and people have been calling it out whenever they spy an American or a Westerner. Everyone seems poised to party, the milling crowds huge, the traffic heavier than ever, but I see not the tiniest indication of any intention to do anything but drive or stand. They've all come out for the event, all these kids, as far as the eye can see, and beyond. They cluster around a laser-light display outside a nightclub, as if not knowing what to do next. Dance music blasts from inside, but nobody dances, sways, even taps a foot or drums a finger.

It reminded me of my first high school dance – boys on one side, girls on the other, both sides afraid to move. Or have I misunderstood? Are the hundreds of thousands of kids driving and driving in circles all dressed up with no place to go – as the song says – or are they truly indifferent to the infinite delights of three chords and a beat? Vietnam seems to have shrugged off the worst of our culture with barely a look back. Is 'living freely', *song tu do*, just driving? Or is it waiting? And for what?

It's *tim ran* time. This time, I'm going to eat something that will, I am assured, make me very, very strong. The strongest. Huong Rung (Flavors of the Forest) Restaurant is a bright beer-garden-like space, enclosed by trellis, its foyer crowded with fish tanks. I enter, sit down, and order a beer right away, steadying myself for what will probably be the most . . . unusual meal of my life so far.

A grinning waiter approaches, holding a wriggling burlap sack. He opens it, gingerly reaches inside, and extracts a vicious, hissing, furious-looking four-foot-long cobra. As I've ordered the specialty of the house, I assume the staff is inured to the sight, but when the cobra, laid on the floor and prodded with a hooked stick, raises its head and spreads its hood, the whole staff of waiters, busboys, and managers – everyone but my cobra handler – steps back a few feet, giggling nervously. My cobra handler, a nice young man in waiter's black slacks and a white button-down shirt, has a sizable bandage on the back of his right hand, a feature that does not fill me with confidence as he lifts the snake with the stick and holds him over the table, the snake training its beady little eyes on me and trying to strike. I knock back the rest of my beer and try to stay cool while the cobra is allowed to slide around the floor for a while, lunging every few moments at the stick. The cobra handler is joined by an assistant with a metal dish, a small white cup, a pitcher of rice wine, and a pair of gardening shears. The two men pick up the cobra, fully extending him; the cobra handler holds him behind the jaws, while the assistant keeps him stretched just ahead of the tail. With his free hand, the handler takes the scissors, inserts a blade into the cobra's chest, and snips out the heart, a rush of dark red blood spilling into the metal dish as he does so. Everyone is pleased. The waiters and busboys relax. The blood is poured into a glass and mixed with a little rice wine. And the heart, a Chiclet-sized oysterlike organ, still beating, is placed gently into the small white cup and offered to me.

It's still pumping, a tiny pink-and-white object, moving up and down up and down at a regular pace in a small pool of blood at the bottom of the cup. I bring it to my lips, tilt my head back, and swallow. It's like a little Olympia oyster – a hyperactive one. I give it one light chew, but the heart still beats . . . and beats . . . and beats. All the way down. The taste? Not much of one. My pulse is racing too much to notice. I take a long swig of *rou tiet ran*, the blood and wine mixture, enjoying it, not bad at all – like the juice from a rare roast beef – robust, but with just a slight hint of reptile. So far so good. I have eaten the live heart of a cobra. Linh is proud of me. Many, many sons. The floor staff grin, the girls giggle shyly. The handler and assistant are busily carving up the cobra. An enormous mass of snowy white snake tripes tumbles out of the cobra's body cavity onto a plate, followed by a dribble of dark green bile.

'This very good for you,' says Linh as a waiter mixes the bile with some wine and presents me with a glass of *ruou mat ran*. It's a violent green color now, looking about as appetizing as the contents of a bedpan. 'This will make you the strongest. Very special, very special.'

I have long ago come to dread those words. I take a long swig of the green liquid and swallow. It tastes bitter, sour, evil . . . just like you'd expect bile to taste.

Over the next hour or so, I eat every single part of the cobra. First, *ran bop goi*, a delicious shredded-snake salad, heavily dressed with citrus and lemongrass and served in a hot pot. *Ham xa*, braised cobra with citronella, is also quite good, though slightly chewy. *Long ran xao*, however, the snake's tripe sautéed with onion, is absolutely inedible. I chew and chew and chew, grinding helplessly away with every molar. My chewing has not the slightest effect. It's like chewing on a rubber dog toy – only less tender. The tripe, while innocuous-tasting, is impossible to break down. I finally give up, hold my breath, and swallow a mouthful whole and intact. *Xuong (ran) chien gion*, the deep-fried bones of the snake, is delightful – like spicy potato chips – only a lot sharper. You might enjoy these at a Yankees game, though very carefully. If one bone goes in at the wrong angle, it could easily pierce your esophagus, making the prospects of lasting through the ninth inning doubtful. *Ran cuon ca lop*, the cobra's meat, minced and rolled in mint leaves, is also delightful – a festive party snack for any occasion.

The manager comes over to present me with a plate containing a large tree grub, white with a black freckle-like mark on one end. It's alive, undulating, bigger than a thumb. Oh, Jesus, no . . . It squirms around, thrashing on the plate. No, I'm thinking. No. Not that . . . Fortunately, the tree grub is cooked before serving, sautéed in butter until crispy. When it arrives back at my table, perched on a little bed of greens, I warily take a nice-sized bite. It has the consistency of a deep-fried Twinkie: crunchy on the outside, creamy and gooey in the middle. It tastes fine. But I would have been much happier not having seen it alive.

Overall, though, not a bad meal. And I've eaten the still-beating heart of a fucking cobra! (I'll be dining out on this story for a while.) For the very first time after eating food that will 'make me strong,' I actually feel something. I don't know if it's just nervous energy and adrenaline, but when I walk out into the street, I feel a buzz, a jangly, happy, vibrating sense of well-being. I think, Yes, I believe I do feel . . . strong.

'Monsieur Fowlair. Monsieur Fow-lairr . . .' someone is whispering.

It's the police inspector in Greene's *The Quiet American*, talking in my dreams. I wake up expecting to see Phuong, the heroine of the novel, preparing an opium pipe for me, and Pyle, the youthful CIA agent, petting his dog in a chair. I'm in my room at the Continental, carved fleurs-de-lis in the woodwork, ornate chairs, yards of intricately carved shelving. I can hear the clack-clacking of shoes on the wide marble floor outside the door, the sound echoing through the halls. Saigon. Still only in Saigon. The French doors leading onto the balcony are open and, though early, the streets are already filling up with cyclos, bicycles, motorbikes, and scooters. Women crouch in doorways, eating bowls of *pho*. A man fixes a motorbike on the sidewalk. Buses cough and stall and start again. At Givral's, across the street, they're lining up for coffee and the short, plump, fragrant-smelling baguettes. Soon, the 'noodle knockers' will come, rapping their mallets to announce the imminent arrival of another yoke-borne kitchen, bowls and bowls of steaming fresh noodles. Linh has informed me of something called 'fox' coffee, *ca-phe-chon*, a brew made from the tenderest beans, fed to a fox (though I have since seen it referred to as a weasel), and the beans later recovered from the animal's stool, washed (presumably), roasted, and ground. Sounds good to me.

I'm leaving Vietnam soon, and yet I'm yearning for it already. I grab a stack of damp dong off my nightstand, get dressed, and head for the market. There's a lot I haven't tried.

I'm still here, I tell myself.

I'm still here.

PERFECT

THE WHOLE CONCEPT OF the 'perfect meal' is ludicrous.

'Perfect,' like 'happy,' tends to sneak up on you. Once you find it – like Thomas Keller says – it's gone. It's a fleeting thing, 'perfect,' and, if you're anything like me, it's often better in retrospect. When you're shivering under four blankets in a Moroccan hotel room, the perfect meal can be something no more exotic than breakfast at Barney Greengrass back in New York – the one you had four months ago. Your last Papaya King hot dog takes on golden, even mythic, proportions when re- membered from a distance.

I'm writing this, these words, from a beach chair somewhere in the French West Indies. My hand is actually scrawling in wet black ink across a yellow legal pad. I'm not here to eat. I'm here to write, and relax, untroubled by phone calls, shoes and socks, visitors, E-mails, or obligations of any kind. I'm here because I've been on the road for over a year and I want desperately to stay put, to dig in, to remain in one place and maybe reacquaint myself with my wife.

I've been coming to this beach for a long time. The first time I visited, back in the eighties, I was still kicking dope, and the blood-warm water felt cold on my skin. My wife and I honey- mooned here, blowing every cent of wedding loot on a two-week kamikaze vacation, which left us tanned, happy, totally in love with the island – and utterly broke. Down here, I like to think that I'm not the brutish, obsessive, blustering blowhard control freak, Chef Tony; nor the needy, neurotic, eager-to-please, talkin-sound-bites Writer Tony – but the relatively calm, blissed-out, sunstroked, amiable Husband Tony – the nicest version of me Nancy is likely to see for forty days at a clip.

After a few lazy hours bobbing around in the warm, gin-clear turquoise water, and dozing on the beach, Nancy was reading me the police blotter from the local paper.

A man, 'G,' from Saint Peters, was detained last night on the Pondfill Road. A gentleman from Domenica complained that 'G' had mistreated him with a pair of nail clippers after a dispute over a game of dominoes at the Dinghy Dock Bar. Dutch side police arrived at the scene and gave 'G' a stern warning and he was released. Two youths from Back Street, 'P' and 'D', were arrested after stealing a gold chain from Kun Shi Jewelers on the Old Street. The youths asked to see a chain in the store, then ran away without paying for it. They were arrested at the bus stop on the Bush Road as they tried to make their escape by bus.

'Jesus,' said Nancy. 'It's a crime wave.'

A while ago, I looked up from my pad, wiped the sweat out of my eyes, and, after consulting my watch, turned to Nancy and said, 'Hungry?' She said yes, as I knew she would. We're creatures of habit down here. We have a routine. That meant a short walk across the hot sand to a thatch-roofed hut with a smoking barbecue grill, a rudimentary bar with five or six kinds of liquor, and two coolers of iced Caribs, Red Stripes, and baby Heinekens. Gus, the proprietor, has known us since 1984, and he had a pretty good idea what we wanted. By the time we ducked under the palm fronds into the shade, he'd already cracked two Caribes.

I ordered the barbecued ribs. Nancy went for the cheeseburger. The service at Gus's is never quick. Our order took about half an hour – normal waiting time on this island. But, uncharacteristically, I wasn't impatient at all. I didn't fidget. I didn't look nervously around. I didn't listen for the telltale sounds of a spatula lifting Nancy's burger off the grill – or the bell signaling an order was ready. I knew Keesha, the woman working the grill, and was aware that she did things at her own pace. I didn't care how long it took. I was happy to wait, drinking the beer in the shade of Gus's makeshift frond-covered shelter, sand between my toes, hair still wet from the sea, Nancy looking brown and happy and a little bit drunk across from me.

My ribs were tender, slightly crispy on the outside and seasoned with the same adobo spice that Gus puts on everything. If the ribs were marinated in something before grilling, I knew not what. Nor did I care. Any critical sensibilities had long ago been put on hold. Nancy's cheeseburger was small, cooked completely through, and topped with a single Kraft cheese slice and a too-large bun, also seasoned with the ubiquitous adobo. She never finishes her food, so I knew that I'd get at least a bite. Both plates were white – plastic, garnished with soggy french fries – just as I'd expected them to be. Gus's new Shaggy CD played on the sound system for at least the fourth time that day. It will, of course, remain the music from this time on the island. From now on, that CD will always and forever bring me right back here to this time and place, the taste of crispy pork and adobo seasoning, Gus's Beach Bar, the look on Nancy's face as she sighed distractedly, yawned, stretched, and then tossed one of my rib bones to a stray dog that'd been lurking by our table. The dog knew the routine.

I've learned something on the road. It doesn't do to waste. Even here – I use everything.

– August 2001

ACKNOWLEDGMENTS

Thanks to: Karen Rinaldi, Joel Rose, Rosemarie Morse, Kim Witherspoon, Panio Gianopoulos, Lydia Tenaglia, Chris Collins, Matt Barbato, Alberto Orso, "Global" Alan Deutsch, Bree Fitzgerald, Michiko Zento, Shinji Nohara, Dinh Linh, Madame Ngoc, Khoum Mang Kry, the incredible Zamir Gotta, Scott Leadbetter, Simon McMillan, Lu Barron, Edilberto Perez and family, Martin Vallejo, Abdou Boutabi, Luis and Virginia Irizar, Chris Bourdain, Jose Meirelles and family, Philippe Lajaunie, Colin and Isabella Cawdor, Mark Stanton, Abdelfettah and Naomi, Jamie Byng, Fergus Henderson, Gordon Ramsay, Thomas Keller, Juan Mari Arzak, Dan Cohen, Kim Martin, Liane Thompson, Christian Gwinn, Dan Halpern, Anya Rosenberg, Sarah Burns, Scott Bryan, Eric Ripert, Michael Ruhlman, Mark Peel, Tracy Westmoreland, and all the people who helped me on the way.

A NOTE ON THE AUTHOR

Anthony Bourdain is the author of *Kitchen Confidential*,
two satirical thrillers, *Bone in the Throat* and *Gone Bamboo*,
and the urban historical *Typhoid Mary*. A twenty-eight-year
veteran of professional kitchens, he is currently the 'Executive
Chef' at Brasserie Les Halles in Manhattan – meaning he gets to
swan around in a chef's jacket taking credit for others' toil.
He lives – and always will live – in New York City.

A NOTE ON THE TYPE

The text of this book is set in Linotype Sabon, named after
the type founder, Jacques Sabon. It was designed by Jan
Tschichold and jointly developed by Linotype, Monotype
and Stempel, in response to a need for a typeface to be available in
identical form for mechanical hot metal composition and
hand composition using foundry type.

Tschichold based his design for Sabon roman on a fount
engraved by Garamond, and Sabon italic on a fount by
Granjon. It was first used in 1966 and has proved an
enduring modern classic.